*

Language, Poetry
and Nationhood

*

J. Derrick McClure

*

Language, Poetry and Nationhood

*

SCOTS

AS A POETIC LANGUAGE FROM
1878 TO THE PRESENT

*

TUCKWELL PRESS

First published in Great Britain in 2000 by

TUCKWELL PRESS
The Mill House
Phantassie
East Linton
East Lothian EH40 3DG
Scotland

ISBN 1 86232 071 3

The publishers acknowledge subsidy from the Scottish Arts Council
towards the publication of this volume

Typeset by Combined Arts, Rushden

British Library Cataloguing in Publication Data

A catalogue record for this book is available
on request from the British Library

Printed and bound by Cromwell Press,
Trowbridge, Wiltshire

Acknowledgements

My thanks are due, firstly, to my colleagues in the English Department at Aberdeen University, and in particular to Thomas Crawford, David Hewitt, Caroline Macafee, Colin Milton, Wilhelm Nicolaisen, Gert Ronberg, Isobel Tait and the late Matthew P. McDiarmid: for taking on the extra work during my period of research leave in which most of this book was written, and, much more importantly, for countless ideas and suggestions given, often unthinkingly, in conversations and discussions over many years.

To friends and colleagues elsewhere in the academic and literary worlds, among them Jamie Reid Baxter, David Clement, Marace Dareau, Beat Glauser, Manfred Görlach, Ronald D. S. Jack, John M. Kirk, John Law, Roderick J. Lyall, Stuart McHardy, Iseabail MacLeod, Douglas Mack, William Neill, George Philp, David Purves, Mairi Robinson, Kenneth Simpson, Harry Watson, Doreen Waugh, the late Roddy MacDonald, and above all, those twin Titans of Scots language studies, the ever-missed A. J. Aitken and David Murison.

To the students of Scots whom I have taught and learned from, in whom individual enthusiasm and commitment provides consolation for their sparse numbers: in particular Alasdair Allan, David Hastie, Dauvit Horsbroch, Steve Murdoch and Kenneth Sadler.

To the living poets, and friends and relations of deceased ones, whose interest in the project was a steady source of encouragement; and especially to John Gray, Bet Mackie, Cath Scott, Heather Scott and Clara Young.

And – of course – to my wife Ann for her everlasting support.

Til the memore o

my faither
JOCK McCLURE

my guidfaither
DWIGHT BOLINGER

an my mentor
JACK AITKEN

'Ye ar the licht o the warld. A toun biggit on a hill-tap canna be hoddit; an again, whan fowk licht a lamp, they pit-it-na ablò a meal-bassie, but set it up on the dresser-heid, an syne it gíes licht for aabodie i the houss.'

Contents

1
Scots and Scotland

That a nation's language should be the vehicle of that nation's poetry is, on the face of it, as natural and predictable as anything can be. However, the concept of "a nation's language" is far from straightforward. Of the nation-states of Europe, some, such as France, have through centuries of existence as independent politically-defined entities cultivated one particular speech form as the principal medium of their administrative mechanisms and their literary creations. Others, such as Germany, have come into being through a perceived common identity which transcends and eventually abolishes political divisions, of which a common language is an integral part. Others still, such as Slovakia, have emerged from a political construction in which a common identity, again intimately associated with a language, was denied the autonomous existence which its members saw as their right. That is, a connection at first merely incidental between a polity and a language may be deliberately raised to the status of a close identification; or a common identity inhering in, or at any rate underpinned by, a common language may lead to the political definition of that language's territory either by abolishing political boundaries within the territory or by establishing them around it. In all such cases, and they of course do not exhaust the possibilities, an intimate association between language and polity becomes institutionalised and – almost invariably – encouraged as a conscious national endeavour. However, neither in any of the three countries mentioned nor in any other European nation-state (Iceland excepted, and disregarding statelets such as Liechtenstein or San Marino) is the association complete. Provençal, Breton and Alsatian are spoken as community languages within France; the *Grossdeutschland* that emerged from nineteenth-century ideals never incorporated all German-speaking territories; the boundaries of Slovakia include areas of Magyar speech.

1

No state in Europe is monolingual: on the other hand, most have a single official language. That is, in most of Europe's countries, some citizens endure the disadvantage of being obliged by political, economic and often cultural necessity to use a language other than that which they identify as their mother tongue. The degree of provision made for speakers of languages other than the official one varies from state to state: Swedish-speakers in Finland, demographically a small section of the population, have by law precisely the same rights as Finnish-speakers; in Spain forcible repression of languages other than Castilian has changed in recent decades to generous government-sponsored encouragement; France, notoriously, continues to this day in its policy of non-benign neglect of its minority languages. There is, however, no predicting the way in which speakers of non-official languages will respond either to repressive or to supportive policies. No national government has made greater efforts to support its minority language than that of the Irish Republic, yet the decline of Irish as a community speech has never been halted; Catalan, by contrast, vigorously resisted a long period of active discouragement to enjoy, in our own time, a cultural efflorescence of impressive scope and quality.

In Scotland, an enduring sense of nationhood survived the loss of statehood, and still survives pending its eventual recovery. The relationship of national to linguistic identity, however, is both more complex and more elusive than in any of the cases hitherto discussed. A paradox which has existed in Scottish history from its beginnings is that whereas a sense of common national allegiance – the concept of the Community of the Realm of Scotland – emerged much earlier than in other European countries, it was never, and never has been, firmly associated with a common language. A fallacy which appears to enjoy almost universal credence – even the reservation "except in Scotland" is not unequivocally warranted – is that the linguistic history of Scotland presents a simple parallel to those of Ireland and Wales: a protracted conflict between a Celtic language and English, with the latter frustrated of complete victory by a sense of patriotic loyalty towards the indigenous tongue. The truth, however, is that since at least the fifteenth century a large part of Scotland, including the principal centres of political power, not only has not been Gaelic-speaking but has demonstrated attitudes towards the

Gaelic language and its associated culture which are the reverse of patriotic loyalty: ignorance, fear and hostility. The linguistic conflict in this part of Scotland has not been between English and Gaelic but between English and Lowland Scots, the language with which the present study is concerned; and not only have the terms of this conflict been much less clearly defined than that which certainly existed (and still exists) between English and Gaelic, but its relationship to the question of national identity has been much less simple and less consistent than that of the parallel conflicts in Ireland and Wales.

Lowland Scots and English are in their internal linguistic structures as mutually distinct as many pairs of speech-forms with the official status of separate languages (Norwegian and Danish, Czech and Slovak, Finnish and Estonian), and have been since at least the fifteenth century: one of the most frequently-quoted of Scottish historical documents is the letter from the Spanish ambassador at the court of James IV, who noted (among many other things) that James's Scots speech was as different from English as Aragonese (i.e. Catalan) from Castilian.[1] Yet this highly individual language, already the vehicle of one of the greatest national literatures in Europe, was not, and never fully came to be, an integral part of the perceived national identity.

The reasons for this are complex, but of fundamental importance to both the later history of Scots and its contemporary developments. During the Stewart period, Scots had developed into the principal language of government and administration, as well as literature, of an autonomous nation-state enjoying both a flourishing cultural life and full participation in the European network of diplomatic and commercial relations. It was not until 1494, however, that the practice of designating it *Scottis* in contradistinction to *Inglis* – until then the latter word had been used unquestioningly to refer to either of the two national languages or collectively to both – is first recorded, in a book "translatit out of fraynche in scottis" by Adam Loutfut. Shortly afterwards, a much greater and more influential writer, Gavin Douglas, made a special point of claiming that the language in which he wrote was *Scottis* and that *Inglis* was, like Latin and French, a foreign language on which he could draw

1. See P. Hume Brown, *Early Travellers in Scotland*, Edinburgh 1891.

3

for loan-words when it suited his purpose. With hindsight it is permissible to say that attitudes towards the Scots tongue were beginning to develop in a way that *might* – indeed, probably would – have led to its attaining the status of a national language: certainly, this was the time when it was best equipped to do so, being the period of its finest literary development and its highest social status, as well as the greatest degree of international importance that Scotland itself has ever achieved.[1]

But the nation, and with it the language, was catastrophically diverted from the course on which it had run in the fifteenth and early sixteenth centuries. The Reformation not only had the effect of flooding Scotland with English theological works and placing an English translation of the Bible in every Scottish household above a certain income level: it replaced France by England as Scotland's strongest political connection and principal cultural model among the European powers. There is no reason to believe that a deliberate policy of linguistic Anglicisation was pursued by the Reforming party; but their success in the religious and political spheres laid Scotland and the Scots tongue open to English influence, which very soon undermined the integrity of both. The loss of the monarchy and court ended the status of Scots as a vehicle for art poetry in the European tradition: this had flourished at the highly literary court of James VI, but his departure left a cultural vacuum at the heart of Scotland which was not to be filled until well after the Union of Parliaments. The seventeenth century – the period of the Covenanters' wars, the Cromwellian oppressions and the Killing Times – saw a steady decline in literary creativity in Scotland; the abolition of Parliament in 1707 led to the extinction of Scots as a language carrying social or political prestige. (Though derogatory statements from English commentators regarding the Scots speech of the new members of the "British" parliament are not to be taken at their face value, they unmistakably show that what had until then been the ruling class of Scotland still spoke Scots, and hence that the language had now ceased to be used for the operations of government.)

1. For a discussion of the concept of "Scottis" in the Stewart period see J. D. McClure, "Scottish, Inglis, Suddroun: Language Labels and Language Attitudes," in In Lyall, R. , and F. J. Riddy eds., *Proceedings of the Third International Conference on Scottish Language and Literature (Medieval and Renaissance), University of Stirling 2 – 7 July 1981*. Stirling and Glasgow: Stirling and Glasgow Universities 1982, 52 – 69, reprinted in *Scots and its Literature*, Amsterdam (Benjamins) 1995, 44 – 56.

Scots, that is, was prevented by the entire course of the nation's history after the Reformation from fulfilling its early potential of becoming the recognised national language of Scotland. (Gaelic had not been the language of the monarchy or government since the thirteenth century: even before the extinction of the Celtic royal line in 1286, the kings had taken ɔ affecting French as a court language.) And in the eighteenth century, when Scottish identity was a matter for intense, searching and painful debate, the potential of the language to serve as a focus for this was again only partly appreciated and fulfilled. Scotland east and south of the Highland Line was essentially a Scots-speaking community, though its more educated members *could* also speak English, until well into the present century; yet the language never, any more than in the Stewart period, came to be widely or consistently recognised as a symbol, still less as an essential component, of "Scottishness". On the contrary, a well-known feature of Scottish intellectual life in the eighteenth century was a strong revulsion against the tongue and a desire to replace it with the London-Oxford-Cambridge standard of literary English: a desire which its proponents saw as entirely compatible with an enduring belief in a Scottish national identity and profession of Scottish patriotic pride.

To regard this as paradoxical would betray a misconception. If such men as David Hume, James Boswell and James Beattie had perceived Scots as a *language* which bore the national name and thus formed an integral part of Scottish identity, it is inconceivable that they would have attempted to expunge it from their speech and writing. But they did not: such a conception had never, as we have seen, been generally held in Scotland; and was much less likely to arise in the intellectual context of the eighteenth century than it had been in the sixteenth. The vernacular speech of Scotland was perceived as being on a level with the provincial and low-class speech-forms of England: Hugh Mitchell in the title of his handbook refers to "Scotticisms, Vulgar Anglicisms, and Grammatical Improprieties" as if they were all of a piece. The feeling that "Scotticisms" were by their nature undesirable arose as a direct result of the influence on Scottish intellectual life of the language controversies of seventeenth- and eighteenth-century England.

The protracted struggle for the recognition of English as a literary language worthy of respect had long been won by the end of the Jacobean period; but its successful conclusion led to a further period of anxious debate on the standards of grammatical and stylistic propriety to which the language should adhere. Faced with the fact that English usages had visibly altered since Shakespeare's time and much more since Chaucer's, scholars and poets were assailed by the fear that their own form of the language would become unintelligible to posterity; and therefore directed their efforts towards refining the language and devising an authoritative grammar which would provide a permanent standard for future generations. An extreme concern for "purity" in language arose, marked by a spate of writings on prescriptive grammar; and the use of "barbarisms", "vulgarisms", "provincialisms" – however vaguely or erratically conceived – was seen as a solecism to be avoided at any cost in serious writing. This attitude, spreading to Scotland, led many people to perceive the entire vernacular speech of the non-Gaelic parts of the country as a mere "vulgar" or "provincial" dialect: something at the opposite end of the scale of respectability from a national language.

The revival of Scots as a vehicle for poetry, associated principally with the triumvirate of Allan Ramsay, Robert Fergusson and Robert Burns, was certainly in part the literary expression of a socio-political reaction to this fashionable disdain of the vernacular. Ramsay, the only one of the three who committed his thoughts on the Scots tongue to print, vigorously expressed his contempt for the snobbish attitude towards the language:

> There is nothing can be heard more silly than one's expressing his *Ignorance* of his *native Language*; yet such there are, who can vaunt of acquiring a tolerable Perfection in the *French* or *Italian* Tongues, if they have been a Forthnight in *Paris* or a Month in *Rome*: But shew them the most elegant Thoughts in a *Scots* Dress, they as disdainfully as stupidly condemn it as barbarous.[1]

– and elsewhere claimed that Scots was eminently well suited for poetry:

> But some Nations speak rough, and their Words are confounded with a Multitude of hard Consonants, which makes the Numbers unharmonious. Besides, their Language is scanty, which makes a disagreeable Repetition of the same Words. – These are no Defects in our's, the Pronunciation is

1. In the Preface to *The Ever Green*. See *The Works of Allan Ramsay* vol. 4, eds. A. M. Kinghorn and A. Law, Scottish Text Society Fourth Series vol. 6, Edinburgh (Blackwood) 1970, p. 237.

liquid and sonorous, and much fuller than the English. . .[1]

Manifestly, Ramsay's choice of Scots as his poetic medium was motivated in part by a fondness for the language, both in itself and as an expression of Scottish identity. Neither Fergusson nor Burns gave direct expression, as far as the records show, to his reasons for writing in Scots; but it is intuitively as clear as anything can be that both poets, as well as enjoying the sense of being "at home" in the language and of having in it a medium of enormous expressive power, found it an eminently appropriate vehicle for displaying their Scottish patriotic sentiments.

On the other hand, the use of Scots was at best only a part of the patriotic manifesto of the poets. Other features of Scotland and its culture, such as its landscape, dress, food, drink, music, folk customs, earlier literary achievements and history including antiquarian history, were regularly cited overtly or implicitly as grounds for national pride; and poetry using those as counters could be, and was, written in English as well as Scots. English was by now fully established as a language used in speech and writing by all classes of Scottish society (the level of general literacy in eighteenth-century Scotland was the highest in Europe): the desire proclaimed by some members of the *literati* to see Scots displaced entirely by English of course never became a reality, but all Scots (outwith the Gaidhealtachd) could read English and understand it when spoken, and many were entirely capable of speaking it when the occasion arose. William Burnes, father of the poet, was renowned for the quality of his English: in view of the dissimilarities between the dialects of his native Kincardineshire and the Ayrshire in which he lived from the age of twenty-nine, he may have found it useful even for everyday social converse with his neighbours. The benefits, indeed the necessity, of possessing English as well as Scots were well recognised: Ramsay, in the second passage quoted above, goes on to claim that his and his countrymen's full command of English as well as their native Scots is a great advantage in enriching their already copious linguistic resources. Furthermore, the *de facto* difference in status between Scots and English was clearly perceived, and no evidence suggests that it was questioned, as a fundamental fact,

1. In the Preface to his 1721 volume of poems. See *The Works of Allan Ramsay* vol. 1, eds. B. Martin and J. W. Oliver, Scottish Text Society Third Series vol. 19, Edinburgh (Blackwood) 1945, p. xix.

any more by the protagonists of Scots than by its detractors. The title of Burns's Kilmarnock Edition of 1786 is *Poems, Chiefly in the Scottish Dialect*; and this title was adopted by many other poets. A "dialect" was assumed to be, in some sense however nebulously understood, a lesser speech-form than a "language": this is still the implication of the word in popular usage; and it goes without saying that recent attempts to give it a scientific and non-judgmental definition based on objective facts – attempts which even now have not rescued the word and its application from controversy – were unknown to eighteenth-century thought. Scots was a fine poetic medium and a worthy and appropriate language in which to express patriotic feelings, but it was not *necessary* for either purpose; and the notion that it could be or become the national language of Scotland could no more have occurred to Robert Burns than to David Hume.

Expressions of Scottish patriotism on the linguistic or cultural plane, too, were almost entirely dissociated from active attempts to restore Scottish political autonomy. The development of Jacobitism as an aspect of Scottish identity had its effect, and in one sense a harmful one, on the status of the language. In the early years of the century, restoration of the Stewart monarchy (by armed force, since no other method was conceivable) was a realistic possibility; and repeal of the Union of Parliaments was a pledge made by the Old Pretender in exchange for Scottish support. The cause was widely popular in Scotland: Allan Ramsay in describing himself as a Jacobite was very much part of a general climate of opinion, and his poetry contains numerous references to the decline in Scotland's social, commercial and political life in the aftermath of the Union. However, he took no active part in the 1715 uprising (which occurred when he was about twenty years of age), nor indeed in any form of party-political activity. In the course of his long and prosperous life, his ideal appears to have changed from the recovery of Scottish independence under a restored Stewart monarchy to the revival of a vigorous and strongly national literary and intellectual culture in the context of renewed commercial prosperity: an ideal which was realised with unequivocal success, and to which his own contribution was of seminal importance.

By the middle of the century, the popular mood was very different. The failure of the Jacobite insurrection of 1745 – 6 had many causes, but a fundamental one was the simple belief that the possibility of political independence was not a sufficiently high stake for the risk of a dangerous and disruptive conflict. Burns, born thirteen years after Culloden, probably never regarded a Stewart restoration as a serious possibility: it is indeed difficult to imagine that he, a radical egalitarian whose calf-ground was a region with one of the strongest Covenanting and Presbyterian Whig traditions in Scotland, would actually have welcomed the prospect. Yet his ardent patriotism was stirred by the heroic aspect of the Jacobite uprising; and it was he who gave splendid inauguration to the literary association of Jacobitism with Scottish national sentiment. Many of the finest, most characteristic and most enduringly popular Scots poems and songs of the period, that is, were associated with a cause which, however dynamically alive as a focus for patriotic feeling and literary inspiration, was recognisably, and soon unmistakably, dead as a political issue.

In the Reformation period, spokesmen for the Roman Catholic church occasionally made a debating point out of the Anglicised language favoured by their opponents: much the best-known instance is the line in Ninian Winget's open letter to John Knox: "Gif ʒe, throw curiosity of novatiounis, hes forʒet our ald plane Scottis quhilk ʒour mother lerit ʒou, in times cuming I sall write to ʒou my mind in Latyn, for I am nocht acquent with ʒour Suddrone". To the extent that this had any effect at all on the status of the language, it may have been negative; since overt support of Scots was thus associated with the defeated party. It is not inconceivable that a much greater, more deliberate and more enduring association which the language acquired, namely with literary Jacobitism, was similarly in the long run a hindrance to its social and political development. Jacobite poems and songs continued to be written throughout the nineteenth and twentieth centuries: many are still popular today. From the first, they have varied in merit; but some are among the finest examples of song and lyric poetry ever produced in the Scots tongue. The positive side of this achievement is that it has contributed to the great corpus of literature in Scots, and helped to ensure the unstinting productivity of the language as a poetic medium; the negative, that it has perpetuated a deep-seated linkage between Scots and a romantic, nostalgic, backward-looking view of the nation and its history. Walter Scott, too, though his achievements in the use of Scots for dialogue and for characterisation are unsurpassed, almost invariably associated it either with the lower orders of society or with the relicts of a passing historical period: a classic instance is *The Bride of Lammermuir*, where the conflict between the dispossessed Ravenswoods and the upstart Ashtons is symbolised by the fact that it is the old retainers and tenants of the Ravenswoods, fiercely and doggedly loyal to a doomed family with only memories to sustain them in the new political order, who express themselves in Scots. And Scott, albeit the staunchest of defenders of Scotland's cultural traditions, never advocated the restoration of political independence.

Nor did this again become a major cause for decades: it was not until 1888 that Scottish Home Rule was adopted as the policy of the Liberal Party; and not until 1927 that the Scottish Nationalist Party (forerunner of the present Scottish National Party (SNP)) came into being. One of the mainsprings of the entire historical development of Europe in the nineteenth century is the growth of nationalism: the search of peoples with a common ethnic or (often associated with the latter, or erroneously equated with it) linguistic identity for a politically-defined territory in which they could govern themselves as autonomous peoples. Nationalism led to the creation of the German and Italian states, and to the destruction of the multi-racial Austro-Hungarian and Ottoman Empires. Scotland presented a very different picture. A sense of national identity existed, though becoming visibly more uncertain in the course of the nineteenth century. The Scots language, too, continued as the mother tongue and the normal means of communication in Eastern and Southern Scotland: remarks on its decline and gradual replacement by English were regularly made and no doubt with some warrant, since the belief that "speaking proper" was necessary in order to further oneself socially was by now a tenet of popular thought; but the lower orders still habitually conversed in Scots, and it is not to be imagined that the local ministers, doctors and schoolmasters would be unable, or unwilling, to use it in conversation with those whom they served. Yet there is very little evidence in Scotland of the militant desire for national independence shown by, say, the Hungarians, Poles or Serbs; and none whatsoever of the common European linkage between language and nationalism. Scottish patriotic sentiment continued, ever more nostalgically, to be associated with romantic Jacobitism; and the Scots language as a literary vehicle with this and also with celebrations of a traditional rural life which was itself rapidly vanishing with nineteenth-century urbanisation and industrialisation.

The concern of the present study is to examine Scots as a language for poetry in the later nineteenth and twentieth centuries. What will emerge is that the development of a more careful attention to the nature and the appropriate poetic functions of the language, and a clearer awareness of the political implications of its use, led to an enormous widening of the range of Scots, both internally by a vastly more creative and imaginative use of its linguistic resources than had characterised most nineteenth-century poetry, and externally by a challenging and deliberately iconoclastic approach to its potential range of topics and functions. It will also become clear that, for the first time in Scotland's cultural history, an overt linkage was made between linguistic and political nationalism: the writing of Scots, in the past (as with Ramsay or Burns) at best a defiant proclamation of an enduring cultural distinctiveness, now became both a symbolic expression of and a weapon in the struggle for Scottish independence. This linkage, however, has remained essentially a literary phenomenon: the political nationalist movement, represented in our time by the SNP, has made very little attempt to exploit the language and its associated literary culture as a focus for nationalist aspirations – and very little attempt, for that matter, to develop a language policy at all as an important part of its political manifesto; a failure (for such it clearly is) for which reasons could be found in entrenched cultural and educational traditions. The political aspect of writing in Scots, too, rapidly developed a variety of ramifications; and the association of Scots with radical socialism as well as nationalism, and later with a socialism which overtly intersected and to an extent conflicted with nationalism – with a class struggle within Scotland itself, as demonstrated by the emergence of a literary form of Scots based on socially marked urban dialects – will be examined and discussed.

The reasons for these developments are various, and with at first sight no obvious linkage between them: the rise of modernism in literature, and the harnessing in other countries (particularly Ireland) of new literary techniques to political causes; the growth in Scotland, as elsewhere in Europe, of interest in dialectology as a scientific study; the increasingly

11

urgent sense that the dialects, with their associated cultures, were in decline and that some attempt to preserve them, in literary and scholarly records if not as community languages, was called for; the developing political voice of the urban working class and the rise of socialism as a doctrine; the growing evidence of Scotland's economically and socially disadvantaged state, particularly in the years following the First World War. However, in the last analysis the contributions of individuals is of irreducible importance. The central figure in the story of recent Scots poetry is Hugh MacDiarmid, a fact which by now requires no special demonstration; but if the amount of space devoted to him in this book is somewhat less than expected, it is not only because a respectable number of scholarly studies of him, his work and his influence are already in existence: it is also because, firstly, his achievements in the linguistic and the literary fields are based on ground prepared by predecessors whose contribution has not been sufficiently emphasised; and secondly, the poets in the extraordinary group who wrote under his direct influence have not, either individually or collectively, fully emerged from his shadow. Even relatively minor poets like Logie Robertson, Pittendrigh Macgillivray and Lewis Spence deserve better than to be remembered (if at all) only as faint stirrings of the breeze which grew into MacDiarmid's storm-voice; and outstanding poets like Sydney Goodsir Smith, Robert Garioch, Alastair Mackie, Tom Scott and Alexander Scott assuredly deserve the degree of serious scholarly and critical attention that any other country would accede to writers of such calibre.

Scots poetry over the last hundred years has developed in ways which would have been wholly unpredictable at the beginning of the period: it is unlikely that any prophet performing in the 1890s or 1900s would even have foreseen that Scots as a poetic language, or as a community language, would by the end of the century still have been in existence at all. A ground-breaking critical study first published in 1898, *Scottish Vernacular Literature: a Succinct History*, by T. F. Henderson, ends elegiacally:

> His [Burns's] death was really the setting of the sun; the twilight deepened very quickly; and such twinkling lights as now and then appear only serve to disclose the darkness of the all-encompassing night.[1]

1. London (Nutt), p. 458.

Yet far from fading quietly into oblivion, Scots as a poetic language took on an astonishing new lease of life. And as one of the most remarkable, and most distinguished, centuries in the history of Scots poetry reaches its close, it is a fitting time to offer an assessment of the linguistic medium and the developments which it has undergone.

2

The Scots 'Language'?

The view of Scots tacitly assumed in the last chapter, that it is in some sense at least a "language", clearly requires to be examined. And the first point which must be understood is this: the word "language" as a count noun (as in "the Russian language" or "How many languages can you speak?") has no straightforward definition; and the concept of a language is not simple but complex and highly elusive. The idea that Scots is a language just as English is a language, and therefore that Lowland Scottish writers may choose between English and Scots as those from the Gaidhealtachd may choose between English and Gaelic, has come to be held as something like a dogma in literary circles and has even generated its own largely factitious reality; yet in the light of academic linguistics it is scarcely warranted.

To arrive at a clearer understanding of the status of Scots as a "language" it is helpful to consider something which is unequivocally and by universal agreement a "language": any of the great world languages such as English, French, German, Arabic, Hindi or Mandarin Chinese. The properties of a speech form in that list include the following:

1. It has a "standard" form with a canonical set of rules for grammar and spelling, used for nearly all writing and as a learning model for foreigners.

2. It is, in its "standard" form at least, mutually unintelligible with any other spoken tongue.

3. It is the normal, everyday speech of a living and functioning community.

4. Its speakers (that is, those of the "standard") regard themselves as using a tongue with its own accepted conventions of "proper" usage and not requiring to be modified according to the standards of any other speech form.

5. It has a tradition of use in all branches of literature, developed over centuries and by now including a corpus of enormous size, range and quality.

6. It is also used in writing for purposes other than literature: it has practical, utilitarian functions.

7. It is the official language of at least one politically-defined, autonomous territory.

As is at once evident, these statements refer to different aspects of a speech-form. The first two are *linguistic*: observations regarding the language itself and describing its state of development as a structured code functioning as a means of communication. The third and fourth are *socio-linguistic*: they state facts pertaining not to the language but to the *users* of the language. The fifth and sixth are *cultural*, referring to the part played by the language in the formation of the distinctive achievement of its community of speakers. The last is *political*, referring to a status bestowed on a language as a result of decisions made in a field wholly external to its structure and cultural functions. Yet they are, in the last analysis, mutually inseparable; for not only has a language no existence apart from the people who use it, but the use of language is integral to all human activity. And since the speech of an individual, like that of a community, is a fundamental and intimate aspect of his entire being, the emotions associated with a speech form, in the minds of those who speak it and of those who do not, are *facts* with which any discussion of the speech form, and still more any practical attempt to alter it in any of its aspects, must necessarily be concerned. (The attitudes of "those who speak it and those who do not" may be a factor of great importance if a well-defined set of representatives of the second group are in direct conflict with those of the first.)

The question of how many languages there are in the world is often asked; and the estimated number is invariably given as being in the thousands. Yet if we ask instead how many languages can be found which possess all the properties listed here, the answer will not be a few thousands, but a few *tens*. Most of the world's spoken tongues have never been put into written form; if we consider all those which existed between the emergence of human language and the development of writing (a number impossible to estimate), the proportion of written to non-written languages is very much further reduced. Mutual intelligibility is a matter of degree and is inevitably subjective, but it is true that a native speaker (or even a proficient learner) of Italian can understand at sight, or at first hearing, the essential meaning of a text in Spanish, and vice versa; and the same is true of Norwegian (Riksmål) and Danish, Polish, Czech and Slovak, and numerous other pairs or sets of speech-forms conventionally identified as "languages". The third feature is absent in the case of artificial "languages" such as Esperanto and effectually extinct "languages" revived for cultural purposes such as Cornish. The fourth, known as "autonomy", is characteristically found in languages with canonical standard forms and accepted official status, and also in some which lack any written form but exist as the normal and unchallenged medium of conversation for the members of a community: the set of speech forms which lack it are those which are close enough to a standard language to be readily assimilable to it, and of which the speakers find themselves to be under some social pressure to adopt the standard language in place of their own. The Italian peninsula alone furnishes numerous examples – Friulian, Ligurian, Piedmontese, Neapolitan, Calabrese, Abruzzese – and this factor is particularly relevant in the case of Scots. Even among "languages" with long-established written forms, by no means all have been developed as vehicles for literature other than oral literature: a noteworthy example is Basque: and the case is by no means unknown of "languages"[1] with highly-developed literary traditions but virtually no application in non-literary writings. Finally, there are hundreds, if not thousands, of tribal or regional "languages" in such places as Africa, South America, the Indian sub-continent and Indonesia of which the domains have no political definition, and the speech community no official recognition whatsoever.

Applying those criteria in turn to Scots, the result would be, in summary:

1: *no*; 2: *doubtfully yes*; 3: *with reservations, yes*; 4: *no*; 5: *yes*; 6: *no*; 7: *no*.

That is, with slightly more elaboration: Scots has no canonical standard written form, though it has a set (or several distinct sets) of conventions

---

1. The quotation marks are not intended to suggest that the tongues referred to are not entitled to claim the status of "languages", but merely to emphasise the lack of a precise meaning or set of implications associated with the word.

from which individual writers may select more or less as they choose; some of its forms at least would undoubtedly present serious difficulties of comprehension to a monolingual English-speaker (and of course there is no other language with which it has even a remote degree of mutual intelligibility); there certainly are still communities where some form of Scots is the normal means of social interaction; even its most accomplished speakers are now not only able to speak English but unquestioningly accept that on some social occasions English, or something more like it than their habitual speech, is what they *should* endeavour to speak; it assuredly has a literature surpassing those of many small languages with a greater degree of recognition; it is *not* used for any practical written purpose (such things as the postings of the Scots Language Society informing members of forthcoming events, which are written in Scots, do not controvert this statement: the practical function of these notices is in no way furthered by the language); and it has absolutely *no* official status. Interestingly enough, if the criteria were applied to Scots in the mediaeval period, when it had reached a level of development from which it could make a much more credible claim than at present to "full" language status, the results would be more conclusive: the first cannot be applied, as no living vernacular was fully standardised in the fifteenth or sixteenth century (though Scots was as near to it as most); but for the others, we would find:

2: *doubtfully, yes*; 3: *yes*; 4: *almost certainly, yes*; 5: *yes*; 6: *yes*; 7: *yes*.

Clearly, therefore, Scots is (so to speak) less of a language now than it was in the Stewart period; on the other hand, it is very much *more* of a language than numerous speech forms which have not been the focus of the same amount of literary and political activity. A failure to appreciate this elementary fact, that the status of a tongue is not a simple "language or dialect" choice but is dependent on a large number of factors both internal and external to the tongue itself, is the reason for the repetitiveness, and also the vacuity, of the discussions (which continue to the present day) of the status of Scots.

Language is a human function, and the status of languages can be changed by human effort. Examples abound of periods in the cultural history of a language when a great literary efflorescence and a powerful growth of patriotic feeling, of which one manifestation may be political nationalism, are so closely interrelated as to be in fact aspects of the same development: one of the clearest and most spectacular instances in European history is the emergence of German in the late eighteenth and nineteenth centuries. In such cases, the language is emancipated from a position of social and cultural inferiority (in the case of German, this was due to the overwhelming dominance of French) to acquire both an extension and enhancement of its range of uses and a position of greater dignity in the eyes of its own speakers and the international community. One of the central aims of the poets of the Scottish Renaissance was to achieve such an emancipation for Scots: to restore the Scots tongue (as they saw the situation) to its rightful place as a national language. This aim was perceived as an integral part of the greater goal of restoring Scotland to a state of full political, intellectual, and cultural autonomy. In examining this movement as a historical phenomenon, the relevant question is not whether or to what extent Scots had in reality ever held the status of a national language, nor whether or to what extent the Scots tongue had ever been a mark of Scottish national identity: it is, rather, what did the poets perceive as unsatisfactory in the existing state of Scotland and the Scots tongue, and how did the results of their efforts to improve it measure against what *could*, under the circumstances, have been achieved?

That Scots should have been seen as in need of such a recovery is not surprising. Its social prestige, declining since at least the eighteenth century, had received a further blow from the 1872 Education Act, which replaced the parish schools established at the time of the Reformation with a uniform, centrally-directed system in which great emphasis was placed on speaking "properly" – that is, speaking standard English. Many accounts testify to the fact that children could be, and often were, punished for using Scots words in the classroom: a situation which prevailed until at least the middle of the present century. The entire ethos of the school system was inimical to the active use of Scots (and of Gaelic), though token attention was paid to the poetry of Burns and occasionally other exponents of Scots in literature. Scots as a vehicle for poetry had remained productive, and (as will be examined in the next four chapters) poetry of a much higher quality than is sometimes acknowledged was being written in the late nineteenth and early twentieth centuries; but the low social prestige of Scots – which by now amounted to a complete loss of recognition of the tongue itself, Scots being regarded as "bad English" by the teaching profession and (as a result) by the wider community – was a factor obviously antipathetic to any attempt at developing its cultural or political importance. The contrast between the status and importance of Scots in the early twentieth century and in the early sixteenth could not fail to arouse in any informed observer, at the very least, a sense of sad and shameful deterioration: there is indeed a case for interpreting the disgraceful neglect of the Scots literary heritage in the education system, and the general failure to recognise the living tongue as "Scots", as, at some level, mechanisms for defence against so painful a reaction.

The "Scottish Renaissance" which began in the 1920s was a literary movement: its links to developments in the Scottish political field, particularly the growth of demands for Home Rule, were at best tenuous. Even though C. M. Grieve and many of his successors in the poetic sphere were at times active in politics, neither then nor ever since have events in Scotland afforded any comparison with the activities which gave rise at the same time to a German literature and a German national spirit; and Scotland in the present era has produced no Vaclav Havel or Zviad Gamsakhurdia. And poets, working in that capacity, clearly cannot (for example) legislate for official recognition of a language, compel its use in education or in any other field, or initiate a language-planning programme with any status other than that of an academic exercise. What they *can* do is extend and develop the use of the language as a poetic medium: a proceeding which, if the social and educational climate is propitious, *may* lead to a greater degree of respect being accorded to the language and thence to an increased desire for a formally-recognised enhancement of its status.

To this extent, there can be no doubt that the Scottish Renaissance achieved not only all that could be realistically expected, but incomparably more than any observer in 1922 – the year when Grieve in his flagship periodical *Scottish Chapbook* first elevated his linguistic and cultural aspirations for Scots to the status of a manifesto – could possibly have anticipated. The scope of Scots *as a language for poetry* has been widened enormously: a contemporary writer such as Tom Hubbard has, in an absolute sense, a medium of greater expressive potential at his disposal than had, say, Violet Jacob; and this is true notwithstanding the fact that Hubbard's native-speaker competence in Scots is of necessity (given the inexorable decline in the demographic strength, social status and fields of use of Scots) slighter than was hers. By unearthing the enormous store of almost or completely forgotten words from moribund spoken dialects and from earlier phases in the history of the written language, by re-establishing a vital link between the literature of the present and that of the Stewart period, and by restoring to Scots the ability to grow and regenerate itself from within by creative use of its existing lexical and grammatical resources, the poets of the present century have successfully challenged the tacit assumption on which nearly all Scots writing since the seventeenth century had been based: namely, that the tongue in its written form can only reflect the linguistic resources and the social and cultural status of whatever spoken form an individual poet chooses to use.

In another respect, that of mutual intelligibility with English, the poets of the Scottish Renaissance have also brought about a change, though perhaps a superficial one, in the status of the language. The natural process of historical language development had given rise to the familiar situation of a number of spoken dialects, mutually differentiated most importantly by phonology but also to a large extent by vocabulary and much less significantly by grammar; all recognisably Scots and sharing many features by which they were collectively differentiated from standard literary English. The most widely-used written form of the language, for much of the nineteenth century, was in effect a continuation of the linguistic register associated with Burns; and as no writer of Scots poetry for decades after his death came near to matching his intellectual keenness or linguistic inventiveness, the medium became relatively enfeebled and limited. An Anglophone reader with no previous experience of Scots could, one may assume, given a moderate amount of application and goodwill, read and even appreciate the poetry of (say) Logie Robertson with little difficulty. Developments which had occurred before the Renaissance, such as the poetic use of strongly-marked dialects and of quasi-archaic language, certainly increased the distance between some registers of literary Scots and standard literary English; but by vastly augmenting the word-stock of Scots available for poetic purposes, Grieve and his successors ensured that not only readers accustomed only to English but even those accustomed to traditional literary Scots would require far more frequent recourse to glossaries and reference works in order to understand their writings. There is no doubt, in fact, that a deliberate attempt to differentiate their vocabulary to the greatest extent possible from that of standard literary English has been part of the technique of many writers in the present century. This practice is open to criticism from several points of view; but it should be noted that a very similar procedure has been followed in several cases of officially-directed language planning: a frequently-cited example is Nynorsk, deliberately distanced from Danish by the replacement of many words of German or French origin by forms derived from Old Norse roots; another is Greek, which in the period following independence was affected by a "puristic" movement aimed at reducing the foreign, particularly Turkish, element in the vocabulary and replacing it with forms derived from the classical language. On another level, attempts (which will be discussed in later chapters) at devising for Scots an orthography, or at least a set of orthographic guidelines, to make the written language both more consistent and more distinctive, have also lessened its apparent similarity to standard literary English.

Furthermore, though poets cannot directly change the political status of their linguistic medium, they may bring the political implications of its use more forcefully into popular awareness. Any use of a non-standard speech-form for literature in a community generally literate in the standard has inescapable socio-political overtones, in that it amounts to an assertion that the dominance of the standard is not complete. However, a non-standard form may have an accepted, if restricted, place in the life of the community, and may be used for literature in a sphere which does not exceed the limitations on the range of social and cultural functions assigned to the tongue itself. This was, roughly speaking, true of Scots in the period from the death of Burns to the Scottish Renaissance: much poetry, including some of high distinction, was produced in the tongue; but the range of topics, genres and poetic forms had become circumscribed, and the connection of Scots with (at best) an unchanging, unenterprising, tradition-bound mode of life was manifest. The association between "speaking proper" and "getting on" – that is, between abandoning Scots for English and making a dynamic change for what was seen as the "better" in an individual's socio-economic position – was so deeply entrenched as to be virtually unquestioned: Scots, though it might be regarded with affection both in itself and as recalling or symbolising a friendly, familiar way of life, carried the inferiority of a backwater culture resistant to social progress. There was no inherent instability in this situation: after all, many people did in fact remain within the conservative Scots-speaking communities, and the popularity of the Scots poetry being written until and beyond the Renaissance period is sound evidence that the nostalgic appeal of the traditional life was great even among those who had left it. However, a major change in the status of Scots occurred when Grieve and his successors insisted on the association of Scots with, not a socially restricted section of the Scottish nation, but the nation itself; and began to use the language as a counter in arguments on Scotland's actual and desired political status. Grieve's vituperative (and utterly misjudged) attack on Charles Murray's medium – "His particular dialect is perhaps the poorest of them all and certainly the least capable of being used to genuine poetic purpose ... Aberdeenshire Scots is certainly the reverse of 'pure': *anything further from the conceivable norm* – anything more corrupt – it would be difficult to find in any dialect of any tongue"[1] – is simply absurd if taken as a comment on it as language; but the real reason for Grieve's hostility is revealed in the italicised phrase: Murray's Scots could not serve as a *national* language because it was so firmly based on a specific local dialect. The Renaissance poets revolutionised the political status of Scots, and the political implications of its use in literature: not by *making* it the national language of Scotland, which obviously they neither have done nor could have done, but by the mere fact of raising the possibility that it could and should be this, and thus engendering a controversy which has remained active to the present day.

If we return to the properties which qualify a speech form as a "language" and consider whether the status of Scots has been altered as a

---

1. In *Contemporary Scottish Studies, Scottish Educational Journal* 10th July 1925; p. 7 of 1975 edition.

result of the literary Renaissance, we may conclude that though there is no case of a *no* having been changed to a *yes*, in some cases Scots is at least *nearer* to the described state than it was in the 1900s, and in others a simple unquestioned negative has given place to an ongoing discussion of what might or could be the case. If there is still no canonical standard form, vigorous efforts have been made to devise one, and the possibility and desirability of one have been, and still are, argued with energy and lucidity; there are now registers of Scots which are much more unlike any form of English than were to be found before the Renaissance; the literary development of Scots, already outstanding, has been still further enhanced; its status as an official national language, though certainly not established, is at least imagined. However, a grave objection can be raised to this seeming record of impressive achievement; and it is that while *literary* Scots has, in respect of its linguistic development, its political importance and its cultural and academic prestige, progressed apace, *spoken* Scots – Scots as the living mother-tongue of an organic community – has continued to decline; and, as a corollary, the written form, in some registers at least, has diverged so radically from any spoken form (past or present) as to have virtually ceased to be the same tongue. The very common reaction of readers who can respond with warm enthusiasm to a writer whose medium is closely related to a living dialect, such as Flora Garry, but feel puzzlement and irritation at the "artificial" Scots of a writer such as Alexander Scott, is adequate testimony to the force of this objection.

The sociolinguistic history and the present state of spoken Scots are not, except incidentally, the concern of this book, which is a study of Scots as a literary medium. It may be noted that recent developments in fields other than that of literature give grounds for a much greater degree of hope in the future of Scots as a community language than seemed possible even ten years ago: the greatly increased attention now being given to Scots speech and writing in the primary and secondary education system, and the growing number and improving quality of writings on and in Scots designed for school use; the recognition of Scots by the European Bureau for Lesser-Used Languages; the campaign, active at the time of writing, to have a question on Scots included in the Census. It can certainly be claimed that, given the conspicuous lack of interest among the political parties in promoting Scots, these initiatives have been impelled at least in part by the qualitatively and quantitatively extraordinary achievement of recent Scots literature. However, the most comprehensive answer to the objection outlined in the preceding paragraph is the following. No written language is a simple reflection of the spoken form from which it is derived, and a mature written language is an autonomous medium: the process of a language's development to full literary maturity is precisely that of finding functions and applications, and devising appropriate modes of expression, distinct and independent from those of speech. At the outset of the modern period in literature throughout Europe, written language virtually parted company with previously-established conventions of grammar and idiom, to an extent inconceivable for spoken language: if the language of *A Drunk Man Looks at the Thistle* or *Under the Eildon Tree* is remote from any form of spoken Scots, that of *The Wreck of the Deutschland* (let alone *Finnegans Wake*) is, quite obviously, very much more remote from any form of spoken English. And the experimental, innovative use of language is simply part of creative writing: any writer may experiment, and run the risk of his experiments being unsuccessful. In the case of the Scots Renaissance poets, their experiments were, as literature, highly successful: they resulted in a challenging, stimulating and linguistically inventive poetry which vastly increased the scope of their medium. They also had, as the poets intended, far-reaching effects in a field other than literature, namely politics: writing (this is uniformly true) as political and cultural nationalists and insistently emphasising the political implications of their use of Scots, they made the language the focus of controversies of which the final results have yet to be seen. But fundamentally, their achievement was with Scots. Mary Symon's medium and Robert Crawford's are registers of the same language, even though Crawford's register was no more available to Symon than T. S. Eliot's was to Christina Georgina Rossetti.

Scots categorically does not qualify from all points of view as a "language". Yet as a medium for poetry, it has attained in the twentieth century a peak of development far surpassing those of many tongues whose claim to that status might seem more soundly based. The nature of, and the reasons for, this remarkable development will occupy our attention in the following chapters.

3

The Curtain Rises:
Logie Robertson and Robert Louis Stevenson

In 1777, the Aberdeenshire poet Charles Keith wrote *An Address in Scotch upon the Decay of that Language*, lamenting the fact that the people of Scotland are gradually abandoning their mother tongue for English.[1] Though his poem ends with a tribute to the citizens of his home town, whom he exempts from his general strictures –

> On gentle fowk o' Aiberdeen
> I cast nae blots,
> For lads and lassies there, I ween,
> Speak guid braid Scots

– his anger, as well as despondency, at the gradual erosion of Scotland's linguistic distinctiveness is forcefully expressed. Yet a century later, in 1878, J. Logie Robertson published a collection of poems[2] including *On the Decadence of the Scots Language, Manners and Customs*: evidence of a somewhat amusing nature that the language had survived. Nonetheless, Robertson's poem, whatever its defects as literature (it is monotonous in its prosody and for the most part banal in its rhymes, the tone of un-relieved lamentation becomes more than a little wearing, the Scots component in the language is at times attenuated to vanishing point), embodies an accurate and comprehensive summary of social develop-ments which were indeed affecting the Scots-speaking communities, with inescapable effects on the language and its status. The absorption of small farms into large estates made many crofters homeless and reduced the social and economic status of those who remained; the growth of capitalist industrialism encouraged large-scale migration from the coun-

1. The poem was written as a prelude to Andrew Shirrefs's pastoral play *Jamie and Bess*, and is included in Shirrefs's *Poems Chiefly in the Scottish Dialect*, Edinburgh 1790, pp.xxiv-xxvii.
2. *Poems*, Dundee (John Leng & Co.).

tryside to the cities, with consequent depopulation of the village communities and disintegration of their social structures; the weakening of cross-generational links led to a decline of traditional components of folk-culture such as singing and story-telling; the advent of railways not only polluted the landscape but formed a new and unpleasant intrusion on the lives of the country people. Robertson does not emphasise (and perhaps did not fully recognise) the connection between these developments and the decline of the language, which he laments as if it were a separate issue: Scots was the language of an organic community and of its individual culture; and as that community was eroded, the language too suffered attrition.

Robertson refers, seemingly as a sign of hope, to the enduring popularity of Scots poetry:

> It lives in Freedom-Barbour's lines,
> In bauld Dunbar it brichtly shines,
> On Lyndsay's page like licht it streams,
> In Border scraps it fitful gleams,
> An' like the shimmerin' spunkie strays
> By Ettrick banks an' Yarrow braes.
> It lives for aye in Allan's play,
> In Coila's sangs, the Shepherd's lay,
> The bird-like lilts fra' Paisley side,
> The Wizart's tales that flew sae wide,
> Forbye the vast an' various lore
> O' later ballants by the score...
>
> (*Poems, op. cit.*, pp.47 – 8)

The references in lines 7 – 10 of this extract are to Allan Ramsay, Robert Burns, James Hogg, Robert Tannahill and Alexander Wilson ("Paisley's twa", as he styles them in another poem), and Sir Walter Scott. The four last, however, died in 1835, 1810, 1813 and 1832 respectively, and it is noteworthy that Robertson makes no individual reference to Scots writers from nearer his own time. The simple fact, whether or not this was his reason, is that scarcely any of them deserve to be mentioned in the company of Wilson or Tannahill – let alone the other four. For most of the nineteenth century, the Scots poetic scene was dominated by a school now inseparably associated with the title of a poetic anthology, first published in 1832 and frequently revised and reprinted: *Whistle-Binkie*.

Despite the derogatory overtones which this term has acquired through its association with one of the most depressing phases in the national literary history (and perhaps also, though only accidentally and *post hoc*, through the phonaesthetic suggestions of coyness and triviality which the name is liable to evoke), it may be observed that "whistle-binkie" not only has a perfectly straightforward meaning but embodies the succinctness and the inventiveness to which the Scots tongue invites its users. As an introductory "Dissertation on whistle-binkies" in the 1878 edition has it, "the name was first conferred on one who, in his attendance upon weddings and other convivial occasions, rendered himself so agreeable to the company by his skill in whistling, that he was allowed to sit at the Bink or board, and partake of the good things free of all expense[.]" (Vol.1, pp.71–2) *Whistle-Binkie, or, The Piper of the Party* was the collection's full title; and it was, in intention, a collection of lyrics suitable for singing or reciting at social gatherings: *refined* social gatherings, for whose members the comment of the editor (John Donald Carrick) "...we have been particularly careful in excluding all pieces of an indelicate or immoral description..." would have been greatly reassuring. This concern for propriety evidently extended to anything which could be regarded as conducive to intellectual stimulation, let alone social or political unorthodoxy or subversion: the *Whistle-Binkie* anthologies are monuments to unimaginative, unadventurous literary and artistic sterility. Many of the songs are eminently singable, no doubt; an occasional lyric rises above the average level of the volume to be genuinely clever and amusing; and once or twice a note of political protest makes itself faintly heard, as in *The Toom Meal-Pock*:[1]

> Tell them ye're wearied o' the chain
>   That hauds the state thegither,
> For Scotland wishes just to tak'
>   Gude nicht wi' ane anither!
>
>   (p.136)

– though this poem, according to the Editor, was written circa 1793, well before the period of the book. Scots is the language of many of the poems, and it cannot be denied that a measure of vitality and linguistic

---

1. Quotations are from the 1878 edition: Glasgow (David Robertson & Co.)

27

ingenuity can occasionally be observed:

> Sic smashin' and chappin' was a' round about,
>   Sic clankin', sic rattlin' an' din;
> Wi' rocks blawn like thunder frae quarries without,
>   And smiddies an' reeshlin' within;
> And wheelbarrows drivin' a' hours of the day,
>   Wi' Eerishmen swearin' like Turks;
> And horses were fechtin' wi' cartfu's o' clay,
>   And plaister and stanes for the works.

> (p.360)

However, what *Whistle-Binkie* offers for the most part is a domesticated Scots: the devitalised language of a people drained of confidence, and making of a specious and manufactured charm, humour and sentimentality a substitute, or a debased token, for a cultural identity. Confidence, that is, in the native language and its value as a mark of nationality. In other respects, confidence abounded, in the economic and industrial developments of Scotland's Victorian age; but a nation which was capable of doing nothing more worthy with the language of Burns, Scott, Hogg and Galt than *Whistle-Binkie* was not in a healthy state.

The Scots tongue as a poetic medium had, to all appearances, come to be inseparably associated with the trivial and banal: a situation, admittedly, to Robertson's advantage, since his own moderate talents as a writer of Scots earned him a reputation which against stronger competition he would scarcely have deserved. Nonetheless, as a popular and capable Scots poet for whom the language was a deliberate aspect of his literary persona, writing when the status of Scots was at a critical stage in its historical development, his linguistic practices require some attention. Robertson's patriotic spirit is manifest in his writings: expressions of love for Scotland abound, a notable example being in *On the Decadence of the Scots Language, Manners and Customs*, referring to crofters who have lately been dispossessed:

> Tho' short his boonds, an' small his gain,
> A BIT O' SCOTLAND was his ain.

> (*Ibid.*, p.49)

It is also clear that Robertson's view of Scots poetry, and of poetry in general, was serious and committed. His advocacy of a more than token

degree of attention to Scottish culture, including literature, in the education system still has relevance today. The posturings of his persona
"Hughie",[1] with his Shakespearean confidence in the immortality of his
verse, are hardly likely to represent Robertson's own estimate of his
poetry:

In vain the future snaps his fangs,
The tyke may rage – he canna wrang's,
I put my haund upon my sangs
    Withoot a swither;
To me this monument belangs,
    I need nae ither.

(*Hughie's Monument*, in *Horace, op. cit.,* p. 44)

– but the poem *Echoes,* if taken as an actual expression of the writer's
sentiments, suggests in language of peculiar intensity his awareness of
the greatness of Scots writing in the past and his desire to meet the
responsibility of his heritage:

'Tis the clamorous Voice of the Past I hear,
    The Sounds of a World gone by, –
The noble speech, and the poem clear,
    And the deed divinely high.
All down the ante-rooms of Time
    They stream and gather and roll;
And with hopes to which I may never climb
    Their echoes vex my soul.
I know that a music of my own
    Their terror-tones might lay,
But what can I, with the wish alone
    To do or sing or say?

(*Poems, op. cit.,* pp.156–7)

However, Robertson's response to these promptings, though far from
contemptible, cannot be described as ambitious or enterprising. His most
important collection of Scots poetry is *Horace in Homespun,* published
under the name of the fictitious speaker of the poems, "Hugh
Haliburton, shepherd of the Ochils", whom Robertson introduces in a
Preface using his own name. In the introduction to the Glossary, he

---

1. *Horace in Homespun: A Series of Scottish Pastorals.* By Hugh Haliburton, Shepherd of the
Ochils, with Preface, Notes and Glossary by J. Logie Robertson, M. A. Edinburgh (William
Paterson).

describes his Scots as "that variety of the Scottish language which is still in vigorous use among the regular inhabitants of the Ochils". In fact, however, there is very little of a local nature in his vocabulary: most of the words he uses could indeed be heard among the Ochil Hills, but also and with equal frequency in any other part of the Lowlands and Borders. Attempting to maintain verisimilitude, Robertson points out (credibly enough) that internal migration, or the influence of literature, might lead to words originating in one part of Scotland being heard in another: "Into this speech words and phrases, which are commonly regarded as peculiar to other districts of the country, may have been imported – in a perfectly natural way. ... Burns, and in a less degree Scott and Wilson,[1] not to mention inferior writers, have enriched and, to a great extent, assimilated the various Scottish dialects". He mentions *callan* as a word which might have been brought from the Borders to the Ochils; though as in his poetry it is used only to rhyme with *Allan*, a device found more than once in poetic tributes to Allan Ramsay, its presence is probably evidence of literary rather than dialectal influence. But his explanation is, in the context of his poetry, really unnecessary: his vocabulary is simply common-core Scots, with very few exceptions: *caulker* (drink of whisky – mostly East and North-East), *gibbles* (tools – similar), and *sprog* (sparrow – as opposed to *speug, spurdie, spurgie*, etc. – restricted to either side of the Tay) account for them all. His Glossary contains some words relating to farming or country life: *feerin'* ("measurement of the rigs, preparatory to ploughing"); *leglen* ("a milk pail with a straight handle"); *nowte* (cattle); several to drink: *greybeard, jorum, tappit-hen, mutchkin* (different measures or vessels); *peat-reek* (a nickname for whisky); *heilant horn* (an expression for a larger glass); some – but very few, considering "Hughie's" frequently-professed love of the Scottish countryside – for trees, plants and birds: *rowan, whin-blume, whaup* (curlew), *lintie* (linnet); a couple for traditional customs: *guizer* ("masquerader (at Hogmanay)"), *broose* ("race (at country weddings)"); but apart from that the words are simply those for life's basic appurtenances and functions.

Like many Scots-writing poets, Robertson frequently lapses into

---

1. Probably Alexander Wilson of Paisley (1766–1813), weaver, packman, traveller and author of an impressive work, *American Ornithology*, as well as a corpus of poetry including some in vigorous if unsubtle Scots.

English: a device which Burns, for example, often applies deliberately for artistic effect; but for which in Robertson the fundamental reason is probably the limited and unadventurous nature of his vocabulary. This too is supplied with an explanation in the introduction to his Glossary: "An unusually elevated or serious train of thought in the mind of a Scottish peasant seems to demand for its expression the use of a speech which one may describe as Sabbath Scotch" – a disarming but unconvincing euphemism for English. Occasionally an English word is used for a rhyme (*control o't - whole o't, Lomon' - no man*), though to his credit this is rare: more often English is associated with romance or sentiment –

> Thee still in dreams by night I view,
>> Thee flying o'er the plain,
> Thee cruel Peggy! I pursue
>> O'er rolling seas in vain!
>
> (*Hughie Thinks Himself now too Old for Love*, in *Horace, op. cit.*, p.52)

– and is often sadly bathetic in its effect.

Robertson's rather thin and unenterprising Scots is not a particularly interesting medium in itself: on the other hand, he generally employs it with skill and confidence. Alliterative tags, some well established in the language through long-standing literary use, appear with some frequency: *douf an' dowie, dreich an' dreary, better sune than syne, as gleg as gley'd*. An occasional Scots idiom like *tak the gress* (fall down) or *drive Shanks Naigie* (walk), or a figurative expression like *I'm no a hair the belder* to refer to a short length of time, enhance the vernacular realism of the language. He uses a variety of metrical forms, including such traditional Scots ones as ballad metre, the Habbie stanza and the Helicon stanza:[1] the last only once, in *Hughie's Advice to Auld Tammy to Tak' the Use o' his Savings*, but quite worthily:

> But hame still, the same still,
>> We've a' to find oor way;
> What maitter tho' later
>> Or earlier in the day?

1. That is, the complex stanza associated with the tune *Ye Bankis of Helicon*, used by Alexander Montgomerie in *The Cherrie and the Slae* and frequently by later poets, e.g. Burns in *Second Epistle to Davie*.

In *Hughie at the Smiddy – a Dramatic Idyll* he achieves the unique feat of writing a dialogue in Habbie stanzas in which the speech-breaks occur within stanzas and lines:

> – Noo, billies, ken ye what's the steer?
> – Dave's listed.
>   – Lowrie's on the beer.
> – Nick's cut his throat.
>   – The gude be here,
>   An' guard an' bless us!
> There's scandal for a lang loup-year –
>   Gie owre your guesses!

Several of his verse forms are clearly suggested by song metres, a probable reason for his notable tendency to end even-numbered lines with an unstressed monosyllable. This occasionally makes for a humorous rhyme:

> He's fairly aff, he's stown awa'
>   A wolf that wore a fleece, man!
> He's cheated justice, jinkit law,
>   An' lauch'd at the policeman.

(*Hughie's Indignation at the Conduct of the
Absconding Elder,* in *Horace, op. cit.,* p.7)

Joke-rhymes, a well-established trick in Scots poetry (Fergusson and Burns being past masters), sometimes appear (*if need is - torpedies*): for the most part, however, his rhymes are commonplace, but in one poem, *Hughie's Belief in Present Duty*, four four-line stanzas, each line rhyming with *men*, end smartly, in contrast to the very feeble conclusions of many of his poems, with "An' noo – produce the tappit hen!" Reminiscences of Burns are unmistakeable: those on the level of the rhymes *fancy - Nancy* or *roarin' - snorin'* are no doubt unintentional, even unavoidable; but the purpose of such obviously deliberate quotations as *ca' the yowes, gie knaves their wine, tak aff your dram*, is presumably to emphasise Robertson's claim to a place among Burns's acknowledged successors.

Logie Robertson is assuredly not a major poet; however, his importance in the history of Scots as a poetic language is far from negligible. His readable and very agreeable poems, expressing an innocent enjoyment of nature and human society, an easy, comforting and complacent philosophy, and a patriotism safely divorced from activity or even discussion on the political dimension ("An' noo, afore I fesh the barley-bree, Nae politics the nicht!"), were widely read and appreciated; and being incontrovertibly in Scots, albeit an unremarkable Scots, they formed a corpus of sufficient scale and appeal to reinforce the status of the language, increasingly under threat from social and educational changes, in the popular estimation. And since his choice of Scots as a poetic medium was clearly deliberate and motivated by his cultural patriotism, his work contributed to the increasingly urgent debate on the place of Scots in the national life.

The suggestion made in the introduction to a poetic anthology[1] that Logie Robertson and Robert Louis Stevenson together might lead a revival of poetry in Scots seems decidedly unpercipient today, in view of the vast disparity in the reputations of the two writers; but the volume *Underwoods*,[2] which contains most of Stevenson's Scots verses, was published the year after *Horace in Homespun*, and the appearance of a second and manifestly finer collection of poems immediately following Robertson's anthology must have been recognised as a favourable omen. It is observable that both poets devote one poem to the decline of Scots, Stevenson's *The Maker to Posterity* being the first poem in the collection and therefore presumably intended to set the tone. The differences in mood and style between the two poems, however, are striking. Robertson's *On the Decadence of the Scots Language, Manners and Customs* is a tearful lament, in which neither remedy nor relief is suggested for the social changes described and the suffering and despondency which they entail, ending:

> But what avails this lang oration,
> This pleadin' an' expostulation?
> Oh, Ichabod![3] – the better plan
> Were just to end as I began –
> To note the waefu' change, an' cry
> The guid auld times are a' gaun by!

Stevenson in his poem, by contrast, though seeming to accept the even-

---

1. Sir George Douglas, ed., *Contemporary Scottish Verse*, London 1893, p. xiv.
2. London (Chatto and Windus), 1887.
3. "And she named the child Ichabod, saying, The glory is departed from Israel. . ." (1 Samuel 4:21.)

tual disappearance of Scots as an inescapable, though regrettable fact –

> Few spak it than, an' noo there's nane.
> My puir auld sangs lie a' their lane,
> Their sense, that aince was braw an' plain,
>   Tint a'thegither,
> Like runes upon a standin' stane
>   Amang the heather –

proceeds in a tone bordering on exultation to express his ironic satisfaction in the prospect of the disappearance of Scots being merely a prelude to the apocalyptic fate of all mankind:

> Your book, that in some braw new tongue,
> Ye wrote or prentit, preached or sung,
> Will still be just a bairn, an' young
>   In fame or years,
> When the hale planet's guts are dung
>   About your ears;
>
> An' you, sair gruppin' to a spar
> Or whammled wi' some bleezin' star,
> Cryin' to ken whaur deil ye are,
>   Hame, France or Flanders –
> Whang sindry like a railway car
>   An' flie in danders.

Whatever else may be said about this attitude, it incontrovertibly denotes a far higher degree of emotional energy and vitality than Robertson's tone of lachrymose resignation. And the language with which Stevenson expresses this challenging thought is correspondingly both more imaginative and more forceful than Robertson normally achieves. Lexically, words and expressions suggesting violence abound – *dung ajee, mangled throu'ther, dung about your ears, whammled, whang, flie in danders*; and a pugnacious, almost insulting tone towards the hypothetical future reader is conveyed by *his mou to steik*, the ironic *puir brither!*, *Ye're nane sae lucky* and the understated *mebbe waur than weel For you, my buckie*. The suggestion of a deprecatory view of Scots in *No bein' fit to write in Greek, I wrote in Lallan* is immediately undercut by the expression of fondness and respect for the language; and the choice of the rhyme-word *Tantallon*, a fortuitous gift to the writer, suggests (in a subtle counter to the ostensible assumption of the poem) the durability of the language, since *to ding doun Tantallon* – a stronghold near North Berwick – is a proverbial expresson for an impossible task. This simile is neatly matched in the following verse by that of *runes upon a standin' stane Amang the heather*, a vivid pictorial image of something potent, mysterious and indestructible. The simile in the last verse, too, is aptly chosen, reinforcing the prevailing tone of irony by reducing the destruction of the world to the crash of a railway car, but also drawing on contemporary impressions of trains as types of daunting speed and power.

If Robertson's view of the state of Scots moves him to invoke Ichabod, Stevenson's rather suggests Samson: if Scots is going down, it will go down with such a fight as to take the whole world with it. And throughout his small corpus of Scots poems, Stevenson shows the same awareness of, and readiness to avail himself of, the vitality of the language. His Scots is consistent, without Robertson's modulations into English (or even "Sabbath Scots"): like Fergusson, he keeps the language of his "poems in Scots" and that of his "poems in English" clearly distinct. His vocabulary is richer and more varied than Robertson's, and the poems contain a recognisably higher proportion of Scots lexical items. A definite feature of his language, and one of the things which impart the unmistakeable sense of physical energy which prevails in his poems, is a preponderance of Scots verbs, appearing in both finite and (frequently) participial forms: these are often suggestive of noise (*craws crangle thegither, the hoastin' rookery, we skelloch "Hang the beast!"*), physical sensations (*snowkit up the reek, nippin Easlan' breeze, crunklin' underclaes*, (with a synaesthesia) *the yammerin' pain*), rapid action (*the steerin' mither, my chitterin' frame, comes linkin' doun the brae, yirks the tüne into the air*) or awkward, difficult or painful action (*hirsle throu, shauchlin' testimony, I sat an' plowtered, the brangled collieshangie*). Scots words often appear in alliterative phrases, or with repetition of a grammatical structure (*your chimleys reek ... your windaes keek; on draigled hizzie, tautit wean An' drucken lads...; the simmer brunt, the winter blae ...; a yowlin' tyke, a glandered mear*). When a forceful lexicon and a carefully-applied set of small-scale rhetorical patterns are combined, as in *Late in the Nicht,* the result is poetry of irresistible exuberance:

Late in the nicht in bed I lay,
The winds were at their weary play,

An' tirlin' wa's an' skirlin' wae
  Through Heev'n they battered,
On-ding o' hail, on-blaff o' spray,
  The tempest blattered.

The masoned house it dinled through;
  It dung the ship, it cowped the coo;
The rankit aiks it overthrew,
  Had braved a' weathers;
The strang sea-gleds it took an' blew
  Awa' like feathers.

– which becomes a deliberate self-parody in *Embro Hie Kirk*, a satirical reaction to the controversy over the installation of a pipe-organ in St Giles Cathedral:

Up, Niven, or ower late – an' dash
Laigh in the glaur that carnal hash;
Let spires an' pews wi' gran' stramash
  Thegither fa';
The rumlin' kist o' whustles smash
  In pieces sma'.

Noo choose ye out a walie hammer;
About the knottit buttress clam'er;
Alang the steep roof stoyt an' stammer,
  A gate mis-chancy;
On the aul' spire, the bells' hie cha'mer,
  Dance your bit dancie.

Ding, devel, dunt, destroy an' ruin,
Wi' carnal stanes the square bestrewin',
Till your loud chaps frae Kyle to Fruin,
  Frae Hell to Heeven,
Tell the guid wark that baith are doin' –
  Baith Begg an' Niven.

On a different level, his much-quoted passage from the introduction to the Scots section of *Underwoods* – "...I simply wrote my Scots as well as I was able, not caring if it hailed from Lauderdale or Angus, from the Mearns or Galloway; if I had ever heard a good word, I used it without shame; and when Scots was lacking, or the rhyme jibbed, I was glad (like my betters) to fall back on English" – again shows the difference between his approach and Robertson's: the latter is at pains to argue for the verisimilitude of his literary dialect, while Stevenson adopts a tone of cheerfully insouciant defiance towards the whole principle of verisimilitude. (The suggestion of a negligent approach to his work – *"not caring* if it hailed from Lauderdale or Angus . . ."* – is as transparent a sham as this master craftsman ever perpetrated.) In fact, it is scarcely more true of Stevenson than of Robertson that his Scots includes words of restricted geographical distribution: what is interesting, however, is his statement that "purity" – that is, dialectal consistency – in literary Scots is unnecessary since the language is in any case on the point of death. "And if it be not pure, alas! what matters it? The day draws near when this illustrious and malleable tongue shall be quite forgotten. . ." Despite the "alas!", the logic of this argument could lead to a conclusion more optimistic than at first appears: a poet is now free to exercise his creative imagination with any and all forms of Scots, since he will no longer incur the responsibility of ensuring that his literary language can be measured against a spoken form. This, however expressed and whether consciously recognised or not, was to become precisely the assumption underlying much of the most linguistically interesting Scots writing of the present century.

4
The Rise of North-East Doric:
Mary Symon and Charles Murray

The North-East of Scotland has always been, in language as in character, distinctive. In the eighteenth century an important, if quantitatively small, contribution to the Vernacular Revival was made by writers from this part of the country; and its two most outstanding representative works, *The Christmas Bawin o' Monymusk* by John Skinner and *Helenore* by Alexander Ross, are in a Scots strongly flavoured with local shibboleths of phonology and vocabulary. These did not establish a tradition of poetry in North-East dialect: verses emanating from the area in the later eighteenth and most of the nineteenth century show little that is distinctive in their language (or in any other respect, it must be admitted). The reputation of the local speech as incomprehensible to outsiders endured, however: John Galt, in 1823, wrote of a character in *The Entail* that "When he alighted from the Edinburgh coach at the canny twa-an'-twae toun of Aberdeenawa, he had some doubts if the inhabitants spoke any Christian language"[1] – an understandable, if perhaps overstated, reaction of an Ayrshire ear to the dialects of the opposite corner of the country. And if poetry, here as elsewhere in Scotland, generally failed in this period to rise above mediocrity, at least one gifted prose writer, George MacDonald, made skilful use of the local speech; and in the later nineteenth century the emergence of a flourishing school of regional journalism led to an astonishingly prolific and sophisticated development of the dialect into a medium of expository and argumentative prose.[2]

In the course of the nineteenth century a unique series of social develop-

1. Vol. III, Chapter 16.
2. The rise of the local press was a phenomenon not unique to the North-East, but it was there that the opportunity to develop the local speech as a prose medium was most extensively and enthusiastically exploited. The full story of this important cultural development is told in two books by W. Donaldson, *Popular Literature in Victorian Scotland* (Aberdeen University Press 1986) and *The Language of the People* (Aberdeen University Press 1989).

ments – in summary, nothing less than the transformation of the landscape from a sparsely-populated wilderness to one of the most productive
areas of arable farming in Great Britain – *ipso facto* transformed the native
peasantry into a prosperous class of farmers and itinerant farm workers
embodying a highly individual culture intimately connected with the land
and the seasonal labour of farming. The opening of a poem written in the
1930s by Flora Garry conveys both the rapidity of the transformation and
the part played in it by the lifelong, dedicated labours of individual men:

> It wis jist a skelp o the muckle furth,
>   A sklyter o roch grun,
> Fin granfadder's fadder bruke it in
>   Fae the hedder an the funn.
> Granfadder sklatit barn an byre,
>   Brocht water to the closs,
> Pat fail-dykes ben the bare brae face,
>   An a cairt-road tull the moss.[1]

Associated with the developing system of large-scale arable farming,
indeed an integral part of it, was the "bothy", or communal sleeping-
quarters of the farm workers. The "bothy ballads", part of Scotland's
unsurpassed tradition of folk song, were preserved and perpetuated in
this society; and the custom among younger farm workers of "flitting"
– moving from one farm to another every few years or "raiths" (terms)
– maintained a unity of the ballad culture throughout the region.

This culture of song and folk poetry, embodied in the dialect of the
area, was the ground from which the North-East's contribution to the
Scots literary revival eventually grew. The first two figures in a quite sudden, brilliant and enduring poetic efflorescence of the North-Eastern dialect were Charles Murray and Mary Symon.[2]

That the local speech (the term "Doric" is uniformly used in the area

1. *Bennygoak*, ll.1–8, in *Bennygoak and Other Poems*, Aberdeen (Rainbow Books) 1974.

2. For an analysis of the reasons for the sudden emergence of the North-Eastern dialect as a
poetic medium, and in particular the ambivalent part played by the 1872 Education Act with its
abolition of parish schools and enforcement of compulsory education, see Colin Milton,
"From Charles Murray to Hugh MacDiarmid: Vernacular Revival and Scottish
Renaissance", in *Literature of the North*, eds. D. Hewitt and M. Spiller, Aberdeen University
Press 1983, pp. 82–108; for a discussion of the emergence of the North-East dialect as a literary
medium contrasting with general Scots, see J. D. McClure, "'Lallans' and 'Doric' in North-
Eastern Scottish Poetry," in *English World-Wide* 8:2 (1987), pp. 215–234.

to refer, not to Scots in general, but to this form of it as contrasted with all others) is to be emphatically the medium of Mary Symon's poetry is evident in the first stanza of *The Auld Fisher: his First Troot*, the first poem in her collection *Deveron Days*[1]: the rhyme *meenits - deen – It's* ... depends on a pronunciation of the word for "done" which is found only north of Angus; and the word *wahnie* ("fishing rod") shows one of the stereotypes of local speech, the ubiquitous diminutive suffix. This is one of the slightest poems in the book; but in some of her more substantial pieces the local element is far more conspicuous. The diminutive appears frequently: *hoosie, hannie, stripie* (from *stripe* "rivulet"), *mullie* (from "mill", viz. a snuff-mill). Phonological features of the dialect abound: [i] as the reflex of Middle Scots [ø (:)] or French [y] (*bleem* "bloom", *bleed* "blood", *fleer* "floor", *Eel* "Yule"), lexeme-specific diphthongisation of [i] (*squile* "squeal", *lye* "leave" (the loss of [v] being a general Scots change), *quine* "quean", the invariable North-East word for "girl"), [f] for initial [ʍ] (*fat* "what", *faur* "where", *futtle* "whittle", *fustle* "whistle"), raising of [e] to [i] before [n] (*een* and *eence, gane* made to rhyme with *e'en* "evening"), [a(:)] causing palatalisation of the preceding consonant (*kyaak* "cake", *myauken* [mjakən] "hare", *fyackie* (from *faik* "plaid", with the diminutive), and numerous pronunciations not attributable to general sound-changes.

Most noticeably, her vocabulary includes a striking proportion of words restricted in their geographical distribution to the North-East, or even to her own region of it. Often these simply appear in their context as the normal words for the thing referred to, with no evident intention of producing a special literary effect: "An' there's the aul' *vricht* (joiner)", "yer hin'maist bit an' *houp* (mouthful of drink)", "Wi' *dosses* (bunches) o' roses meanderin' roon". Even local words with a greater measure of emotive force than those may be used in this unemphatic manner: the humour or the irony in "An' his bodygaird was a *fozelin'* (wheezing) tyke As ready to row's to run" and "He'll be *mirkier* (cheerier) at his burial Tho' he winna look as droll" or "Ay, it wasna that ye ca'd him, or ye *bunged* (became angry or petulant) a month yestreen" is not dependent on the presence of the dialect words. By contrast, in "Aul' Carnies *ree-misht* (noisily and awkwardly shoved) in a hearse", the word, evocative

1. Aberdeen (Wyllie) 1933.

though it is, only acquires its full significance in the context by association
with its object. And in many cases the specifically local status of a word
makes it peculiarly apt. In *An Appeal*, one of several poems on the theme
of the exile's longing for his calf-ground, the line "I *stouf* ("walk with a
slow, dull, heavy tread"[1]) aboot the city street", by containing a word
which is not only powerfully emotive in itself but the first (and only)
markedly North-Eastern word of the poem, closely associates the speaker's North-Eastern identity with his frame of mind (indicated by his gait)
as an exile in Glasgow. The lines

> Its canny jow gaed throu' the hoose
>> Like some laich-chanted spell.
> It cried, "Ye jaud, ye *fuged* [skipped] the school,"
>> It speired, "Fa *bosied* [embraced] Bell?"

in another nostalgic poem, *The Aucht-day Clock*, emphasise the tone of
sentimental regret by including two markedly local words in the lines
imagined as spoken by the clock. A contrasting effect is obtained in *A
Recruit for the Gordons* (the Great War and its effect on the local community is another of her recurring themes), where North-Eastern dialect
words are chosen and positioned with notable skill to suggest the speaker's complex mixture of pride and ironic self-depreciation: the vivid and
dramatic

> Wi' Huns upon wir *thrashel-stane*
> An' half the world red wud

pointedly includes the local word for "threshold", but immediately afterwards in

> An' sae I *paumered* back an' fore,
>> Practeesin' in my kilt,
> An' Sownock fae the bothy door
>> Kame-*sowfed* a martial lilt

the undignified action suggested by *paumered* ("walked clumsily and
heavily") and the unimpressive *kame-sowfed* ("played on a paper and
comb") undercut the cheerfully vaunting tone with which the poem
opens. A few lines later the following passage occurs:

> ... Lord sake! That wasna me,

---

1. Definition as in the *Scottish National Dictionary*.

> The eat-meat sumph that kissed the quines
>> An' took a skyte at Eel;
> I was the heir o' brave langsynes,
>> A sodger, head to heel.

The first half of the stanza contains no fewer than four local dialect features: the expression *eat-meat* (an idler or parasite), the special sense of *skyte* (here meaning a drink), the word *quine* and the pronunciation *Eel*; the second half, none at all, all the Scots features being common to the whole Scots-speaking area. The suggestion of a light-hearted ferm-loun consciously transforming himself into a dedicated soldier, and aware of the somewhat ludicrous contrast between what he has been and what he is awkwardly but sincerely trying to become, is suggested with delicacy and poignancy by the change in language.

A similar device is used in her finest poem, *The Glen's Muster Roll*, an elegy for the young men of a parish, known to the Dominie (the speaker of the poem) as former pupils, who have served in the War and in many cases suffered injury or death. Among the boys whom the master recalls with pride, an entire stanza is devoted to one remembered as "the Gaup" (a predominantly North-East word meaning, as a verb, "to stare stupidly" and as a noun, by implication, a fool): the derogatory nickname is immediately made to alliterate with "a Gordon wi' the 'Bydand'[1] on his broo". A concentration of dialect words appears in the lines evoking "the Gaup" in his school days:

> Nae *murlacks* (crumbs) *dreetlin'* (trickling) fae his pooch or owre his
> grauvit noo,
> Nae word o' *groff-write* (large clumsy script) trackies on the "Four best
> ways to *fooge*" (play truant) –

and his remembered words "But – bizz! A *dhubrack* lowpit as I passed the muckle pot" include a word of markedly local distribution for a smelt; but no local vocabulary is to be found in the master's tribute to his courage –

> He steed his grun' an' something mair, they tell me, oot at Hooge...
> Ay, ye didna ken the classics, never heard o' a co-sine,
> But here's my aul' lum aff tae ye, dear gowkit Loon o' Mine

– though the dialect *phonology* is as consistent as ever. Elsewhere in the

---

1. The motto of the Gordon Highlanders, incorporated in the regimental cap badge.

poem, the line "Some *tyaavin'* wi' the 'Rule o' Three,' some *widin'* throu 'Mensa'[1]'" uses two dialect forms (the first meaning "working laboriously" and the second being the local pronunciation of "wading") to suggest the boys' painful efforts in the classroom; and the mixture of affection and disapproval with which the master regarded his charges is touchingly suggested by phrases like "Dysie's *sheemach* (tousled) head", "twa lang *stilpert* (lanky, long-legged) chiels", "Dick McLeod, his *sanshach* (smart, wily) sel'". No particularly noticeable words appear in the last verse, however, though again the dialect is consistently represented by its phonology: the almost unbearable sadness of the conclusion is suggested by the very ordinariness of the language. The unexpected English line "Not mine but yours to question now! You lift unhappy eyes – " serves simply to emphasise the heart-touching familiarity of the immediately-resumed dialect. Mary Symon's poetry includes banal, clumsy and maudlin passages; but her use of Banffshire speech in this poem is sufficient to earn her an unchallenged place among the major poets of the Great War.

Mary Symon's use of her local Doric is, in fact, a carefully-controlled artistic tool. This is demonstrated in reverse, as it were, by her poem *Burns Nicht in the Glen*, which, though its language throughout is a locally-accented Scots abounding in interesting words, consistent in grammar and phonology, and effectively manoeuvred to convey the speaker's changing emotions, in fact contains remarkably few words which would not be recognised beyond the North-East. In a poetic tribute to Burns, a poet regarded throughout Scotland with unmatched respect and affection, this is surely not accidental:

> Oh, English speech for English yird!
> We ken it's grand an' fine:
> But ah! It tak's the dear Scots word
> To grip your heart an' mine.
> Ill-faured, an' rude, an' roch it's ca'ed,
> Wanworth an' a' the rest;
> But – hands across the heather, lad –
> We ken oor ain kens best.

1. The word traditionally used as a model for the Latin first declension. The practice was to recite the declension with a heavy stress on the inflectional syllable: the word here rhymes with *raw* "row", pronounced [raː].

Mary Symon here is clearly identifying her own medium with that of Burns: to do which she requires to understate the characteristics of North-Eastern speech which make it conspicuously unlike Burns's Ayrshire. And the handsome tribute to Charles Murray which forms the conclusion of the poem –

> Oh, Robin's chair for lang's been teem,
>> Let Charlie tak' it noo –
> An' twine the heather an' the breem –
>> A laurel for his broo.

– though it includes a reference to Alford as Murray's birthplace, by implication claims him as a poet for all of Scotland, not exclusively the North-East.

In view of Murray's enduring local popularity and well-established reputation as the archetypal poet of the North-East, it is somewhat surprising to observe that the distinctive linguistic features of the "Doric" are much less conspicuous in his poetic language than in that of Mary Symon, and often absent altogether.[1]

The poem which typifies Murray's achievement for most casual readers (perhaps unfortunately, since it is far from his most serious, most subtle or most linguistically inventive work), *The Whistle*, demonstrates many of his most individual and attractive qualities. The unforgettable opening line "He cut a sappy sucker from the muckle rodden-tree" at once seizes the reader's attention with its tripping rhythm, alliteration, internal rhyme (*suck*er – *muck*le) and familiar vocabulary. The natural life within and around the farm – birds, and wild and domestic animals – is evoked, often by Scots words: *teuchat, mavis, puddock, futt'rat, bawd, kye, foalie*. Scots vocabulary furnishes the onomatopoeia in "He wheepled on't at mornin' an' he tweetled on't at nicht"; the compressed expressions "he was beddit boss" (sent to his bed hungry) and – better still – "he had clawed the caup" (scraped the dish for the last remains of the porridge which had been finished by more active members of the farm) add force to the language; such features as the alliterative tag "he cared na doit nor docken" and the use

1. *Hamewith: the Complete Poems of Charles Murray*, Aberdeen University Press 1979. This contains the poems originally published in the collections *Hamewith* (1900), *A Sough o' War* (1917), *In the Country Places* (1920) and the posthumous *The Last Poems* (1969).

of physical detail to convey the sense "he was up earliest of the household" by "he had his bonnet on afore the lave had breeks" suggest the ready creativeness of a fluent and articulate dialect-speaking poet. One of the remarkable successes of the poem, too, is the subtle suggestion of the busy lives of the farm personnel proceeding with their routine work as a background to the "wee herd's" musical displays: harrowing, milking, preparation of food, attending to the animals, even supervising the boy himself, are conducted unobtrusively by unspecified "they" or "the lave". Yet this quintessentially North-Eastern poem, though abundantly demonstrating its author's humour, sympathy and linguistic fluency, proves to contain only two words, *futt'rat* (weasel) and *baillie* (cattleman) with a strongly local colouring, and very little in grammar or phonology that locates it firmly within the area: even the instrument is a *whistle*, not a *fussle*.

Many of the other poems in *Hamewith* (his first collection) demonstrate the same engaging realism and fluency of language, in a Scots which in its vocabulary and phonology shows only hints of a North-Eastern colouring. In a loosely-defined set of poems consisting of masterly portraits of local worthies, the degree of dialect markedness in the language appears to vary with the subject. In *Jeames* and *Skeely Kirstie*, creations (or sketches from life?) whose provenance is only incidental (in the sense that they, as individuals or as types, are not *necessarily* associated uniquely with Murray's Howe of Alford), the Scots includes only a sprinkling of Doric words and local allusions: Kirsty can treat a *scrat* (scratch) or *scob* (set) a broken bone; Jeames got drunk at *Scuttrie Market* (a district fair held near Alford): but most of the Scots words are general, and some of the rhymes assume a pronunciation *other* than the characteristic local one: *bane, ane* and *nane* must have [e], instead of the North-Eastern [i], to rhyme with *wean* (itself not a common word in this area, where children are *bairns* or *littleens*); *brew* must have the general Scots pronunciation (which is the same as the English) to rhyme with *fou* (saxifrage) and *mou'*, although a very distinctive local dialect feature is the use of a diphthong like that in English *cow* in this and similar words. When, by contrast, an abundance of Doric terms occurs in *The Antiquary*, the effect is to emphasise the whimsical and old-fashioned nature of the "little mannie" and his house:

The horn-en' fu' o' craggins, quaichs an' caups,
Mulls, whorls an' cruisies left bare room to stir
Wi' routh o' swourds an' dirks a' nicks an' slaps,
An' peer-men, used langsyne for haudin fir.

The picture here is of a microcosm of the material culture of a bygone age: the last line (referring to a primitive stand for resinous branches burnt as candles) suggests that Murray's own original readers might require an explanation for some of the articles, and their names, in the old man's collection. Some of the local words in this poem are simply terms for items known by other names in different parts of the country: *leems* (unspecified tools), *fleerishes* (pieces of shaped steel for striking sparks from flints), the *horn-en'* (the inner room); others refer to distinctive items of local culture: the house itself is *stob-thackit*, a mode of thatching characteristic of the area, the straw being held in place by forked sticks. The antiquary's accomplishment of *trailin' the raip*, though the words themselves are common Scots, is a mode of bringing bad luck on a house to which all references are from the North-East. It is noteworthy, too, that his dying wish begins *"Gweed grant..."*: Murray does not regularly use this dialect form of *good*; but when an aged man is quoted as using it as a euphemism for *God*, it is entirely appropriate. In *The Miller Explains*, a dramatic monologue, the supposed speaker likewise uses a rather higher proportion of Doric words, idioms and pronunciations than in many of Murray's other poems: *bishop* (a tool for firming the earth round fence posts, or the action of using one), *displenish* (sale of household possessions), *roup* (auction), *sids* (oat husks); *fa' tee* (get going); *shaltie* (local form of *sheltie*, pony), *oonslockened*.

In this collection of poems, Murray's achievement is to evoke, in Scots verses of abounding vigour, fluency and linguistic richness and authenticity, the life and local culture of the North-East: its characters with their work, their preoccupations and their idiosyncracies, and the seasonal round of change in their daily activities. Consistent use of North-Eastern dialect, however, is a device which he uses only for specific poetic purposes. The poem *Winter* opens with a stanza which might have been by Fergusson or Burns:

Now Winter rides wi' angry skirl
On sleety winds that rive an' whirl,

An' gaberlunzie-like plays tirl
   At sneck an' lozen.
The bairns can barely bide the dirl
   O' feet gane dozin.

The use of Scots here shows impeccable skill and taste: the emotive rhyme-words, the phonaesthetically memorable *gaberlunzie* with the combination of humour and menace in the personification, the metonymic use of the Scots words for "door-catch" and "pane", the suggestion of stress and fractiousness reinforced by alliteration on plosives in the lines referring to the "bairns". It is not North-Eastern Scots, however: no part of this verse would not be entirely familiar throughout the Scots-speaking part of the country. When the scene moves to the interior of the house, local pronunciations appear –

The ingle's heaped wi' bleezin' peats
An' bits o' splutterin' firry *reets*
Which shortly thow the ploughmen's *beets;*
   An' *peels* appear
That trickle oot aneth their seats
   A' ower the *fleer.*

– and an occasional vocabulary items such as *shank* (knit stockings), *moggins* (footless stockings), the suggestion being of a transition from a description of a general Scottish winter to one more sharply focused on an Aberdeenshire ferm-toun with its large coterie of family and workers and its music by Neil Gow and William Marshall (local players and composers of fiddle music who flourished in the eighteenth century, and produced work of seminal importance in the development of the Scottish fiddle tradition).

Murray's classical translations in this book show the same presence in only a slight degree of local dialect features, though the naturalisation of the poems by the use of Scottish personal and place names is both charming and convincing. It is of interest to observe that his spirited rendering of the Virgil passage (*Aeneid* III, 588 – 640) is in the same metre and style as the very first piece of verse to be published in North-Eastern dialect, Robert Forbes's rendering of a passage from Ovid's *Metamorphoses* as *Ajax his Speech to the Grecian Knabs* (1742), and even contains some verbal echoes of it:

Sall then these arms be deny'd
  To me, wha in this bruilzie
Was the first man that drew my durk,
  Came flaught-bred to the toulzie?
An' sall this sleeth come farrer ben,
  Wha was sae dev'lish surly,
He scarce would gae a fit frae hame,
  An o' us a' was hurly?
                      (Forbes, ll.85–92)

A Greek was he, wha short afore
  At Troy was in the brulzie,
An' tho' a halflin then, he bore
  A man's pairt in the tulzie.
As soon's he spied our Trojan graith
  He nearhan' swarfed wi' fear;
But maisterin' his dread o' skaith
  At last he ventured near.
                    (Murray, ll. 17–24.)

In other poems in this collection where the theme and setting have no particular connection with the North-East, local dialect features may be absent altogether from the language: his somewhat disappointing poetic tributes to Stevenson and Burns are examples.

In his later collection *A Sough o' War*, a definite development is visible in Murray's poetic technique: instead of the more or less audible, but never overwhelming, presence of a North-Eastern accent in poetry which is otherwise in general Scots, a clear and unmistakeable contrast is now visible between a rich and vigorous, but not regionally determined, Scots for some poems and a Doric dialect far stronger and more consistent than is ever found in *Hamewith* for others. Instead of a "Scots" and an "English" voice, as can be (simplistically, of course) observed in many Scottish poets, Murray in this collection varies between a "Scots" and a "Doric" voice. The contrast between

Ye're better men, ye're baulder men,
  Ye're younger men forby,
Mair fit we ken than aulder men
  To answer Scotland's cry.
Yet mony a chiel that's beld an' grey,
  An trauchlin' at the ploo,

Would fain fling up his tack the day
    To face the frem't wi' you.
Gey short o' breath, but keen an' teuch,
    It's but his birn o' days
That hauds him here by closs an' cleuch,
    Lythe haughs an' heathery braes.

("Ye're Better Men")

and

Ye hard the claik hoo Germany gied France the coordy lick,
An' Scotland preen't her wincey up an' intill't geyan quick –
But fouk wi' better thooms than me can redd the raivell't snorl,
An tell ye fa' begood the ploy that sae upset the worl'.
I ken that I cam' here awa' some aucht days aifter Yeel,
An' never toon nor fee afore has shootit me sae weel;
They gie me maet, an' beets an' claes, wi' fyles an antrin dram –
Come term-time lat them flit 'at likes, *I'm* bidin faur I am.
Tho' noo an' than, wi' dreepin' sark, we've biggit dykes an' dell't –
That's orra wark; oor daily darg is fechtin' fan we're tell't.

(Fae France)

is recognisable from the first glance.

Associated with the two contrasting registers is a contrasting set of out-looks on the War. In the untitled introductory poem in the collection (from which the first extract is taken) the tone is of a courageous Scottish patriotism, and the emphasis is on the strength of the bond between the soldiers in the trenches and their families and other fellow Scots at home. The language, in the last quatrain, is presented (most touchingly) as a visible symbol of this bond –

An' in the tongue we never tine,
    In words as bairns we spak',
Here's Scotland's biddin' in a line,
    "Hing in an' haiste-ye-back."

– but there is no suggestion that North-Eastern Doric as contrasted with any other form of Scots is intended: apart from an unimportant rhyme of *een* with *gane* [gin], the only conspicuously local word is, again touch-ingly, "Tak' then for kain these *strouds* o' rhymes" (a *stroud* is a piece of trivial verse or doggerel). The title poem *A Sough o' War* with its refrain "Auld Scotland counts for something still", and *Wha Bares a Blade for Scotland?* with its allusions to Scotland's military exploits in the past,

49

express the same mood; and in both, the language is strongly Scots with only traces – single words or rhyming syllables – of local dialect. These are poems which appeal to the hearer's Scottish patriotism as a motive for playing a worthy part in the national conflict. In striking and revealing contrast to these, poems such as *The Wife on the War, Fae France, Hairry Hears fae Hame* and (best of all) *Dockens Afore his Peers* evoke the individual reactions of sharply-characterised North-Eastern folk to the war and its effect on themselves. The speaker of *Fae France*, on his own showing a violent-tempered and ill-conditioned young man who finds trench warfare eminently suited to his disposition, recalls rescuing his wounded officer:

> "Ging on an' leave me here, ye gype, an' mak' yer feet yer freen'."
> "Na, na," says I; "ye brocht me here, I'm nae gyaun hame my leen."

The last phrase could not have been uttered by any Scot born outwith the region bounded by Dee and Deveron; and his reminiscence of flinging grenades into a German trench "Like loons that's trued the squeel to stane young puddocks i' the stank" is as realistic in terms of the supposed background and personality of the speaker as it is in its representation of the language: the words and rhythms fall into the iambic heptameter with absolute ease and conviction. Similarly, John Watt o' Dockenhill addresses his tribunal in language which reproduces in poetic form not only the words and sounds but the idioms, cadences and conversational style of the North-East:

> O ay, I'll sit, birze ben a bit. Hae, Briggie, pass the snuff;
> Ye winna hinner lang wi' me, an' speer a lot o' buff ...

Murray's use of language adds a very considerable degree of complexity to this collection of war poems. It is in Scots that we hear the rousing, patriotic call to arms; it is in Doric that the self-interest of Dockens, the naive pugnacity of "the wife" or the barely-controlled anxiety and loneliness of the soldier's fiancée in *Hairry Hears fae Hame* are heard to reveal other aspects of the war and its effects on the lives of the people. Indeed, though this can scarcely have been his intention, within the collection the Doric voice certainly calls in question, if not actually undercutting, the pronouncements of the Scots.

That Murray was a poet of exceptional talent, and the supreme portrayer in verse of the life of the North-East farming communities, has scarcely been questioned by anybody except, notoriously, Grieve; but his changing use of the Doric, first as simply a means of adding local colour to a poetic language not essentially different from traditional Scots, and later as a highly-developed medium contrasting strongly with the latter both linguistically and in its social and psychological implications, has been less often observed. It is when Murray places his Doric in a poetic context in which it and his Scots are made to form a contrast, in their linguistic features and in the nature of the poetic statements made in and by them, that the true extent of his poetic skill is most evident.

5

The Advent of Mediaevalism:
Pittendrigh Macgillivray and Lewis Spence

In December 1925, a letter from one H. Brown was published in the *Scottish Educational Journal*, headed "Mr Grieve's Creed?" The writer, attempting as he said to give a quasi-canonical form to C. M. Grieve's cultural and political philosophy as it appeared to emerge from his articles, proposed the following among his items of "Mr Grieve's Creed":

10. The object of the Scottish Renaissance is to create out of the wreck a new culture, which shall be a living force in Catholic world culture.

11. It is impractical and undesirable to rear this culture upon a Celtic foundation.

12. Neither is it desirable to found it upon modern English culture, which is decadent.

13. Nor can it be founded upon Post-Reformation culture, which is hopelessly provincial.

14. What is possible and desirable is a creative modern development of the interrupted Scots-English culture of the fifteenth century.

Grieve's response, which (in view of his well-known combativeness) must have astonished many of the *Journal*'s readers, was to suggest a couple of tiny emendations to Brown's wording and conclude "Otherwise his Sixteen Points admirably describe my position and programme".[1]

The literature of the two centuries from Barbour to the Castalian Band of James VI has exerted a potent influence on Scots poetry of the present

---

1. Grieve's weekly articles were published in the *Scottish Educational Journal* between June 1925 and February 1927. A selection was published in book form under the title *Contemporary Scottish Studies* in 1926. The complete series, with the associated correspondence and a new introduction by Grieve, was published by the *Scottish Educational Journal* in 1976: references in this and subsequent chapters are to this edition. The passages here referred to are on pp. 68 and 72.

century. This is in a straightforward sense entirely to be expected: the opulent resources of Middle Scots, and the skill with which the poets exploited them, make of Stewart literature an inspiring study for any reader capable of appreciating poetry of merit. But besides the quality of the poetry itself – and this is indisputably the greatest period of sustained literary achievement in the Scots language – a subtler reason can be suggested for the attraction of modern poets to the works of their mediaeval confrères: Scotland under the Stewart kings was a sovereign power, capable of pursuing an independent policy among the nations of Europe, and the Scots language and the literature embodied in it therefore acquired a symbolic value as those of a free people. A poetry deliberately reminiscent, in language or style, of Scotland's late-mediaeval and Renaissance period could instil in modern Scottish readers a desire to restore the nation to the proudly independent status which it had once enjoyed: or at any rate, could remind them of their responsibility to maintain the distinctiveness of Scotland's cultural heritage.

Two poets whose opus includes work in an archaising style are Pittendrigh Macgillivray and Lewis Spence.[1] (It is of interest to note that neither of these was a poet except as a sideline to his life's main vocation: Macgillivray was one of the most gifted sculptors of his time, statues of Burns in Irvine and Byron in Aberdeen, and the Gladstone Memorial in Edinburgh, still bearing familiar witness to the quality of his work; and Spence was a folklorist and anthropologist, with a special interest in magic and the supernatural, whose books on Celtic mythology and on the religions of pre-Conquest Mexico are landmark studies in those fields.) For Macgillivray, experiments with archaic language represented only a small part of an output which is mostly in either English or the Scots of his own time. In the introduction to his collection *Bog Myrtle and Peat-Reek,*[2] he made it clear that the language of his Scots poems was firmly based on his knowledge of the spoken tongue: *"I have used the North and South dialects of our Scottish Vernacular in so far only as I have a living knowledge of their words, idiom and accent; and I have done nothing in*

1. Both are discussed in K. Buthlay, "An Awkward Squad: Some Scots Poets from Stevenson to Spence", in *Scotland and the Lowland Tongue*, ed. J. D. McClure, Aberdeen University Press 1983, pp. 149 – 169.
2. Privately printed by J. Skinner (Edinburgh), 1922.

the way of making a curious mosaic of 'auld-farran' *and obsolete words, such as no Scot of any period or district ever spoke*".[1]

The poems in the book are arranged in three groups headed "The Nor' West", "The Nor' East" and "The Lowlands". The first of these sets contains poems which are for the most part in English, though their themes are Scottish; most are either romantic "Celtic twilight" visions or laments for the lost Jacobite cause. *After Culloden* is in a somewhat thin and inconsistent Scots:

> We wile them ow're mosses an' pine covered braes –
> We cheat them by nicht and watch them by days,
> Till wan'ert we hae them where deil kens the ways,
>   Syne hame owr a linn we maun bid them awa.

But otherwise, an occasional *wae* or *sairly*, or in the poem *Tears* the Gaelic line *Ochoin, ochoin, O chridh!* and a subtitle *Deoir, Deoir, O Dheora Shearbh* (translating the opening line "Tears, tears! O bitter tears…"), are all that differentiate the language from standard literary English. The other two groups, however, are in Scots, and quite clearly differentiated in dialect. The language of the "Nor' East" poems includes several phonological shibboleths (initial *f-* corresponding to *wh-*: *far, fatever, files, fup*; a fully close vowel corresponding to the half-close one of most other dialects and to [u] or [ju] in English: *peer, gweed, teen* "tune"; frication instead of loss of *w* in initial *wr-*: *vrutten*) and a few local vocabulary items (*queyn* "girl", *tyauve* "struggle", *staig* "stallion"); besides numerous references to local topographical features:

> Whar UGIE wynds to meet the DON,
> And BENNACHIE tours up ayon…

The "Lowlands" poems are in a more general Scots, almost the only local feature being the spelling of *süne, düne, shürely*, where the umlaut presumably is intended to suggest the rounded vowel (as in French *deux*) of Eastern Border dialects. Macgillivray was born near Inverurie, and no doubt was more intimately aware of the distinctive characteristics of his own dialect.

1. I reproduce Macgillivray's use of various type-faces. Throughout the book, he makes pointed use of contrasts between Roman and italic type, and between capitals and lowercase: this is a patent imitation of the practice in eighteenth-century texts such as the Kilmarnock Edition of Burns.

His interest in Scots as a language is shown by his meticulous differentiation of the dialects of his poems, and also by his extensive and detailed glossary: as with Burns, on whose practice he is clearly modelling his own, his entries sometimes take the form of short notes:

> Bourtree, *an elder tree; often grown round farms in Scotland as a screen.*
>
> Fey, *under the shadow of death or madness; subject to occult influences.*
>
> Norlan', *Northland, generally meaning in Scotland the north-east quarter of the country.*
>
> Strathspey, *a dance in which two persons are engaged – the name being that of the district of its origin.*

A familiarity with folk-literature is suggested by the remarkable range of metric forms found in his work: besides staple fare like ballad metre and Habbies, many of his poems (like those of Logie Robertson) are in song metres, including some which can scarcely be appreciated without a knowledge of the tune:

> My bonnie bairn,
> My bonnie bairn,
> My bonnie bairn, there's *blessing's* in yer e'e.
> An' O ye hae a dainty mou, dainty mou, dainty mou –
> I wat ye hae the sweetest mou'
> That ever kiss't wi' me.

The measure of this poem, *A Mither's Lilt*, is taken, according to Macgillivray's note, from "an old Aberdeenshire Nursery Rhyme".

Like Robertson and Stevenson, he refers to the decline and (as he predicts) eventual demise of Scots: "*For a time yet, in remote districts like* BUCHAN *in* ABERDEENSHIRE, *or between the* Pentlands *and* Ettrickvale *in the* LOWLANDS, *where in simple ways the work and worth of our old peasant life continue, our dialects may linger on; but the levelling, mechanizing forces of the day are as surely turning down the old things and expressions as the four-fold motor-plough and the machine reaper are eliminating the more human* horse-plough *and the* rhythmic scythe". Nonetheless, the first of his "Nor' East" poems is the reverse of pessimistic in tone. Entitled *The Norlan Fiddle*, it includes a listing of the poets currently writing in the local form of Scots (Charles Murray, Mary Symon, Violet Jacob, "And ALEXANDER, – be't in prose, Our *fiddle's* gamut shrewdly knows");

and expresses both pride and satisfaction in their achievement and confidence that the life of the dialect is assured:

> They say our *fiddle's* auld an' deen,
> Or neen o's now that ken the teen
> O' *Lallan Scots* or *Aiberdeen*
>   To kittle up
> An' prink the thing as ticht an' keen
>   As crack o' fup.
>
> But na; I'll nae believe't just yet,
> That a' our *loons* hae tint the wit
> To stent the *strings* in tune to fit
>   Our native MUSE –
> Tho' she's a mark that's ill to hit,
>   Ye may jalouse.

Abounding in exclamations (*nyod*; *An' Och!*, *But Hoot!*, *Na fy!*) and occasionally making an imaginative use of rhyme words –

> There's wheedlin' sleekit CHARLIE MURRAY,
> He tigs the *strings* wi' funny hurry
> Till kittlan rhymes flee roun' an scurry
>   Wi' *cantrip* words
> That jouk an' jink an' baffle worry
>   Wi' lauchan dirds.

– the poem shows a greater degree of vigour and inventiveness than many in the collection.

Mercy o' Gode, a poem first published not in *Bog Myrtle and Peat-Reek* but in Grieve's short-lived monthly magazine *Scottish Chapbook* (Vol.1 no.11), shows Macgillivray's adeptness in handling his contemporary Scots at its best: avoiding the bathos and banality to which his work is often prone, he combines an unusual stanza form with a sparse but carefully-selected Scots vocabulary to produce a grim and haunting poem in which a vein of bleak and angry irony is maintained with notable skill:

> Twa bodachs, I mind, had a threep yae day,
>   Aboot man's chief end –
>   Aboot man's chief end.
> Whan the t'ane lookit sweet his words war sour
> Whan the tither leuch oot his words gi'ed a clour,
> But whilk got the better I wasna sure –

I wasna sure,
An' needna say.

The casual *I mind* and *yae day*, the undignified word *threep* and the rare *bodachs* (in Gaelic *bodach* is simply the regular word for "old man", but in Scots it is infrequently used, indeed scarcely naturalised, and sometimes has sinister or supernatural overtones) create a context in which "Man's chief end" is ironically robbed of its dignity and respectability.[1] Unattractive similes and comparisons ("like wearyfu' craws", "a crackit bell") reinforce the cheerlessness of the graveyard setting, as does the pointed use of aptly-chosen Scots words with negative connotations: "A flash i' the pan In darkness smored", "They may hae been bitter, an' dour, an' warsh". The wretchedness of the tramps' situation – "Twa düne auld men – naither bite nor bed" – is contrasted in one direction with the grandiose theme of their conversation, in the other to the poet's use of humorous nicknames, "baldy" and "stumpie"; and the resulting tone of sustained irony is effectively broken by the passionate expletive "Mercy o' Gode!" with which the poem ends.

Macgillivray published only two poems in archaic language; and one, *Abasshyd*, is a mere trifle:

I toke hyr heid atween my hondes
  And kyste hyr dusky hair;
I lyghtly touchte hyr luvely cheek
  Syne kyste hyr mouth so rare.

His intention in this poem was evidently not to write in a language clearly identifiable as Scots, or at any rate not to emphasise the Scots component: such spellings as *ane*, *sum* and *lityll* certainly suggest Middle Scots, but *hondes* and *commaunde* are more reminiscent of Chaucerian English, and *aschamte* ("ashamed") and *abasshte* (thus in the text) are not authentic. The question arises, indeed, what was gained by the archaic spellings, for both the technical structure and the literary quality of the poem, such as they are, would have been unaffected if it had been written in contemporary English. Much more interesting is *Ane Playnt of Luve*:

1. "What is Man's chief end?" – "Man's chief end is to glorify God and enjoy Him for ever." The opening of the Shorter Catechism, on which generations of Scottish children were brought up.

O hart, My hart! That gyves na rest,
Bot wyth luve madness dois dismaie;
For all thingis ellis, ye haif na zeste,
Nor thocht; bot luve may drive awaye.
   Deir hart, be still,
   And stay this ill,
Thi passioun sall me slay!

Here Macgillivray has been at some pains to ensure not only the authenticity and consistency of his Middle Scots forms (though *hairt* is a more usual spelling than *hart*), but to maintain a style and sentiment consistent with the supposed historical period: by suggestion, that of Queen Mary or James VI. The opening formula, repeated in each verse and echoed in the "Deir hart" of the wheel, recalls the technique of love poetry of that period (Alexander Scott springs to mind); and the strictly regular metre, the reference to "all hir partis", and the convention of addressing one's own heart, are all details in which Macgillivray adheres faithfully to the poetic practices of the later sixteenth century. Only the rhyme of *disdeyne* with *schyn* and *myne*, which would have been false then as now, strikes a seriously jarring note. *Ane Playnt of Luve* is scarcely a major poem, but it is emblematic of Macgillivray's interest in the literary achievement of Scotland in earlier times, and in the language of those times as a legitimate source for poetic experimentation.

Macgillivray's poetry attains sometimes to merit but rarely to distinction: his interest in language, his vigorous expressions of Scottish patriotism, and the fiercely satirical tone, directed at the Scottish artistic establishment, of a few of his poems, would no doubt have appealed to Grieve, but the latter's attempt to claim for him the status of the greatest contemporary poet in Scotland[1] is an aberration remarkable even for that unpredictable critic. Nonetheless, as an individual and determinedly independent figure in the literary world of the early 1920s he exerted a not unimportant influence; and his efforts at any rate went a short way towards demonstrating the experimental interest of writing in a language influenced by pseudo-Middle Scots.

Whereas Macgillivray ventured only rarely to use an archaic language,

1. In the article on Macgillivray in his *Contemporary Scottish Studies* series, August 31 1925, pp. 13 – 16 of the 1976 edition.

in the Scots poetry of Lewis Spence it is an essential feature of his technique: many of his poems are in pastiche Middle Scots throughout; and even those in a more contemporary language show unmistakable influence from the language and style of a much earlier period.[1]

Spence's fascination with legend and romance, and with the past as reflected therein, is manifest in his poetry. His English poems – accomplished and very attractive specimens of their kind – are uniformly in the vein of late-Victorian romanticism, abounding in lines like "The moon-swan on the night's enchanted lake" or "The phoenix-fabled burning of the year", in exotic place-names (Trebizond, Samarcand, Thrasymene, Famagusta), names from classical and mediaeval lore (Helen, Jason, Broceliande, Beatrice), mythological references (nereids, naiads, dryads; "the moony-painted unicorn, the nyx...", "of griffin or of gorgon..."), words relating to wealth and splendour (*pageants, banners, oriflamme, amethyst, emerald*), images of sun and moon, of palaces, forests, armour and the like, and obsolete and highly-charged words (*swards, merle, sere, glaive, purpure, levin*). Though without intellectual rigour or emotional profundity – the impression given is of what in Middle Scots was referred to as *anammalyng*, skilfully applied but amounting merely to a colourful surface – they show a high degree of sensitivity to the emotive power of words and imagery. A recurring theme is the splendour of Edinburgh: "Royal maiden city", "A city carved from mountain and romance!", "this Naples of the sky", "this high place Wrought for our joy by Time's own grace"; and the poem *Prologue to Festival* ends on a stirring note:

> Now in full stature of Athenian might
> Let us arise and make the nations see
> Where great things were still greater things shall be!

Other poems, too, express Spence's patriotic sentiments in the same manner: Angus and "many-birded Gowrie" are the objects of his expressed romantic attachment, and in the poem *Claymore!* a call to arms is couched in verse which, it must be acknowledged, is scarcely as rousing as the title leads a reader to expect:

1. *Collected Poems of Lewis Spence*, Edinburgh (Serif Books) 1953.

My heart shall never sleep,
　Nor shall my soul be free
Of shadows till our Scotland keep
　Her tryst with Liberty.

It is, indeed, easy to recognise in Spence's English verse the author-
ial talent and cast of mind which, in alliance with an interest in Scots
as a medium for literary effect, would readily produce the works by
which he influenced the development of Scots poetry. Such flights of
fancy as Edinburgh descending like a dragon to drink at the sea (*The
Gray Etin*) or sailing "like an enchanted ship" to meet other great
cities and "ding them a'" (*The Prows o' Reekie*), "the wee May of
Caledon (*Regina Scotorum*)" saying her Pater Noster while four "oufant
wifies" utter grim oracles, or mermaids praying to the "royal lyon
prow" of King Elshinner's wrecked ship are clearly of a piece with
those found in the English poems, and the dominant imagery is the
same. Spence's attraction to what he called "the strange remoteness
of the ballads and of Celtic poetry, that 'otherwhereness' so characteristic of the weird and supernaturally beautiful Scottish verse of the
past", is manifest throughout his work: however, whereas in his
English poetry the suggestion is at best of a continuation of the artificial mediaevalism of the Pre-Raphaelites, in his Scots work the device
of using language and poetic techniques from earlier periods could be
taken as at least a gesture towards presenting his mediaeval inspiration
in a more authentic guise.

A clear illustration of this is his renowned and justly-praised sonnet
Portrait of Mary Stuart, Holyrood. The central theme of the poem, a
beautiful portrait which is nonetheless far excelled in beauty by its living subject, is of course one which occurs frequently in mediaeval and
post-mediaeval romance; though, unusually, the portrait here in question is an actual one, often reproduced, and depicting a woman whom
both contemporary portraits and verbal accounts show to have been
indeed of exceptional beauty. "Sancts and angells" belong to pre-
Reformation Christian thought; the conceit of the stars and planets
as the abode of heavenly beings and their visible light therefore having spiritual as well as merely aesthetic potency is pervasive in mediaeval writing (an example with which the present poem, audaciously,

invites comparison is the opening of *The Kingis Quair*; a connection reinforced by the shared suggestion of the poet contemplating the skies during a sleepless night); roses and lilies as similes for the hues of a beautiful face had become hopelessly clichéd long before Spence but were not in the time of the Stewart monarchy. The persona of the poem, that is, appears to speak from a period remote from its actual date. This impression is reinforced by the language, which abounds in quasi-mediaeval forms: the spellings *hir*, *sancts*, *Scottis*, *mirour*, *spirituall*; the indefinite article *ane*, *haf* for "have"; *bydand* meaning "waiting", which combines a possible (though in fact atypical) Middle Scots spelling of the stem with the familiar *-and* ending of the present participle, also seen in *vivand*; *pleasaunce*, an archaic spelling for a word itself restricted by this date to literary use; the use of *glamour* in its historical rather than its weakened contemporary sense, and again with a quasi-mediaeval spelling; and the rare word *balas* (which appears in *The Kingis Quair*) for a kind of rose-pink ruby. Not all the quasi-archaic or otherwise unusual forms in the poem have definite precedents: *seraphy* appears to be Spence's invention, and *sake*, whatever it means (apparently "image", but for the poem's reprinting in Douglas Young's *Scottish Verse 1851–1951* it is glossed as "self") is either an idiosyncracy or a plain error. A linguistic fault, too, is that neither in Middle nor in Modern Scots can *moon* and *noon* rhyme with *croun*. Despite these questionable details, however, the mutual appropriateness of language, method and subject matter, and the skilful execution, result in a poem of undeniable merit.

Other poems likewise show, though not always with the same success, a mediaeval colouring to language, subject or both. By evoking the ballad of *Sir Patrick Spens* (with references to "King Elshinner" and "the tempests gray o' Norroway") and the scrap of doggerel surviving from the event to which it refers –

> Maydens of Inglande, sore may ye mourne
> For your lemmans ye have lost at Bannocksbourne,
> With heave a lowe!

– Spence produces a fine poem, *The Lost Lyon*, in which the patriotic feelings evoked by those references are enlisted in the service of its optimistic call: "O see anither ship be biggit...":

King Elshinner a ship he biggit,
   Wi' a heave-a-lowe, ye ho!
Cut frae the guid pine-wood and riggit
   Wi' hemp frae the Lowlands low,
Whare the lyart lint doth grow, ye ho!
And the lilt o' the loom is slow.

The Unicorn not only uses an abundance of archaic spellings (*chainyeit, hui-fis, regioun, horss*) and allusions ("Herauld nor pursuivant nor trumpet-tour...", "the desarts Pers and Ynd"), but employs two devices which instantly recall Dunbar: a recurring refrain as the last line of each verse (*Suthely is the Unicorn the roy of all beasts!*) and the extended portrayal of a heraldic animal seen both quasi-realistically and as it appears on a specific blazon (his precedent is the Lion in *The Thrissil and the Rois*). Inventive touches appear in the vocabulary of this poem: *raxters* ("the gowden raxters of the sand") is a rare word of Norse derivation, of which the meaning presumably intended here, a stretch of barren land, is mostly restricted to northern dialects; *farrach* ("this farrach land") is not historically an adjective but a Gaelic-derived noun meaning vigour or energy; *staik* ("than he staiks the shaws") is a rarely-attested (and normally intransitive) verb meaning "to walk with a slow stately step"[1]; *siles* ("...whan the mune she blaws Out of the siles of shaddaw...") is puzzlingly ambiguous, either of two normal senses of the word, "filters" or "rafters", being conceivable (in a figurative sense) in the context. A poem written with a degree of verbal elaboration that again recalls Dunbar (if only as the model which Spence is conscientiously trying to imitate) is *The Pavone*, in which archaic spellings and vocabulary combine with a wealth of alliteration and internal rhymes, mythological references (Tyton, Apollo, Fata Morgana), imagery of lights, jewels and sparkling ornaments and a splendidly mediaeval central conceit (the sub-title of the poem is "In the quhilk the makar compares Juno's bird with Hope") to form as ingenious an example of pastiche-mediaevalism as any in Scottish literature.

Spence's other "sonnets in Scots" are less consistent either in language or in the association of language with subject, and are therefore less suc-

---

1. This is the definition in Walter Gregor's *The Dialect of Banffshire*, a classic work of dialect lexicography, in which *farrach* also appears: could Spence have used this as a source? Gregor was also the author of a short work entitled *Notes on the Folk-Lore of the North-East of Scotland*, which Spence would certainly have known.

cessful. *The Queen's Bath-House, Holyrood*, clearly intended as a companion piece to the *Portrait* poem, lacks its underpinning factor of a striking visual image as the focus for a coherent, if neither profound nor original, idea; and its language includes fewer archaisms (*hald* and *hie* instead of the modern *haud* and *heich*, the -*es* ending (though in Middle Scots it would have been -*is*) in *toures* and its rhymes, the ending on *withouten* and the word *diamant*) and, indeed, fewer Scots features of any kind: there is no obvious reason why *not* is used instead of mediaeval *nocht* or modern *no*, why *hand* and *stands* instead of the well-established Scots *haun* and *stauns*, or why *all* and *walls* should appear alongside *fa'*. The opening line "Time that has dinged doun castels and hie toures" contains an amusing grammatical error: the verb *ding* is invariably strong (conjugated like *sing*); and it can be for no other reason than a consideration of propriety (which assuredly never worried writers of earlier periods) that has led Spence to invent a spurious weak past participle rather than to use the correct form *dung*! (This form occurs in other poems, for example *The Embers o' Embro'*:

> Plotcock had cam' oot to play
> And doon the Castel dung like strae –

but the imagery of this poem is of apocalyptic destruction, very unlike the decorous tone of the sonnet.) *Eidolon* suffers from the opposite error, a concentration of archaic forms for which neither the central thought nor the imagery of the poem provides any particular warrant: *swa*, *fra*, *ane*, *scho*; *saith the buke* (with an obsolete English, not Scots, ending to the verb); *lyre* (complexion), *wilroun* (savage – really a noun in Middle Scots meaning a boar or some other fierce animal, but used inventively by Spence in the collocation *wilroun ways*), *hatrent* (hatred), *felloun frekes* (cruel men – an unfortunate choice, since the word *freke*, common in mediaeval alliterative poetry, being now entirely obsolete will inevitably be misinterpreted by uninformed readers as the homophonous but unrelated *freak*), *barrets* (seemingly an error for *barrace*, rampart).

Spence's verbal dexterity and imaginative fecundity are frequently shown by other means than the use of linguistic and literary archaisms. His fondness for alliteration, often merely as an embroidery, is sometimes turned to impressive onomatopoeic effect, as with the repeated plosives in "No' the greediest gled i' the glebe, no' the corbie nor kae" (*The Haantit Hoosie*), or the last verse of *Craigentinnie*:

> Snell is the wind upon the lea,
> A grue frae aff a dreid despair,
> The nicht brings dule, and bitter sair
> The gurly whisper o' the sea.

His metrical effects can range from gracefully-tripping anapaests –

> As the thrall to the lochan that laved him the fere o' the free,
> Eprile and a sorrow o' waters, to thee sall I gang...
>
> (*Glenshee*)

– to an invigorating concoction alternating hammer-beat stresses with irregular sprinklings of unstressed syllables –

> Awa' wi' diddles on the pipes and the fiddles,
> Awa' wi' yer ballats and yer flings sae free!
> Hey for the smiddy whaur the auld toun hiddles,
> And the lilt o' the hammer in the North Countree!
>
> (*The Sang o' the Smiddy*)

Scots words from the contemporary language are often well selected for their expressive force: the verse just quoted from *Craigentinnie* contains several examples, and others are "To gar it shog wi' dunts o' Hell" (*The Embers o' Embro'*), "She turnit wi a foumart's girn And yammert..." (*The Gyre Carline*: echoes of a much more recent literary source, namely Stevenson's *Thrawn Janet*, can be detected in this poem), or

> A pibroch's sough, a clarsach's tang
> Were plaidings to the saul o' a sang.
>
> (*The Ferlie*)

Spence's approach to politics was deliberately emotional: in the introduction to a pamphlet entitled *Freedom for Scotland* which he wrote as President of the Scottish National Movement[1] (in fact a detailed, reasoned and carefully-organised summary, presented with considerable rhetorical force, of arguments which are as valid today as when the pamphlet was produced, containing historical interpretations of which some are now discredited but others are both accurate and relevant) he wrote: "I have not burdened this narrative of Scotland's record and wrongs with a great array of facts. I have chosen rather the medium of sentiment, for I know

1. Scottish National Party Publications, undated.

that by sentiment we Scots live and die". (Had this approach been maintained by the protagonists of the cause, it would probably have succeeded long ago: it is no very profound or abstruse observation that feelings are a far more powerful motivating force than factual arguments. The fact that from that day to this opponents of Scottish independence have invariably chosen to deride the cause as "sentimental" or "emotional" or "romantic", and still more the fact that its proponents have seemed to accept the implication that this aspect of the case is indeed without value and therefore concentrated their arguments on the practical, material benefits of independence, is one of the saddest and strangest features of Scottish politics.) As a poet, Spence's intention was probably again to appeal to the emotions, by way of the ear and the sensory imagination; but though he can bring the evocative power of words and images expertly to life, his work, even at its most skilful and most imaginative, is in no sense profound: a reader of his poetry can admire his verbal ingenuity, but will not be touched in the intellect or the deeper emotions. In 1929, by which time most of his poems had been published, Spence wrote in despondent terms of the failure (as he saw it) of both himself and Grieve, who had tried different methods of reviving Scots as a poetic language: "Two distinct efforts have been made to render it [Scots] more sophisticated and suitable for the higher flights of poetry, one rather more elaborate than the other. Speaking frankly, neither has been successful..."[1] Yet Spence's influence has been profound; and he deserves to be remembered, not only for the two or three individual poems that regularly appear in anthologies, but as a seminal figure in the Scots Renaissance. By re-discovering the language of the mediaeval period – not its relatively superficial (and sometimes erroneously presented) features such as spellings, but part at least of its vocabulary and its poetic techniques – and utilising it in an arresting and highly controversial body of poetry, he stimulated not only further experiment but an active debate which kept the issue of Scots poetry in the attention of the literary public.[2] And despite his misgivings, the vein of mediaevalism

1. "Scots Poetry Today", in *Nineteenth Century and After*, 106 (1929), pp. 253–68.

2. The pages of the *Scottish Educational Journal* furnish lively illustrations of this: issues of July and August 1926 included an exchange of long and impassioned letters in which the main players were Spence, Grieve and one Donald MacKenzie, a determined critic of the other two. (MacKenzie, it must be acknowledged, kept his temper and his dignity in the debate much more successfully than Spence.) See pp. 114–124 of the 1976 edition.

which he more than any other poet added to his contemporary poetic Scots has remained as an integral part of the medium ever since.

6

Traditional Scots Continues:
Marion Angus, Violet Jacob, Helen Cruickshank, Alexander Gray

As the strongly regional school of poetry in the North-East was adding its distinctive contribution to the development of Scots poetry, a noteworthy group of poets – all, as it happened, from the same area of Scotland, but less inclined than Murray and Mary Symon to emphasise the local characteristics of their language – continued to enhance the national poetic scene with work in traditional Scots: a language showing neither archaisms nor innovations, and one in which regional shibboleths were incidental rather than essential to the desired poetic effect; but a language which the talent of the writers was able to develop for poetry of impressive force and beauty.

In some respects the most individual of the group, and indeed one of the most distinctive voices in modern Scots poetry, is Marion Angus.[1] The quality which pervades almost all her work was summarised in an obituary notice published on 19 August 1946:

> She caught the note of "gramarye" which is the peculiar distinction of the Scottish ballads; she possessed the gift of "natural magic" which Matthew Arnold regarded as the chief contribution of the Celt to English poetry; and she understood what Mr de la Mare has called "poor mortal longingness," especially the longingness of ageing and forsaken women, and expressed it in verse of rare subtlety, tenderness and sweetness.[2]

1. A collected edition of Marion Angus's poems is long overdue, though *Selected Poems*, ed. Maurice Lindsay, Edinburgh (Serif Books) 1950, contained an adequate representative selection. Her individual collections are *The Lilt and Other Verses*, Aberdeen (Wyllie) 1922, *The Tinker's Road and Other Verses*, London (Gowans and Gray) 1924, *Sun and Candlelight*, Edinburgh (Porpoise) 1927, *The Singin' Lass*, Edinburgh (Porpoise) 1929, *The Turn of the Day*, Edinburgh (Porpoise) 1931, *Lost Country and Other Verses*, Glasgow (Gowans and Gray) 1937.

2. A copy of this is held in Aberdeen University's archive of papers relating to Marion Angus, but the source is unidentified.

In all features of its phonology and grammar, her Scots is consistent, and used with the easy and natural grace of one born and bred to speak it. A couple of shibboleths identify the dialect as Eastern (except in one poem, *George Gordon, Lord Byron*, in which the language is made to harmonise with the Aberdeen setting by North-Eastern touches such as *fan* (when), *fatna* (what: *whitna* in most other dialects), *fussles* (whistles) and *steens* (stones: instead of *stanes*). Intriguingly, however, the "haunting, elfin note"[1] of Marion Angus's poetry is not associated with obviously inventive uses of Scots, but, on the contrary, by a sparse language in which peculiarly Scots vocabulary items are rare and almost wholly restricted to words with physical referents.

The poem *Mary's Song* illustrates several recurring features of her language and style:

I wad hae gi'en him my lips tae kiss,
Had I been his, had I been his;
Barley breid and elder wine,
Had I been his as he is mine.

The wanderin' bee it seeks the rose;
Tae the lochan's bosom the burnie goes;
The grey bird cries at evenin's fa',
"My luve, my fair one, come awa'."

My beloved sall ha'e this he'rt tae break,
Reid, reid wine and the barley cake,
A he'rt tae break, and a mou' tae kiss,
Tho' he be nae mine, as I am his.

Though the language is Scots in its phonology (except for *goes* and *break*, apparently rhyme-forced, and the seemingly unmotivated *one*), scarcely a word belongs to the distinctively Scots lexical stock: *lochan* is a Gaelic diminutive, rarely used in Scots (though occurring elsewhere in Marion Angus's poetry); and *burnie* is the only instance of a Scots vocabulary item. The language is of the simplest; and the startling emotional force of the poem is achieved by means which are, superficially at least, easy to identify: the negative implication of *wad hae gi'en* and the following (repeated) negative conditional; the emotionally charged images of the second verse, with the metaphorical *bosom* and the diminutives *lochan*

1. Obituary notice in *The Bulletin*, August 1946.

and *burnie* reinforcing the sense of tenderness; the juxtaposition of the parallel phrases in *A he'rt tae break, and a mou' tae kiss*, conveying the suggestion that the first refers to an action as simple and literal as the second; the recurrence of words and phrases from the first verse in the last, with the heightening addition of an overt reference to the *he* as *my beloved* and the emotional as well as visual intensity suggested by the repetition of *reid*. If it is assumed, as it generally is, that the "Mary" of the title is Mary of Bethany,[1] a whole field of potent implications is generated; but none of the details cited depends *entirely* for its effect on this or any specific identification of the speaker. This poem is, in fact, an outstanding example of a writer's skill in exploiting the inherent evocative power of simple, direct statement and images with automatic emotional connotations: Marion Angus here merits comparison with Burns in several of his songs.

The Lilt, another of her best-known poems, is similar in style and method. The language is unequivocally Scots: the words show the phonological developments by which Scots and English have been mutually diverging since the Old English period (*lane, ain, gane; nicht, licht; heid, threid; saft, sang;* and so on); and the phrasing too is Scots: *a' her lane, aye she minds o'. . ., the years that's bye and gane.* The easy, fluent rhythm, disyllabic and trisyllabic feet alternating with the randomness of colloquial speech, serves to foreground the refrain *the sma', sma' rain* with its succession of stressed syllables. As in *Mary's Song*, repetitions abound: *a' her lane* is emphasised by the presence of *lane* as a rhyme word in each verse (though once, in *Lovers' Lane*, it is a different, homonymous word). The sudden sensual intensity of *your lips were flamin' reid* contrasts arrestingly with the muted tone of the first two verses; the vocative "Oh! Lass" and the dramatic change from third to second person bring the "young lass" of what is in the poem's time-frame the past more immediately within the reader's awareness than "Jean Gordon" of the poem's present; the demonstrative in *yon rose* (no rose has been mentioned hitherto) suggests that the memory of the events described is already fully shared by the reader. However, words for which a monolingual English-speaker would require a glossary are almost completely absent.

1. See Luke 10.38 ff., John 11.1 – 45 and 12.1 – 8.

This is clearly deliberate: one would not have to venture into the more obscure reaches of the Scots vocabulary, for example, to find words which would express the senses of *stealin'* and *slippit*, words which Scots shares with English, by "Scotland-specific" words (the verbs *snuive, smool, jink, link*, leap to mind). Yet Marion Angus's choice of "common Anglo-Saxon" rather than peculiarly Scots words in this context serves two definite poetic purposes. First, since the actions referred to are covert and clandestine, words which pointedly drew the reader's attention to themselves, and hence to the actions which they describe, would defeat the intended effect. Second, the only strongly-marked Scots lexical item in the poem, *smoory*, is thus reserved to qualify the word *hill* on the last of its four occurrences, positioned as the final word of the fifth line – the only unrhymed one – in each stanza except the last.

Certainly, there are several poems in Marion Angus's opus where Scots vocabulary is much more conspicuous than in those two. Scots words may be used for their emotive force: the title poem of her collection *The Tinker's Road* is an example:

> The broon burn's speerin',
> Frettin' a' the wye,
> "What gars ye gang
> Auld Tinker's road,
> Whaur there's naither fouk nor kye [...]

In this poem almost all the Scots words – *dour, unco, dule, smoored, dowie, sough* – in one way or another suggest gloom, sadness or menace; and they are judiciously placed, often being highlighted by her characteristic repetition of grammatical and rhythmic patterns:

> Stannin' stanes bloomin',
> Grim an' straucht an' dour –
>
> Ghaist or witch or deil,
> Stanes o' dule an' ill [...]

Frequently a Scots word forms part of a pattern of assonance or vowel harmony, a device which Marion Angus uses with great delicacy: the poem *Treasure Trove* has, among other examples, "liltin' and linkin' on the steep hill heids" and

> Reistlin' the heather, an' keekin' 'naith the weeds,
> Seekin' and greetin' in the cauld weet days [...]

In the same poem, however, the line "Steek the door; the munelicht's on the lone hill heids – ", the reason for *lone* instead of the Scots *lane* is almost certainly for the sound: the vowel-harmony with *door*, and the closer approximation to the vowel of *mune*. (One consistent feature by which Marion Angus reveals her dialect is that words like *mune* and *dune*, which she sometimes, but not consistently, spells *müne* etc., are made to rhyme freely with words like *doon* and *croon*. The rhyme is not perfect in any dialect, but in Angus and the Mearns, where the original rounding of the *mune*-vowel has been retained giving a sound like the [ø] of French *deux*, it is at least closer than in dialects where the pronunciation is *min* (Central and Western dialects) or *meen* (North-Eastern).)

Marion Angus, in fact, is one of the clearest exemplars to be examined in this book of the truth that it is possible to write in a language which is, on any showing, unequivocally Scots without making any effort whatever to exploit the distinctive Scots vocabulary. Much of her unique charm inheres precisely in the contrast between the simplicity of her language, at all levels, and the intense emotional charge of the scenes or events which she evokes: in this, and in her recurring use of external details to convey an emotional state, her poetry is strongly reminiscent of the ballad tradition, by which it is obviously influenced. The pathetic fallacies which recur in her verse, and which contribute to the supernatural aura which it often conveys, arise naturally from her method, and are scarcely to be seen as a fault:

> Lassie, think lang, think lang,
> The trees is clappin' their han's,
>
> (*Think Lang*)

> The Corbie Burn's ayont the Dee –
> Wi' cauld white lips it girned at me;
>
> (*The Blue Boat*)

Her poetic effects *may* be dependent on the use of Scots words, and are certainly often enhanced by them; but the characteristic features of her style – repetitions of words, particularly rhyme words, and of rhythmic and grammatical patterns; pervasive though unobtrusive use of alliteration and vowel harmony; references to the scenery of hills and moors, and to birds (with their calls), flowers and conditions of light and weather; frequent use of colour words (*grey* and *gowden* being a favourite

71

collocation) and of references to things with intense colours ("Whaur the rose burns bricht, An' the berry burns reid" (*Patrick*)); use of personae with definite, but unspecified, identities (as opposed to a neutral anonymity) – are in no sense conditional on her using Scots, and in fact are regularly found in her English poetry too. Yet neither is her use of Scots merely incidental: Scots and English in her work are different languages, each with its own individual nature and range of proper uses. An interesting and curious confirmation of this is found in the original version of *Mary's Song*. The version discussed earlier, familiar from numerous anthologies, is not the form in which this poem first appeared: when published in *Scottish Chapbook* Vol. II no. 1, August 1923 (the year before its appearance in the collection *The Tinker's Road and Other Verses*) the three stanzas, enclosed in speech marks, were preceded by the couplet

Mary sings by her candle's light
In the quiet night – the quiet night –

and followed by

So soft she sings by her candle light
In the quiet night – the quiet night.

The title was *So Soft she Sings*. (A few other, very minor, variations require no discussion.) The reasons for the alteration can only be conjectured: a possible one may have been simply to lessen the frequency, amounting to a habit, with which candle light occurs in her poetry: but what is particularly striking is the obvious contrast between the Scots of the song and the English (*light* and *night*, *so*, *soft* and *quiet* instead of *licht* and *nicht*, *sae*, *saft* and *quaiet*, all forms which appear elsewhere in her works) of the framing couplets. By implication, Mary's words in Scots are transmitted to the reader by an unidentified English-speaking observer. Since the style and register of the frame is no different from that of the song, something must have been intended by the language change: Scots itself, conceivably, has a deeper emotional resonance for a poem of unrequited love than English.

The poetry of Violet Jacob, Marion Angus's almost exact contemporary, contrasts with hers in several respects. Conspicuously, Violet Jacob identifies herself much more overtly as a poetess of her region, as is clearly shown by the titles of her two volumes of poetry: *Songs of Angus* and *More Songs of Angus.*[1] References to actual places are frequent; and much literary capital is gained from the local patriotism of the personae of the poems: in *The Howe o' the Mearns* and *The Wild Geese* the exile's longing for his calf-ground is poignantly evoked; in *Baltic Street* the speaker, while acknowledging that Montrose is objectively not particularly impressive –

> Oh, Baltic Street is cauld an' bare
> An' mebbe no sae grand,

– vigorously expresses his affection for it; and in *"Kirrie"* the speaker's love of home is expressed in language which, to an outsider, would seem comically exaggerated: "For it's fules wad bide in London when they kent o' Kirriemuir." In her poems of the Great War, the tone of local pride is skilfully combined with another frequent theme in her poetry, a literal and unquestioning belief in the Christian afterlife, to intensely moving effect: in *Jock, to the First Army* the voices of friends killed in action speak to a young recruit:

> "We've sic a wale o' Angus men
> That we canna weary lang."

And in *Montrose* a soldier prays to be allowed, in the event of his death, a brief visit to his beloved home town:

> Heaven's hosts are glad,
> Heaven's hames are bricht,
> And in yon streets o' licht
> Walks mony an Angus lad;
> But my he'rt's aye back
> Whaur my ain toon stands
> And the steeple's shade is laid when the tide's at the slack
> On the lang sands.

Even in poems where no specific place is named, a strong sense of locality pervades the writing, suggested by frequent references to landscape features, landmarks, and directions: "Beside the doo'cot up the braes The fields slope doon frae me..." – "As I gaed doon by the twa mill dams i' the mornin'..." – "They turned their faces southward frae the glens they aye had kent..."; and changing seasons are regularly evoked, often

1. London (Murray) 1915 and London (Country Life) 1918; collected in *The Scottish Poems of Violet Jacob*, Edinburgh (Oliver and Boyd) 1944.

with strongly-emphasised emotional overtones:

> When spring comes loupin' doon the braes
> And nakit trees are gettin' claes...

> When the clouds hang laigh wi' the wecht o' their load o' greetin',
> And the autumn wind's asteer...

> There's snaw i' the wind, an' the weepies
> Hang deid on the shaw...

Her language, too, contains rather more identifiably Eastern features than that of Marion Angus, causing John Buchan to remark, in his introduction to *Songs of Angus*, "The dialect is Angus, with unfamiliar notes to my Border ear, and in every song there is the sound of the east wind and the rain". *Ane* rhymes with *plane* (instead of the *yin* of Central and Western and the *een* of North-Eastern dialects) and *fa'* with *Na, na!* (instead of the "faw" sound of further south and west). A scarecrow is a *tattie-dulie*, a term whose domain almost precisely defines Angus and the Mearns; a lapwing is a *teuchat*, a word heard from the Tay to the Spey; *arn-tree* (alder), *weepies* (ragwort, a common weed), *kep* (meet), *haver* (not only in the general Scots sense of "talk idly or foolishly" but in the much more locally restricted sense of "saunter about") are likewise words which mark the user as belonging to the district north of the Tay. In *Pride*, one of her most scathingly satirical poems, two local words with strongly adversative meanings serve to reveal the spiteful and envious nature of the speaker:

> For there's him noo wi' his neb to the sky
> In yon deil's machinery *swiggit* [swinging] by...
> But oh! the he'rt o' a body bleeds
> For favours *sclarried* [plastered] on sinfu' heids.

(The use of dramatic monologues in which the speaker unconsciously reveals more than he intends is a device which Violet Jacob uses frequently; and it is observable that her personae are frequently (though not in this poem) male: Marion Angus, by contrast, almost never adopts a male persona.)

Violet Jacob's Scots has the authentic ring of a mother-tongue, abounding not only in distinctive words but in unobtrusive details of grammar: *let me hame, there's him* (another Eastern feature: elsewhere one hears *there he's*), *what a years!* (i.e. "how many years!"), *what grand's the smell ye'll get*: and idiom: *Auld Kate's awa'* (i.e. dead), *she'd sort him weel* (put him in his place), *ye'd up wi' yer windy, an' it's lang, lang waitin' while I sit my lane.* In contrast to the fey, elusive quality of Marion Angus, references to the scenes, events and personae of her poems are usually clear and overt: the seasonal activities of farming, and such aspects of social life as courting and convivial drinking, are evoked with appropriate Scots words and expressions: "We've stookit the hairst an' we're needin' To gaither it in...", "I'm fairly disjaskit, Christina...",

> The stars will drap ayont the hill
> An' Charlewayne turn tapsalteerie,
> Fu' mony a lad has got his fill
> And gane his gate or we be weary.

As with Marion Angus, however, emotional intensity is often conveyed by means other than the use of powerful Scots words: metrical effects, for example, are a conspicuous part of her stock-in-trade, as for example in *Tam i' the Kirk*, where the mood of erotic exultation is suggested by the surging rhythms of the long lines:

> Oh Jean, my Jean, when the bell ca's the congregation
> O'er valley and hill wi' the ding frae its iron mou...

and at the other end of the emotional scale, in *The Field by the Lirk o' the Hill* – as moving a piece as any in the repertory of Great War poetry – where frequent weighting of the two-beat lines with a third pitch-prominent syllable imparts a slow, dirge-like movement to the verse:

> Daytime and nicht,
> Sun, wind an' rain
> The lang, cauld licht
> O' the spring months again...

In both these poems, too, the simple device of verbal repetition – "Crying 'Jean! Jean! Jean!'" , "Aye, bairn, nae mair, nae mair" – conveys precisely the note of joy or despair.

Of the remarkable trio of Angus poetesses, Helen Cruickshank, the youngest, was also the most intimately associated with the Scottish Renaissance; not only because of her friendship with Grieve and other members of the movement and her own active contribution to it, but because, unlike Violet Jacob and Marion Angus, she continued to write and publish poetry almost to the end of her life, by which time the Renaissance was a fact of Scottish literary culture.[1] She is the only one of the three, too, whose poetry shows any degree of "modernist" influence. Whereas the other two invariably follow traditional principles of rhyming and scansion (though their metres are often both inventive and conducive to delicate literary effects), Helen Cruickshank occasionally (much more frequently in her English than in her Scots poetry) uses unrhymed and free verse:

> Frost, I mind, an' snaw,
> An' a bairn comin' hame frae the schule
> Greetin', nearly, wi' cauld,
> But seein', for a' that,
> The icicles i' the ditch,
> The snaw-ploo's marbled tracks,
> An' the print o' the rabbits' feet
> At the hole i' the wire.
>
> (*Background*)

Sudden momentary shifts of focus occur in this poem: the word *marbled* – a word which the child *seein'* these things would not have used – repositions the description as one embellished by the remembering "I"; and the present tense of "...frostit fingers rubbed Till they *dirl* wi' pain", besides emphasising the Scots word, brings a distant recollection to immediate reality. In *The Ponnage Pool*, the contrast between the precision, beauty and intensity of the images of nature (one of the most striking and most pervasive features of Helen Cruickshank's style) and the strange indefiniteness of the speaker's identity creates a similarly disorienting effect:

> I am the deep o' the pule,
> The fish, the fisher,
> The river in spate,
> The broon o' the far peat-moss,
> The shingle bricht wi' the flooer
> O' the yellow mim'lus,
> The martin fleein' across.

(The final line, "Ae day I'll faddom my doobts", is, in the context of the

---

1. *Collected Poems*, Edinburgh (Reprographia) 1971, and *More Collected Poems*, Edinburgh (Wright) 1978.

poem, a weakness, reducing the mysterious speaker to the status of an ordinary individual with problems.)

Helen Cruickshank's Scots is for the most part a straightforward version of the traditional literary language, with an occasional Eastern word: examples include *ted*, a term of endearment – actually the same word as *taid* "toad", but the form is that favoured in Angus and the Mearns; *sacket* "rascal" (used of a child); *pillydacus*, a jocular word with the sense of "heid bummer", entertainingly applied to Grieve in her *Epistle for Christopher Murray Greive on his 75th birthday*: "Chief pillydacus o' the haill clanjamphray!" – the last word in this line is an obvious allusion to its use in one of Grieve's lyrics. *Yorline* "yellowhammer", in "But I ken whaur the yorline biggs" (*Keepit In*) also suggests a literary usage, however inappropriate – to be pedantic – to the schoolboy persona, as this is a Border word (the source, conceivably, being Hogg's *Kilmeny*): the bird is known in the East as a *yella-yite*. Once or twice the accent becomes North-Eastern: *mith* instead of *micht*, or (as in *The Weird Wife*) the well-known initial *f*: *Far are ye gaun. . . Fat wull ye fin. . .* Her manifest love for and sensitivity to the natural world leads to the appearance of several Scots names for living creatures: *clok-leddy*, *ettercap* and *moudiewarp* appear in the poem *Beasties*; *whaup*, *mavis*, *cushie*, *gorlin* and *hoolet* in *Voices from the Waterside*. Insult words are used to good effect in *Lizzie*:

> Bess is a thowless shilpit quean,
> Mary is mim and primsy. . .

and still better in *Fause Friend*:

> Ye're dooble-jinted, soople-sawled,
> An' slithery as an eel. . .

– and in *Coontit Oot* the lines of traditional children's counting rhymes are woven into the verse to produce a delightful bairnsang:

> *Eenerty, feenerty, fickerty, feg,*
> I saw a man wi a crookity leg,
> *Irkie, birkie, story, rock,*
> Airmin a wife wi a raggity frock. . .

Once, memorably, she produces an experiment in archaic language: *A Lang Guidnicht* not only imitates Middle Scots spelling conventions but recalls the Castalian poet Alexander Montgomerie, addressed in the first line "Montgomerie, I rede thy solemn sang. . ." in its use of internal rhymes (each end-rhyme being repeated in the second foot of the following line).

The extent to which Marion Angus, Violet Jacob and Helen Cruickshank saw their practice of writing in Scots as contributing to a political cause, or as having political significance at all, is not always easy to determine. Marion Angus, though keenly interested in the developments in Scottish letters being initiated by Grieve,[1] left no recorded remarks from which a personal *credo* regarding the use of Scots could be deduced; and it is noticeable that Scottish patriotism is not, to any extent, a theme of her poetry. The intense love of home which pervades Violet Jacob's poetry is focused on Angus, or a specific place within it, rather than on Scotland as a nation: the last voice heard in *Jock, to the First Army* says:

> "We're near, we're here, my wee recruit,
> And we fecht for Scotland still."

– but this is in the special context of a war poem; and in the work of both poetesses their choice of Scots for their medium suggests a natural, joyful and grateful availing themselves of the resources of a fondly remembered mother-tongue, rather than a means of making a political gesture. Helen Cruickshank stands to some extent in contrast with the other two, since the social and political condition of Scotland forms the theme of at least a few, mostly later, poems: in *A Lang Guidnicht* the elegance of the pseudo-archaic verse masks an angry reproach to a personified Scotland for its inability to stem the loss of its citizens by emigration; the English poem *Lines for Wendy Wood's Scottish Watch* ends

> We will not rest, till Scotland rings again
> With her children's songs.

Dry Stane Dykes includes an overt call for independence:

> And lang may Scotland haud her ain traditions,
> Yet claim her richtfu place in League o Nations.

– and poetic tributes to Grieve and Lewis Grassic Gibbon express strong sympathy with their patriotic aims. In her *Octobiography*,[2] too, she expressed her thoughts in terms strangely reminiscent of Allan Ramsay's

---

1. See "A Personal Note" by Helen Cruickshank in Maurice Lindsay's *Selected Poems of Marion Angus, op. cit.*
2. Montrose (Standard Press) 1976.

two centuries previously:

> During sporadic outbreaks in the national press there were even Scottish
> correspondents who boasted that they could not read the Scots language.
> Why this mental blockage? Would we respect a Frenchman who repu-
> diated all desire to know anything about Breton dialect and literature? –
> or a German who similarly rejected platt-Deutsch? Our Scots language is
> so colourful, graphic, economical, pungent or poignant that I am con-
> stantly surprised it is not oftener used by poets. Does the blame lie in the
> schools, or further back in the standards laid down by the Scottish
> Education Department? As the Orkney poet George Mackay Brown says
> in "The Orkney Tapestry": "Decay of language is always the symptom
> of a more serious sickness." (p. 77)

The last poet to be examined in this chapter left his views on Scots in
no doubt. The contribution of Alexander Gray to the literary development of the language in this period is of greater extent than his contemporary reputation, or lack of it, would suggest. Except for *Scotland*,
regularly included in anthologies, his poetry is not widely known:
whereas Violet Jacob, Marion Angus and Helen Cruickshank are recognised as poetesses of stature and importance, Gray is virtually overlooked
in current assessments of Scottish literary history.[1] Yet not only does his
Scots verse demonstrate a high degree of skill and inventiveness, but his
writings on the status and legitimate uses of Scots formed, and still form,
a major contribution to the debate.

Gray's original poetry is nearly all in English, though an occasional
Scots word (for example the name of a bird or a tree) may occur. In
Drawing Houses, a tree mentioned earlier in the poem is identified in the
last stanza as a rowan; and for the last two lines the language changes to
Scots, the words *hoose* and *burn* pointedly contrasting with the *house* and

---

1. C. M. Grieve in 1926 (*Scottish Educational Journal*, September 18: see *Contemporary Scottish Studies*, 1976 edn.,p.35) expressed the view that among his contemporaries were ten poets of equal merit to any whom Scotland had produced in all its history and that Gray only just failed to attain to membership of that exalted company; by contrast, in the recent *Aberdeen History of Scottish Literature* he is not even mentioned in the index (neither, incidentally, are most of Grieve's ten).

stream used previously in the poem. His Scots poetry consists entirely of translations, appearing in five books published at wide intervals of time.[1] A full discussion of the status of poetic translations would clearly be out of place in the present context; but since there is no question that, firstly, a good poetic translation is a poem in its own right, and like any other poem a demonstration of the literary resources of the language in which it is written, and secondly, translation is an accepted (indeed a traditional) means of expanding the literary range of the target language, it follows that in a discussion of a poetic language at a particular period in its history translations furnish precisely the same kind of material for examination as original poetry.

Gray was a native of Dundee, and his poetic idiolect is firmly rooted in the dialect of this area. To a greater extent than Marion Angus or even Violet Jacob, he uses spellings which clearly indicate a specific dialectal pronunciation: *han'* and *weet*, instead of (among other possibilities) *haun'* and *wat*; *grite* and *sweit* (i.e. "great" and "sweat"), suggesting a diphthongal pronunciation; rhymes such as *lane/teen*, *ta'en/een*, showing the Eastern raising of [e], from OE long *a*, to [i] before [n]; the rhyme *wey/ gude-bye*, suggesting a fully open diphthong in the first word ("way") instead of the more general close one. These features identify his dialect at least as emanating from north of the Tay: a more precise geographical demarcation is possible from his rhyme *deid/see'd* ("dead/see it"), showing a voicing of the cliticised pronoun not heard in true North-Eastern dialects, and by an orthographic feature which he shares with Marion Angus (though Gray is more consistent): the use of *ü* – *düne, schüle, blümes, müne* – for the characteristic front-rounded vowel of the Eastern dialect. His vocabulary too, though in the main common-core Scots, contains a few words, if only a tiny handful, which would be unfamiliar to a reader from south of the Tay: *sipin* (soaking), *plisky* (mischievous trick), and *glame* (flame). A more individual feature of Gray's vocabulary, though one which might readily be overlooked, is a preponderance of

---

1. *Songs and Ballads, Chiefly from Heine* (Grant Richards, London, 1920), *Arrows: A Book of German Ballads and Folk-Songs Attempted in Scots* (Grant and Murray, Edinburgh, 1932), *Sir Halewyn: Examples in European Balladry and Folk-Song* (Oliver and Boyd, Edinburgh and London, 1949), *Four and Forty: A Selection of Danish Ballads Presented in Scots* (University Press, Edinburgh, 1954), and *Historical Ballads of Denmark* (University Press, Edinburgh, 1958).

words which are, in a specific and limited sense, "poetic": though by no means rare in conversational speech, they had by Gray's time acquired a poetic patina from their frequent (in some cases over-frequent) use in verse. A small selection might include *caller* (fresh), *canty* (cheerful), *couthy* (friendly, companionable), *crouse* (Gray's gloss is "confident," though it has other meanings), *dule* (sorrow), *ferlie* (marvel), *laverock* (lark), *puirtith* (poverty), *skaith* (injury), *vauntie* (proud). Gray's deliberate use of such words is a definite feature of his style, and most appropriate to his practice: the tradition of German folk-poetry is remarkably similar to that of Scottish, and in Germany, as in Scotland, many poets have been strongly influenced by the folk tradition; and Gray's translations from German ballads, and from poets such as Müller, Herder and Heine who were strongly influenced by the themes and conventions of folk-poetry, contain deliberate reminiscences of works from the Scottish tradition into which he is transplanting them.[1]

Gray himself, in the introduction to *Four and Forty*, clearly states his attitude to his medium, both in itself and in its appropriateness for his purposes. It is, he argues, inherently fitting that ballads should be translated into a *dialect*. He candidly admits to being unable to discern precisely why this should be so, but appeals to the experience of earlier translators who have shared his intuitive conviction. This is the reason for his choice of Scots as his medium: Scots, he goes on to argue, is *not* a "language". The controversy regarding its status, he observes, "recurrently strains the correspondence columns of *The Scotsman* and *The Glasgow Herald* to bursting point": forty years after he wrote this, it still does. Rather, it is one of many distinct but closely related forms which the ancestral Anglo-Saxon has taken in the British Isles and beyond, and the only one, except for standard English, with a long-established literary tradition which has included some of the greatest and most widely-renowned writers in the entire canon of "English" literature – surely, Gray suggests, a perfectly sufficient source of justifiable patriotic pride without attempting to make the further claim that it is (or should be, or

---

1. For discussion, see J. D. McClure, "Alexander Gray's translations from German folk-song", in *Appropriations and Impositions: National, Regional and Sexual Identity in Literature. Proceedings of the Fifth International Conference on the Literature of Region and Nation*, eds. Igor Navrátil and R. B. Pynsent, Bratislava (Národné literárne centrum) 1997, 83 – 93.

could be made to be) a language as distinct from English as is Dutch. Gray's arguments for this view of Scots are, firstly, that it is and always has been closely related to English; secondly, that there is no clear boundary between the two, speakers and writers of Scots having always regarded themselves as free to adopt English, or to modulate between Scots and English, when this is felt to be appropriate on either social or literary grounds; thirdly, that Scots has never been spoken throughout Scotland, is far from uniform within its speech area, and merges at the Border into Northern English dialects which have more in common with Scots than with the dialects of southern England; fourthly, that some of the greatest of mediaeval Scottish poets quite clearly regarded their language, which they called *Inglis*, as being one with the language of Chaucer. All this, of course, is incontrovertibly true. It should be noted, too, that this preface of Gray's was published in 1954, by which time not only had his own credentials as a writer of Scots been long since established, but in the other camp, the second wave of "synthetic Scots" writers – Sydney Goodsir Smith, Robert Garioch, Douglas Young, Tom Scott, Alexander Scott, Alastair Mackie – had followed MacDiarmid in proving beyond controversy that a Scots more artificial than he had ever used could be not only a credible but a superb literary medium. Gray, though assuredly not denying the value of the poetic effusions of that group, firmly rejected any linguistic or historic credibility for the claim that their Scots could or should ever become a national language, and the need for any such case to be argued on patriotic grounds: "Do we really need for our national self-esteem a language all our own, shared by none other – not even by our Scots brothers in Nova Scotia?"

Gray's view of the Scots tongue itself, and of the literary-political controversy surrounding it, may be characterised as eminently realistic. Thoroughly familiar with his local dialect as actually spoken, and seeing in it and in the great Scots literature of the past a just, firm and sufficient ground for patriotic pride, he was wholly unconvinced of any need to venture beyond the bounds which intra- and extra-linguistic history had set for the tongue. His attitude to Scots was closer to that of Murray or Violet Jacob than to that of Grieve and his successors. And his actual poetic practice is precisely in accordance with this estimate of Scots, its status and its capacities: his translations from German and Danish balladry recall the original Scottish ballads, and the poetry which they influenced, with such impeccable accuracy as to set a standard for not only translation, but "transplanting" of a foreign poetic product into native soil. One example will suffice:

That you're my ain true love
Weel can you see.
Come in the nicht, come in the nicht,
Whisper: "It's me."

Juist come straicht ben, my lad,
When it stricks twel'.
Faither sleeps, mither sleeps;
I'm by mysel'.

Tirl at the chawmer door;
Lift the sneck high.
Father says: "What a wind."
Mither says "Ay."

(*The Invitation*, in *Arrows*, p.50)

What the achievement of these four poets clearly shows is that though Scots indubitably received a galvanic new lease of life from the innovative practices of Grieve and his successors, it did not *need* those to maintain it in being – still less to bring it again into being – as a viable poetic medium. Violet Jacob and Marion Angus were already writing excellent poetry in Scots before the publication of Grieve's first collection, and continued to do so in a language and style effectively uninfluenced by him for many years after this; Helen Cruickshank and Alexander Gray, despite their enthusiastic interest and active participation in the literary and linguistic controversies of the Scottish Renaissance, continued their use of what was essentially a Scots based on ancestral spoken dialects, wrought into poetic forms in use since the Vernacular Revival, for decades after the MacDiarmid revolution had been established. Despite the fascination of the experimental poetry in Scots in which the twentieth century has abounded, it would be a grave mistake to overlook the fact that poetry of which both the language and the style are in a more conservative vein forms an integral part of the recent Scottish poetic achievement.

7
The MacDiarmid Revolution

That Christopher Grieve did not initiate the revival of Scots as a poetic medium in the twentieth century – as is by now clear – is in no sense a denigration of his achievement, which is of fundamental importance. The potent combination, in Grieve as an individual, of a capacious intellect and phenomenally retentive memory, a fascination with language and its possible effects, a passionately-held commitment to Scottish political and cultural nationalism (albeit idiosyncratically conceived) and to radical socialism, a total fearlessness in expressing his beliefs combined with a cavalier disregard for mere consistency or factual accuracy, and a degree of literary genius rarely encountered in any time or place, enabled him to produce a poetic corpus containing some of the most stimulating, challenging and linguistically imaginative work ever produced in Scots. Equally important, he brought the implications of Scots as a literary language forcibly and inescapably into the political arena, making public and explicit questions which had been ignored or even unrecognised for generations.

Grieve's, or MacDiarmid's, first Scots poem was published in the third number of his monthly magazine *The Scottish Chapbook* in October 1922. This magazine, founded, edited, published and to a large extent written by Grieve, had begun by proclaiming, on the opening page of its first issue, its programme:

> To report, support, and stimulate, in particular, the activities of the Franco-Scottish, Scottish-Italian, and kindred Associations; the campaign of the London Burns Club for the revival of the Doric; the movement towards a Scots National Theatre; and the "Northern Numbers" movement in contemporary Scottish poetry.

> To encourage and publish the work of contemporary Scottish poets and dramatists, whether in English, Gaelic or Braid Scots.

To insist upon truer evaluations of the work of Scottish writers than are usually given in the present over-Anglicised condition of British literary journalism, and in criticism, elucidate, apply, and develop the distinctively Scottish range of values.

To bring Scottish Literature into closer touch with current European tendencies in technique and ideation.

To cultivate "the lovely virtue."

And, generally, to "meddle wi' the Thistle" and pick the figs.

Grieve's manifesto, starting with a comprehensive claim of intent to emphasise and develop Scotland's national literature with its international connections and ending with a wittily iconoclastic epigram, can hardly have been seen by contemporary readers as being significantly furthered by the first issue of his magazine. In fact, *The Scottish Chapbook*, vol.1 no.1, is a motley and for the most part undistinguished collection of writings, including Grieve's fiery and mystical *A Moment in Eternity* but also some very unremarkable poems by other hands (all in English), and a vituperative but ill-focused "Causerie", also by Grieve, more notable for emotive language ("Scottish literature, like all other literatures, has been *written* almost exclusively by blasphemers, immoralists, dipsomaniacs, and madmen, but, unlike most other literatures, has been *written about* almost exclusively by ministers...") than for informative content. Grieve's penchant for confrontation and controversy was clearly revealed in this magazine, but not his genius for writing in Scots. Even "Hugh M'Diarmid" [sic, at this point], the nominal author of an extraordinary dramatic dialogue, by turns obscure, banal and vacuous, entitled *Nisbet, an Interlude in Post-War Glasgow*, would scarcely have been seen on the strength of this contribution as a future pivotal figure in Scottish letters. Indeed, Grieve's most credible and most intellectually respectable prose contribution to this issue is a review of a book entitled *Histoire des Lettres Françaises de Belgique*, in which he compares Scotland to Belgium as a country eclipsed by a more powerful neighbour with a common language and predicts "What Belgium did, Scotland can do. . . . the next decade or two will see a Scottish Renascence as swift and irresistible as was the Belgian revival between 1880 and 1910". The second number of *Chapbook*, though the selection of poems was somewhat better (it included two by Alexander Gray and Marion Angus's *The Lilt*), was essentially another helping of the same mixture: equally strong on polemic and weak on either literary merit or serious debate.

Despite this somewhat unpromising beginning, however, *The Scottish Chapbook* then went on to introduce "Hugh M'Diarmid" in his first appearance as a poet, with a lyric which has come to be regarded almost as the touchstone of Scots Renaissance poetry:

> *The Watergaw*
> Ae weet forenicht i' the yow-trummle
> I saw yon antrin thing,
> A watergaw wi' its chitterin' licht
> Ayont the on-ding;
> An' I thocht o' the last wild look ye gied
> Afore ye deed!
>
> There was nae reek i' the laverock's hoose
> That nicht – an' nane i' mine;
> But I hae thocht o' that foolish licht
> Ever sin' syne;
> An' I think that mebbe at last I ken
> What your look meant then.

And in view of the common (but, as will become clear, naive) charge that much of Grieve's Scots is visibly derived from reference books, it is of interest to note that this first exercise in Scots poetry was directly acknowledged to have been inspired by his study of a book on language: *The Watergaw* had been published a month previously in the *Dunfermline Press*, in the context of an article by Grieve, as one of two poems allegedly by "a friend" (unnamed) who had been inspired to write them by a perusal of Sir James Wilson's *Lowland Scotch as Spoken in the Lower Strathearn Dialect of Perthshire.*[1]

MacDiarmid's use of reference works, in fact, was never any secret.

1. Oxford University Press, 1915. Incredibly, the *other* poem consists of three stanzas of sheer doggerel, beginning
The blaward and the skelly
   Are bonny as of yore,
But bonnier far was Nelly,
   Whom I shall see no more ... !
Blawward ("blue cornflower") and *skellay, skellukh* ("wild mustard, field mustard, charlock") appear in Wilson's list of "trees and plants" (pp.158–9).

The true significance of this aspect of his work, and not the least interesting facet of his achievement, is that he was the first Scottish poet to write
in the intellectual context of the nineteenth-century revolution in language studies, which had begun with the observations and deductions
by Jakob Grimm and his followers regarding the nature and status of dialects. In Scotland as in France and Germany, the spoken vernacular was
beginning to change, in the perception of academic language scholars
(though not in that of educationists or arbiters of social taste), from a
mere vulgar patois to a proper object for systematic study. A seminal contribution to the development of dialectology, and for a long time the only
important Scottish one, was made by Sir James Murray's monograph *The
Dialects of the Southern Counties of Scotland*,[1] with which Grieve was
acquainted; and other less scholarly works which he knew and used
included Walter Gregor's *The Dialect of Banffshire* and George Watson's
The Roxburghshire Word Book:[2] the latter no doubt of particular interest
because it describes a Border dialect whose domain includes his native
Langholm.[3] These books, and others like them, attempted to present serious and credible records of the dialect vocabulary of a particular area, in
some cases also including comments on local pronunciation and grammar and information on other aspects of life in the dialect-speaking community: a valuable result of the new realisation that vernacular speech
could be regarded from other viewpoints than those of bourgeois contempt or nostalgic affection. Wilson's *Lowland Scotch*, one of three[4] by
which the author established his place as a pioneer of Scots dialectology
and one of its most skilful practitioners before the advent of scientific linguistics, contains not only detailed accounts of Perthshire pronunciation,
described by means of an invented quasi-phonetic orthography, but a
wealth of proverbial expressions, idioms, local songs and rhymes, and

1. Published as the 1872 issue of *Transactions of the Philological Society*, and as an independent
book the following year.
2. London (Asher) 1866 and Cambridge University Press 1923.
3. Langholm is in Dumfriesshire, but according to the dialect map in the *Scottish National
Dictionary* the greater part of that county is included with Roxburghshire and Selkirkshire in
the domain of the South Scots dialect: though of course as in all the Scottish dialect areas, local
features of pronunciation and vocabulary characterise the various communities within the
region.
4. The others are *The Dialect of Robert Burns* (Oxford University Press 1923) and *The Dialects
of Central Scotland* (Oxford 1926).

lists of words arranged under topic headings (trees and plants, crops and farming, weather, games, ceremonies, etc.): a small-scale thesaurus, in fact. MacDiarmid, regrettably, did not acquire from his reading of Murray and other dialectologists the realisation that spoken dialects are historically respectable forms of speech deserving of, at the very least, tolerance: his notorious attack on the Aberdeenshire dialect of Charles Murray, already referred to, is an uncomfortably clear demonstration of this. He assuredly did, however, regard the lexical archives in their books as a legitimate source for expressive words with which to enrich his native Scots, and availed himself of this liberty with great skill and discrimination.

By far the most important of the reference books used by MacDiarmid as a word-mine, however, is a much earlier work, John Jamieson's *An Etymological Dictionary of the Scottish Language* (first published in 1808, augmented by a two-volume supplement in 1825, and thereafter reprinted several times in various editions).[1] The historical importance of this dictionary, until the completion of the *Scottish National Dictionary* by far the most comprehensive listing of the Scots vocabulary ever compiled, is enormous, as it represents one of the first systematic compilations of data on any speech-form other than the national standard languages. Many of the words which it includes are rare, many (since his intention was to cover all periods in the history of Scots) are long obsolete, and a few are doubtfully authentic – Jamieson could be uncritical of his sources, and on a few occasions was hoaxed by humorous informants – but for the most part his *Dictionary* is the exemplary result of careful and painstaking research; and in providing not only an enormous number of Scots vocabulary items but detailed definitions sometimes amounting to brief essays, illustrative quotations and etymological notes (if sometimes fanciful ones), it is to this day not only a landmark in the history of Scottish, and indeed of European, language study but a fascinating reference work in its own right. As the achievement of a single scholar it fully merits comparison with its model, Dr Johnson's *A Dictionary of the English Language*. For MacDiarmid, it was nothing less than a treasure-trove of

1. For an illuminating discussion of MacDiarmid's debt to Jamieson, see Colin Milton, "'Shibboleths o the Scots': Hugh MacDiarmid and Jamieson's *Etymological Dictionary of the Scottish Language*", in *Scottish Language* 14 – 15, 1995 – 96, 1 – 14.

potent words. His remark in Vol. 1 No. 7 of *Chapbook* that "We have been enormously struck by the resemblance – the moral resemblance – between Jamieson's *Etymological Dictionary of the Scottish Language* and James Joyce's *Ulysses*" must be read as a natural wordsmith's reaction to the enormous hoard of hitherto unknown, but marvellously suggestive and evocative, words to be found in Jamieson: Norman MacCaig's frequently-repeated observation that Christopher Grieve crawled in at one end of Jamieson's Dictionary and Hugh MacDiarmid crawled out at the other is a not unjust estimate of the importance of the *Dictionary* in at least the early development of his poetic language.

The debt which MacDiarmid in *The Watergaw* owes to Wilson is evident: *yow-trummul*, *waatur-gaw* and *oan ding*, defined as "cold weather in July after shearing", "indistinct rainbow" and "beating rain or snow", are to be found in the "weather" section (p.168 – 9) of his vocabulary lists, *yow-trummul* and *waatur-gaw* being adjacent entries; and his list of "Proverbs and sayings" includes the expression *"Dhur'z nay reek ee laivruk's hoos dhe-nikht.* – There's no smoke in the lark's house to-night (said when the night is cold and stormy)". Yet the trick which he performed in *The Watergaw*, and many times thereafter, is one of which the easy reductive analysis is shamed by the result. On one level, he happened to find some interesting words and expressions and wrote a poem to demonstrate them. On another, he produced a lyric which in its visual clarity, masterly sound-patterning and delicate combination of intensity and elusiveness in its emotional suggestion ranks among the greatest in modern Scottish literature. And many of his early Scots poems demonstrate the same technique: individual lyrics continued to appear in the next few issues of *Chapbook*; all of them were reprinted in the volumes *Sangschaw* (1925) and *Penny Wheep* (1926)[1] which soon followed; and several of the poems in those collections are patently showcases for a memorable word or phrase of specific and identifiable provenance. Another of his most celebrated lyrics opens with an entire line taken almost verbatim from a story in *Blackwood's Magazine* (November 1820): "In the how-dumb-dead o' a caul' har'st nicht"; and a key word in the poem, *hazelraw* (a kind of

---

1. Both published by Blackwood, Edinburgh. See the standard edition of MacDiarmid's poems, *Complete Poems*, eds. M. Grieve and W. R. Aitken, London (Brian and O'Keeffe) 1978.

lichen), has almost its only attestation in Jamieson. "There's no a ressum
to the fore" and "I'se warran' ye're rawn for the yirdin'", other opening
lines, are exact quotations from Jamieson's entries for *ressum* "A small
fragment" and *rawn* "Afraid; timid".

> Ilka hart an' hind are met
> 'Neath Arcturus gleamin bonnie,

the beginning of the poem *Reid E'en*, was suggested by Jamieson's note
"On *Reid-e'en* [i.e. the eve of Rude Day, May 3] ... the hart and the hind
are believed to meet for copulation"; and

> Time'll meissle it awa', it seems,
> An' smell nae must.

from *Au Clair de la Lune* recalls the entry for *meissle* "To waste impercept-
ibly; to expend in a trifling manner": "It is said of one with respect to his
money, *He meisslit it awa, without smelling a must*; He wasted it, without
doing any thing to purpose." *Bear-meal-raik* in *To one who urges more ambitious flights*, like *yow-trummle* an expression which concentrates a set of
potent overtones into a short phrase, is also from Jamieson, whose explanation is "A fruitless errand; supposed to originate from the disappoint-
ment of one who goes out in quest of oatmeal, and is obliged to satisfy
himself with barley-meal". "White as a loan soup was she" (from *Sabine*)
suggests a saying in James Kelly's *Complete Collection of Scottish Proverbs*
(used by Jamieson as a quotation): "You are white as a loan soup [a drink
of milk given to strangers]. Spoken to flatterers who speak you fair." The
magnificent line "There's teuch sauchs growin' i' the Reuch Heuch
Hauch" appeared in Murray's *The Dialects of the Southern Counties of
Scotland*, and before that in a pronunciation manual by Alexander
Melville Bell. Besides whole phrases, several instances occur of rare and
striking words which MacDiarmid almost certainly found in Jamieson
(the evidence being that few or no recorded attestations of them occur
elsewhere), many of them being skilfully placed to call attention to themselves by occurring in the opening lines or some other conspicuous position in their poems:

> *Knedneuch* land
> And a loppert sea ...
>
> (*In the Pantry*)

(*Knedneuch*, "A peculiar taste or smell; chiefly applied to old meat or musty bread"); by forming a pattern of alliteration or other sound feature:

> The muckle white pig at the tail
> O' the midden *slotters* and *slorps* ...
>
> (Farmer's Death)

(*Slotter* "To make a noise like a duck gobbling in swallowing food", *slorp* "To swallow any thing ungracefully, by making a noise with the mouth or throat");

> The auld men o' the sea
> Wi' their *daberlack* hair
> Ha'e *dackered* the coasts
> O' the country fell sair.
>
> (Hungry Waters)

(*Daberlack* "A kind of long seaweed ... the hair, when hanging in lank, tangled or separate locks", *dacker* "To search; to examine; to search for stolen goods"); or by belonging to a particular semantic field (the best example of this being the musical terms *whuram*, *spatril* and *airel* in *Ex Vermibus*: here his source is probably Watson rather than Jamieson). The most flagrant example of dictionary-pillaging in his early poems is from *Gairmscoile*, a long poem in *Penny Wheep* which amounts to a poetic statement of his linguistic and political manifesto:

> Ablachs, and scrats, and dorbels o' a' kinds
> Aye'd drob me wi' their puir eel-droonin' minds,
> Wee drochlin craturs drutlin their bit thochts
> The dorty bodies! Feech! Nae Sassunuch drings
> 'll daunton me. – Tak' ye sic things for poets?
> Cock-lairds and drotes depert Parnassus noo.
> A'e flash o' wit the lot to drodlich dings.
> Rae, Martin, Sutherland – the dowless crew,
> I'll twine the dow'd sheaves o' their toom-ear'd corn,
> Bind them wi' pity and dally them wi' scorn ...

where the words *dorbel*, *drob*, *drochlin*, *druttle*, *dorty*, *dring*, *drotes*, *drodlich*, *dowless* and *dally*,[1] rarely-attested words for the most part, are to be found in the same few pages of Jamieson – almost adjacent entries in some cases.

The issue of *Chapbook* containing *The Watergaw* also has another feature by "M'Diarmid", entitled "Following Rebecca West[2] in Edinburgh: a Monologue in the Vernacular". Here Grieve's exploitation of Jamieson has had much less satisfactory results:

> "She's an allagrugous auld city in this allerish licht! .. I'm no blamin' Miss West – but ye canna play Beethoven on an Almanie whistle! It tak's an almark like Joyce tae write aboot Edinburgh. The lassie never gets amidward. She canna be fashed wi' a' its amplefeysts – she hesna' got the necessary *animosity*. Mebbe Edinburgh
>
> 'Wes in his yhowthyede
> A fayre, sweet, pleasant childe,
> At all point formyd in fassoun,
> Abil, of gude condityione.' ..."

Allagrugous "Grim, ghastly", *allerish* "Chilly; rather cold", *Almanie whistle* "A flageolet of a very small size, used by children", *almark* "A beast accustomed to break fences", *amydwart* "in or toward the midst of", *amplefeyst* "A sulky humour; a fit of spleen; unnecessary talk", *animositie* "Firmness of mind; hardihood"[3] are all on the same few pages of the *Dictionary*; the four lines of poetry (from Wyntoun's *Originall Chronykil*) are cited in the entry for *abil* "able". *Allagrugous* and *almark* are rare words with a restricted local distribution (respectively the North-East and Shetland); *amplefeyst* and *allerish* are among many words for which Jamieson is the only authority. Fortunately, Grieve never repeated this particular experiment. Even in fiction, the notion that anybody could actually have *said* this (and it is only a fraction of the "monologue") is

1. "Any thing unseemly in appearance", "To prick, as with a needle or other sharp instrument", "Puny; feeble; indolent", "Applied to a horse or dog that often stops on its way to dung in small quantities", "Pettish; apt to be sullen", "One in a servile state; perhaps expressive of equal contempt with the designation *slave*", "Used in derision for uppish yeomen or *cocklairds*", "A useless mass", "Feeble; without energy; unhealthy", "The stick used by one who binds sheaves, for pushing in the ends of the rope, after they have been twisted together".

2. Author of *The Judge*, a novel set in Edinburgh, of which a review had been published in the previous *Chapbook*.

3. Jamieson gives no quotation or reference to illustrate this sense of the word. The *OED* gives the meaning as "obsolete" (the date of the last quotation is 1678), but makes no mention of it being a Scottish usage, and none of the quotations is from a Scottish source.

altogether too outlandish; and the narrator's apologia "He was purposely using many obsolete words . . .", which leads to a brief explanation and defence of the procedure, does not make it more convincing. If a speech loaded with obscure and dubious words is beyond credibility when assigned to a fictional character (even an unidentified one), however, the skilful and judicious use of such words in *poetry* is another matter. The essential reason for the success, as it clearly is, of MacDiarmid's experiments in the poetic use of rare Scots words is the almost unerring skill with which he chooses a word with the appropriate phonetic, phonaesthetic or semantic value, and often a pointedly relevant overtone from its previous use, for the immediate context: or alternatively, devises the perfect context in which an unusual word can display its intriguing and enticing qualities of sound and meaning to the full. Even the notorious passage from *Gairmscoile* succeeds as invective – the comparison which suggests itself is with the mediaeval Flytings of Dunbar and Kennedy or Montgomerie and Polwart, with their imaginative vocabularies – all the words (except *dally*) are carefully chosen for their insulting implications; and the alliteration on [d], which continues (with more Jamieson-derived words) over the next few lines, invites a forceful delivery.

This fact – the skill with which MacDiarmid exploits his words for their poetic effect – is one counter to the charge that has been directed against him from the dates of his first Scots poems to the present: that his Scots is a mere conglomerate of words from all accessible sources. That he availed himself of reference books was never in doubt; but his poetic acumen was such that even rare and obsolete words spring to a vibrant new life in his poems. No doubt readers who are prepared to take the trouble to discover their meanings will arrive at a clearer appreciation of the poems than those who are not; but a passage in *Gairmscoile* expresses the clear realisation that even readers who have not the words in their own active or passive vocabularies can share his imaginative response:

> It's soon', no' sense, that faddoms the herts o' men,
> And by my sangs the rouch auld Scots I ken
> E'en herts that ha'e nae Scots'll dirl thro'
> As nocht else could – for here's a language rings
> Wi' datchie sesames, and names for nameless things.

Indeed, it is by now a commonplace of MacDiarmid criticism that throughout his work, including his later "scientific" poetry in English, a sensitive response to words *pur sang* – to the auditory quality, imaginative and evocative force and intellectually stimulating capacity of a rare, obscure, archaic or technical word – was developed in him to an extraordinary degree. In his early poetry, it was principally Scots words which attracted him, and from which he produced some of his finest work. A few memorable lines in *Gairmscoile* convey his imaginative reaction to the power of words:

> ... And there's forgotten shibboleths o' the Scots
> Ha'e keys to senses lockit to us yet
> – Coorse words that shamble thro' oor minds like stots,
> Syne turn on's muckle een wi' doonsin[1] emerauds lit.

But it has long been recognised that the same basic trait of MacDiarmid the poet is illustrated in

> All is lithogenesis – or lochia,
> Carpolite fruit of the forbidden tree,
> Stones blacker than any in the Caaba,
> Cream coloured caen-stone, chatoyant pieces,
> Celadon and corbeau, bistre and beige,
> Glaucous, hoar, enfouldetred, cyathiform,
> Making mere faculae of the sun and moon,
> I study you glout and gloss ...
>
> (*On a Raised Beach*, 1–8)

as in

> Brent on or boutgate or beschacht,
> Bellwaverin' or borneheid,
> They mimp and primp, or bick and birr,
> Dilly-dally or show speed.
> Brade-up or sclafferin', rouchled, sleek,
> Abstraklous or austerne,
> In belths below the brae-hags
> And bebbles in the fern.
>
> (*Water Music*, 21–28)

1. A rare word glossed by Jamieson as 'very', but according to MacDiarmid's gloss an adjective meaning 'dazzling'. Since in Jamieson's only illustrative quotation for the word it appears in the phrase 'doonsin white', MacDiarmid's interpretation of it is arguably as legitimate as Jamieson's own.

– though the former is neither in Scots nor, at least on the surface, a specifically Scottish poem at all.

Another rebuttal of the charge of excessive "artificiality" in MacDiarmid's Scots is the fact that the language of his early poems is, except for a quite well-defined section of the vocabulary, simply traditional literary Scots, often with a strong flavour from MacDiarmid's native Border dialect. "There has been much debate in many quarters during the past decade as to the artificiality – the dictionary-dredged character – of the Scots in which most of my poetry is written; but the fact is that Scots was my native tongue – I can still speak it as easily as I speak English, and with far greater psychological satisfaction," he later wrote in his autobiography;[1] and he is at pains throughout that work to emphasise that Scots as a poetic medium came to him with the natural ease of a mother tongue. Another of his best-known poems, *The Bonnie Broukit Bairn* (the opening poem of *Sangschaw*), is a masterpiece of imaginative imagery and one of the best examples of his characteristic habit of compressing a vision of cosmic magnitude into an impossibly small poetic compass; but its Scots lexis has nothing recondite about it. *Broukit* and *clanjamfrie* are (of course) in Jamieson's *Dictionary*, but they are familiar words: the only word which is unlikely to have formed part of his active vocabulary as a Scots speaker is *crammasy*, and it is by no means unknown in earlier literature. A few words in the poems, such as *pitmirk*, have a ballad-like ring; but real archaisms are almost absent: *skrymmorie* "terrifying" in *Gairmscoile*, for which Jamieson's source is Gavin Douglas, is the only certain example in the two collections. (Grieve is on record as arguing that "Scots writers should adopt the idioms, vocabulary, etc., of Dunbar and Henryson and the other old Makars",[2] but he showed very little sign of adopting his own prescription.) Any reader is bound to be startled into attention by the auditory effect of the line "There's teuch sauchs growin' i' the Reuch Heuch Hauch", and by the poet's audacity in using what is (or originally was) clearly a joke line as the opening of a poem which, though in a familiar Scottish vein of fantastic humour, is by

---

1. *Lucky Poet: a Self-Study in Literature and Political Ideas, being the Autobiography of Hugh MacDiarmid.* First published 1943; quote from 1972 edition (Jonathan Cape, London) p.17.

2. In a letter in *The Scottish Educational Journal*, September 18 1925, reprinted in the SEJ's 1976 edition of *Contemporary Scottish Studies*, p.38.

no means a mere jest; but once he has recovered sufficiently to read the poem with care he will recognise that none of the words (except the Jamiesonism *amplefeyst*) is individually at all unusual, and that the power of the poem inheres first in the wildly imaginative vision by which the sauchs (willows) become boisterously and menacingly animated versions of Yggdrasill, and then in the masterly harnessing of prosodic effects to mirror the impression both of frenetic energy (the swirling anapaests of "Like the **sauls** o' the **damned** are **they**" ... "But they **rin** richt **doon** thro' the **bod**dom o' **Hell**") and of unshakeable solidity (the sequences of pitch-prominent monosyllables in "the **deil's ain hert**" ... "**nane kens hoo fer un**der" ... "**God's ain sel**". *O Jesu Parvule*, despite its origin in a passage from the *Gude and Godly Ballattis*, suggests neither the language of the Reformation nor that of scholarly dialect studies, but a living Scots employed to convey a vision of the Incarnation truly glorious in its combination of an affectionate evocation of a mother and her baby ("the bonnie wee craturie" ... "she's drawn Him in tae the bool o' her briest") and the placing of the event at the centre of all creation ("An' a' the starnies an' he are sib": the emotional loading of the diminutive here is almost overwhelming); and the poem which follows it, *The Innumerable Christ*, likewise relies on the vivid imaginative presentation of a challenging idea rather than on any special feature of his Scots as a language. In *Overinzievar*, words such as *hullerie* (here, with feathers ruffled against the cold), *sook-the-bluid* (a red beetle), *switchable* (earwig: seemingly an idiosyncratic spelling of the more usual *switchiebell*) and *cleisher* ("whopper") have a markedly Border ring; *hanlawhile* (short time) in *Teuch Sauchs* and *scoogie* (apron) in *Cophetua* are likewise words of Border provenance; and the spellings *dooks* (ducks) and *guissay* (a young pig) in *Country Life* may be intended to suggest the pronunciations heard in the Borders: the Scots word for "duck" in most other dialects has an initial *j*- or *dy*- sound; and the *ui* suggests the front rounded vowel which appears in this word (and others) as a characteristic Border shibboleth. Many more of the poems in *Sangschaw* and *Penny Wheep*, including some of his finest such as *Crowdieknowe* and *Empty Vessel*, achieve their effects without the use of a single Scots word which would not be familiar to any native speaker or reader of Scots poetry.

M'Diarmid, according to Grieve (in his "Causerie" in the third issue of

Chapbook), had become "the first Scottish writer who has addressed himself to the question of the extendability (without psychological violence) of the Vernacular to embrace the whole range of modern culture – or, in other words, tried to make up the leeway of the language". The fact that Grieve made a forcefully and frequently stated plank in his literary-political platform of the need to enlarge the scope and range of the Scots tongue has undoubtedly misled many readers and critics into the delusion that his Scots, considered purely as language, is much more "synthetic" than is actually the case. Given that the works of Gerard Manley Hopkins, published not long before MacDiarmid began his poetic career, had earned him the status of a pivotal figure in the history of poetry precisely through his assuming the licence to invent new words, revive obscure, archaic and dialectal words, use existing words with idiosyncratic extensions of their normal meaning and radically distort conventional grammatical patterns, it is somewhat inequitable that this charge should be brought against MacDiarmid with the air of an accusation; but even in itself, it is of extremely limited validity. The Scots of *Sangschaw* and *Penny Wheep* is the rich native dialect of a Borderer, handled with enormous technical skill in the service of a dazzling poetic imagination, and enlarged to incorporate a selection of evocative words and phrases discovered in the course of his voracious reading and woven almost seamlessly into the fabric of his poetic medium.

In *A Drunk Man Looks at the Thistle*, the influence of Jamieson is much less in evidence. MacDiarmid's Scots in this poem, except for a few of the more highly-charged passages, is not notable for rare words nor even for an unusually high proportion of lexical Scotticisms of any kind: a fact which, it could be argued, makes the achievement of the poem still more extraordinary, in that such a long, rhapsodic flight of imaginative and intellectual fantasy could have been expressed in what is essentially a fairly common, even colloquial Scots. The opening section, indeed, arrests the reader's attention by features which in 1926 must have seemed fairly radical for other reasons: its metrically rough-hewn lines, rhymes which are in several cases faulty (*gless - wes*, *hert - fur't*) or obtrusively "jokey" (*thrapple - Adam's apple*, *knock-knee - Cockney*), and expressions clearly drawn from a colloquial register ("Forbye, the stuffie's no' the real Mackay"; "No wan in fifty kens a word Burns wrote"). Something of the "modernism" of, say, T. S. Eliot – the deliberate use of language which breaches the conventional canons of poetic usage – is in evidence here; but not the exuberant playing with the Scots lexicon found in *Sangschaw* and *Penny Wheep*. On the other hand, the meanings or sounds of Scots words are carefully selected for their effect: the heavy fall of *deid dune*, the juxtaposition of Scots words for body parts (*elbuck, sheckle, thrapple*), the sudden change of tone from low-keyed grumbling to angry denunciation marked by the words suggesting violent action, *whummle* and *souse*.

As the poem progresses, the critical, sarcastic voice speaking in a fluent, almost conversational Scots employs the reductive devices familiar in vernacular dialogue. Regularly, flights into an imaginative stratosphere are rudely bought down by the use of Scots words with derogatory or insulting senses: "O gin they'd stegh their guts and haud their wheesht" (l.65), "In wi' your gruntle then, puir wheengin' saul" (125), "...like gealed And runkled auld bluid-vessels in a knot!" (379 – 80),

> Mary lay in jizzen
> As it were claith o gowd,
> But it's in orra duds
> Ilka ither bairntime's row'd. (64 – 7)

These passages are contrasted, however, with others in which the density of the Scots increases: some, though not all, of these also show a more lyrical style and maintain, at least for a few lines, a serious and dignified mood. Occasionally more obscure words come into evidence: a case in point is the section beginning "Abordage o' this toom houk's nae mowse..." (l.873), in which the first word is a Jamiesonism and the presence of *munk* "To diminish, so as bring any thing below the proper size" and *munkie* "a small rope, with a loop or eye at one end, for receiving a bit of wood called a 'knool' at the other..." likewise points very clearly to his source. (But as elsewhere, the use MacDiarmid makes of his words is very much his own: a "munkie wi' munebeam for knool in't".) In some of the poem's most memorable self-contained passages, however, potently expressive Scots words take their place in the discourse with consummate ease and appropriateness: the superb imagery in the section "Ballad of the Crucified Rose" (1119 – 1218) is highlighted by adjectives like *camsteerie, feckless, orra, ugsome, thrawn, grugous*; and the even more brilliant "To the Music of the Pipes" (411 – 434) has its climax in a verse where alliteration and vowel-harmony, words suggesting fast energetic movement, and the onomatope *heich-skeich* (seemingly MacDiarmid's own concoction, though fully conforming to the patterns of the onomatopoeic words which Scots possesses in abundance) combine to astonishing effect:

> Or a muckle bellows blawin'
> Wi' the sperks a' whizzin oot;
> Or green tides sweeshin'
> 'Neth heich-skeich stars,
> Or centuries fleein' doon a water-chute.

It is a matter of ready observation that native Scots speakers are often able to combine a well-developed skill in flyting, backchat and "winding up" with extravagant creativity of imaginative expression: arguably the latter is the main factor that has enabled Scots as a spoken language to survive, albeit in mutated form, the transition from a language of rural agricultural communities to one of crowded urban slums. In this poem, Scots in its full range – that is, not only the phonetic and semantic power of the words and idioms but the whole set of habits of Scots speakers – is drafted into the task of expounding one of the most wide-ranging and most challenging poetic visions in all Scottish literature – arguably in all the literature of twentieth-century Europe. After this poem, the status of Scots as a poetic medium was changed irrevocably.

MacDiarmid wrote much more in Scots before changing to English (an English often as experimental as his Scots ever was) as his medium; and his exploration of the possibilities of different styles and registers continued with undiminished vigour and panache. *The Parrot Cry* evokes the rhythm of a broadsheet ballad and the vocabulary of a political argument in a pub; *Lourd on my Hert* returns to the lyrical mode of the early poems with a sparse and simple Scots; *To Alasdair MacMhaighistir Alasdair*[1] confirms his cosmopolitan vision by decorating its basically vernacular Scots with abundant foreign references and polyglot rhymes; *Water Music* shows his fondness for playing with rare and recondite words at its most extreme. Collectively, they demonstrate with total

1. Since few readers will be acquainted with this poet, it is worth pointing out that his place among the outstanding figures of European literature is evident – overwhelmingly evident – to anyone who reads his works with even an imperfect knowledge of Gaelic.

and triumphant success MacDiarmid's tenet that modern Scots is fit for use in a poetry of an intellectual and imaginative scope equal to anything it had ever attained in the past.

MacDiarmid revolutionised Scots as a vehicle for poetry by both precept and example; but his precept and his example do not precisely coincide. When writing *about* Scots, he argued vigorously and repeatedly that the stupendous expressive power latent in the language could and must be liberated by the revivification of its treasure-hoard of lost lexemes and idiomatic expressions. When writing *in* Scots, he used a medium which never (except perhaps in *Water Music*) lost touch with his ancestral Border dialect and the poetic language of the post-Union tradition of which Burns is the central figure: despite his slogan "Not Burns – Dunbar!", the influence of the Makars on his Scots is almost negligible. That MacDiarmid wrote in a wholly "synthetic" language, or even one which is, as language, much more recondite than that of his immediate or his eighteenth-century predecessors, is simply untenable: as will be seen in subsequent chapters, several of his successors ventured much further than he ever did in the direction of a language artificially aggrandised with rare or archaic words. His revolution consisted, fundamentally, in proving that Scots could be used for modernist poetry: in breaking irreparably the hold which the traditional styles, topics and sentiments of the two preceding centuries had on the assumptions and practices of Scots poets; and his success in this is due not primarily to the fact that he explored in dictionaries for his vocabulary but to the fact that he was a poetic genius.

Equally important, however, for the subsequent course not only of Scots poetry but of the entire cultural life of the nation – though its full effects were not felt for some time to come – was another aspect of his influence: his overt linking of Scots with political and cultural nationalism. Prior to him, the association of Scots as a poetic language with Scottish patriotic feeling was, at best, a tacit assumption: now, for the first time (incredibly) in Scottish history, the Scots language was to be a strongly-emphasised symbol of Scottish national identity, and its liberation a preliminary to, or indeed an integral part of, the liberation of Scotland. Scots in the hands of MacDiarmid and his successors was no longer simply a language, but a weapon.

8

The Tradition Revitalised:
Albert Mackie and
William Soutar

After MacDiarmid, as David Murison was the first to remark, Scotland would never be the same place again. By bringing the Scots tongue to the leading edge of experimental methods in European poetry, and associating the growing demand for Scottish Home Rule overtly with the new direction of the country's literary and cultural development, he struck a death-blow at the lingering association of Scots with romantic nostalgia. The much-quoted concluding lines of *Gairmscoile*:

> For we ha'e faith in Scotland's hidden poo'ers,
> The present's theirs, but a' the past and future's oors.

were a proclamation of confidence in the enduring life of the nation and in Scotland's capacity to regenerate itself not only politically but culturally and linguistically. In the emergent Scotland of MacDiarmid's vision, there was no place for defeatism or sterile laments for a lost age: Scotland's past was not to be mourned but brought into service as a living and vivifying source of inspiration.

By no means all poets whose careers began after the publication of *Sangschaw*, *Penny Wheep* and *A Drunk Man Looks at the Thistle* ventured on the kind and degree of linguistic experimentation which MacDiarmid employed; but his influence was acknowledged, and to some extent manifested, even by relatively conservative poets. Albert Mackie, no major poet but a competent and confident artisan in a vigorous dialect based on that of Edinburgh and the Lothians, was among the first to give public voice to the realisation that with MacDiarmid Scots poetry had taken an irreversible step into a new era:

We seem to be at the beginnings of a national literature. We cannot see the work of Hugh M'Diarmid without believing this. The race of makars cannot perish after a work like "A Drunk Man Looks at the Thistle."[1]

And in a poem entitled *To Hugh M'Diarmid*, he expresses the combined sense of shock and delighted emancipation which the master-poet's work had given to Scots writers:

Guidsakes, I never thocht tae see
The Scottish Muse stravaig sae free
Through a' o' Yirth and Hell and Heeven
And oot-and-in its ainsel even,
And in my tongue and in my time
Hear life's bambaizement set tae rhyme.

Mackie's own poetic voice is somewhat eclectic. In *Edinburgh Sabbath Morn*, written in the stanza form of *The Cottar's Saturday Night*, the inevitable comparison detracts from a poem which, though perfectly respectable as a domestic description, makes no attempt to touch on such moral and social issues as are raised in the original; by contrast, *Elegy*, though beginning in the vein of Logie Robertson, soon develops an acerbic tone from which the latter would have shied away:

The auld toon pub will be chynged a'thegither a'maist,
The auld cheat himsel will be gowpin' a' nicht at the flair;
For nae mair he'll be telt hoo his beer o' the burn has a taste
Or his cheese is a' hair,
Or his pies are gey auld in the meat or gey wersh in the paste –
He'll be missin' ye sair.

In *Trees in the Wind*, MacDiarmid's own influence is unmistakeable; but if the poem is clearly modelled on *Somersault*, the carefully-placed Scots words evoking noise and violent movement, and the daring combination of this with the suggestion of religious revelation, raise it above the level of a mere copy:

Wi' stramash o' trees
And stishie o' win'
The Spirit o' God
Comes breenjin' in. ...

1. *Poems in Two Tongues*, Edinburgh (Darien Press) 1928.

Yae man gliffs up
At the wallopin' host,
And yae tongue's lowsed
In a Pentecost.

Mackie in his preface draws a contrast between his and MacDiarmid's approaches to Scots: "I write on the basis of a living dialect, even indicating this in my spelling, whereas he sets his face against all dialect and writes mainly on a basis of aggregate vocabulary and idiom". Mackie's spelling indeed shows details which suggest attempts to represent a specific pronunciation rather than a general etymologically-based orthography: *abin* and *shin* for *abuin* and *suin*, *yellie* and *uncae* for *yella* (or *yellow*) and *unco*, *yince* for *aince*, *foremist* for *foremaist*; and though his vocabulary is mostly common-core Scots, he also resorts to an occasional localism such as *lummy* (chimney fire), *buffy* (dishevelled) and *clipshears* (earwig: a Scots-speaker's preferred name for this insect is often sufficient to locate his place of origin quite precisely, as MacDiarmid's *switchable* also demonstrates). By contrast, in the poem *Deid 'Oor* (which suggests a jocular parody of MacDiarmid's metaphysical passages) he draws for trick effects of rhyme or metre on nonce mediaevalisms (*permansible*) or fanciful concoctions (*titivilliaries*); and in *To Hugh M'Diarmid* the word *liddenin'*, otherwise attested only in *A Drunk Man*, may or may not be a deliberate echo of the original. On the whole, however, Mackie's vocabulary does not suggest a poet concerned with experimentation or innovation, but simply with the opportunities for racy and energetic writing afforded by the characteristic sounds and words of Scots. His rhymes and alliterations are, perhaps, decorative rather than revelatory of any more profound meaning ("... or wipes at his nose, or blipes at his een" – "Baukies in the bauks / May flaughter..."); and his exploitation of the Scots vocabulary is forceful rather than subtle ("Grumphin' away wi' her gruntle deep in the glaur..." – "Black thochts ben in his dernest places prowl / Like rottens jinkin' by ...").

It is certainly to be regretted that Mackie did not, until much later in his life, further develop his poetic talent: after this single volume, his long and productive career as a man of letters was devoted mainly to journalism, literary criticism and essays; though his enduring fascination with Scots gave rise, much later, to some entertaining short monographs and a stirring long poem *Sing a Sang o' Scotland*. His contribution to the Scots Renaissance in poetry, slight as it is, is nonetheless significant of the conscious attention to the power, and the symbolic function, of Scots as a medium which was henceforth to affect the practices of Scots poets; and of their overt recognition of the new horizons which had been opened for Scots poetry, in principle and in practice, by MacDiarmid's work.

A much greater contribution to the regeneration of the language and its literary status was made by another and more accomplished poet writing under MacDiarmid's influence, William Soutar. The inspiring story of Soutar's years of unflagging literary and intellectual activity conducted while a bedridden invalid is well known;[1] and his enduring friendship with MacDiarmid, initiated when he sent some poems to him as editor of *Northern Numbers* and maintained till Soutar's death, undoubtedly influenced his use of Scots as his medium. He gave potent expression to the association of devitalised speech with diminished national pride in a satirical poem entitled *Lines Suggested by the Voice of a Scottish Wireless Announcer*, which opens with a cacophony of animal noises:

> Nae bubbly-jock blairs like a cuddie,
> Nae cuddy like a bubbly-jock,

proceeds to a riotous evocation of divine ridicule:

> Yet, certes, God maun haud his hurdies
> An', wi' his gowden croun agee,
> Gar a' the haly hurdy-gurdies
> Wheesh, an' his harpers stan abee;
> As, aince mair, roun the sternie reenge
> Wheeps up yon peelie-wally wheenge. ....

– no other words, certainly no English words, could convey the contempt in "peelie-wally wheenge" – and finally modulates from laughter to anger at what is represented by "this Edinburgh parton":

> For in his mankit wurds we hear
> The douncome o' a race, sae blate
> As hansel noo twa hunner year
> A mongrel's hungersome estate.

1. The most authoritative account is *Still Life: William Soutar, 1898–1943* by Alexander Scott, Edinburgh (Chambers) 1958.

And his belief in the central place which the language was to hold in the national recovery was expressed in a lyric which first appeared in his diary (Tuesday 9 September 1937):[1]

Caledonia's near a corp

Caledonia's near a corp;
   Puir auld Caledonie:
Scrog and skrank wi English slorp
   And English parsimonie.

What can mak our Scotland hale:
   What mak her braw and bonnie?
Hamely brose and hamely kail,
   Bannock and baup and sconie?

Wauk her wi a Doric sang;
   Dirl her wi the dronie:
She'll come tae hersel or lang
   And gang as gleg as onie.

Gin she were hersel aince mair
   (And this is no a ronie)
A' the world wud wark to share
   The rowth o' Caledonie.

A degree of ironic humour is obvious in this poem, in the palpable forcing of the rhymes and the hint of exaggeration, even parody, in the obtrusive juxtaposition of *scrog and skrank* and the use of *slorp* principally for its unattractive sound (none of its literal meanings makes sense in the context, though something like "unpleasant and unwholesome food" is clearly suggested); but the effect is not to undercut the sentiment: the tone of angry mockery is directed not at the idea of a Scots revival, but at the state of a country so degenerate that such a revival has become necessary. Lines 7–8 are a pointed dig at the crippling nostalgia of recent Scottish literature, with the repetition of *hamely*, the diminutive on *sconie* and the emphatic positioning of *kail* suggesting a satiric reference to the "kailyaird". This poem, interestingly enough, almost immediately follows an entry (September 2) expressing with fervour and imagination his feeling towards the language:

1. Quotations from Soutar's diaries are from *Diaries of a Dying Man*, ed. Alexander Scott, Edinburgh (Chambers) 1954, unless otherwise specified.

One cannot hope to isolate the true tap-root of nationalism, it goes down too deeply into the racial unconsciousness, but sometimes one can sense as if a portion of oneself has flowered upon the strength which rouses along a fibre of this root. One begins to be more conscious of the atavistic constitution of one's being; life still flows up from the loam of the past and stimulates the branches of one's blood. I feel this particularly in speech. English is *not* natural to me; and I use it "consciously" even in conversation; it is always something of an effort for me to find my words; and not uncommonly I labour as if I were speaking in a foreign language. It is as if one had come out of the past with only a fragmentary memory of one's true tongue, and yet this broken speech remained as rocks which disturb the flow of modern speech.

Soutar had experimented with Scots, prompted at first by his admiration for Grieve's lyrics in the *Scottish Chapbook*,[1] for some years before the publication of his first collection. His "Triolets" combine strict observance of the metrical rules with careful and deceptively simple use of Scots vocabulary: in *Epiphany* or the poem on a tattie-bogle cheekily entitled *Resurrection*, lines like "My auld banes knockit at the sicht" – "His een bleezed wi an eldritch licht" – "Clap a deid man's hat abune" – combine a sharp clarity of sensory impression with the tone of simultaneous humour and horror long familiar in Scottish poetry. His first anthology, however, and in some respects his most influential work, appeared in 1933: *Seeds in the Wind: Poems in Scots for Children*,[2] a collection of "bairnsangs". These, and the children's poems in later collections, show a degree of sophistication which belies the expected limitations of the genre. Appropriately, the best of his bairnsangs make an immediate appeal to the ear by combining simple and "catchy" rhythms with conspicuous and abundant rhyming. More unexpectedly, they employ a rich and highly evocative vocabulary. If Soutar's purpose was to imprint the Scots tongue firmly and enjoyably on children's ears and minds, his poems are admirably suited for the purpose: many of them have a memorable quality which would serve (and has served) to forge a lifelong association of Scots words with the interest and delight of an early literary experience. One poem may employ onomatopes:

1. Alexander Scott's conjecture: *Still Life, op. cit.*, p.54.
2. *Poems of William Soutar*, ed. W. A. Aitken, Edinburgh (Scottish Academic Press) 1988. All quotations are from this edition.

An auld man stands abüne the hill:
Crick-crack, crick-crack.
He's unco comfie gin he's still:
Crick-crack creeshie.
> *(The Auld Man);*

another show an imaginative development of the words of a traditional singing game:

And it's round a' the world when ye gang wi' me
Round the merry-metanzie
> *(A Bairn's Sang);*

another make use of a nursery rhyme -like refrain:

Three wee bit puddocks
Sat upon a stane:
Tick-a-tack, nick-a-nack,
Brek your hawse-bane.
> *(The Three Puddocks);*

and another (this is a frequent device) show close symmetry between the syntactic patterns of successive lines or stanzas. Very often, rhymes serve to reinforce a rhythmic pattern:

Somebody nippit me,
Somebody trippit me,
Somebody grippit me roun' and aroun'
> *(Bawsy Broon);*

and an unmistakable poetic trick is the frequent recourse to Scots words, often ones with a notable degree of semantic or phonaesthetic force, to provide some or all of the rhymes in a stanza: *stishie - hishie, grumphie - humphie, blowf - howff, doukie - droukie, shoggle - bogle*; or in a pattern of internal rhyme: *hallachin' an' yallachin', routin' an' boutin' an' loutin'*. Similarly, sequences of memorable Scots words are often arranged in an alliterative pattern: *bluff blew the blowthery blaw, clabber-claich't as ony caird, frae raggity rungs the fluffers flap, the floichans flurr'd like feathers*.

The most remarkable feature of *Seeds in the Wind*, however, is perhaps the individual nature of the vocabulary. At once noticeable is the density of the Scots: the first poem in the collection, *Coorie in the Corner*, has five Scots lexemes (*coorie, chap* [knock], *winnock, greet, goloch*) and as many words that are phonologically Scots (*a', alane, nicht, juist, rin*) in its six

lines. On several occasions the close juxtaposition of a group of Scots
words in the form of a list –

> And the dominie, wabster, souter and miller
> Cam out wi' gear and cam out wi' siller...
>
> (*The Fiddler*)

– or a set –

> "Noo, by my troth, sin I'm a mither
> I'll name fower reavers," said the hen:
> "The whuitterick's ane, the tod's anither,
> The rottan, and auld Nickie-ben."
>
> (*The Herryin o' Jenny Wren*)

– gives the impression of a subtly-conceived mnemonic device. Much
more interesting is the strongly-emphasised association of Scots with
the natural world, and, linked to this, the prevalence of onomatopoeic
or phonaesthetically appropriate words. Many of the poems are miniature animal fables (clearly designed to appeal to children), and names of
living creatures appear in abundance: *mowdie, bawkie bird, corbie, houlet,
merle, mavie, gowk, laverock, cushat, peesie, stirrie, lintie, puddock, puddle-doo,
goloch, wabster, emmick*. Words for noises are chosen with unerring aptness: a hen *chickers*, a duck *gaggles*, a scurrying rat *reeshles*, a gnawing
mouse *charks*, a bell *dunnles*, a windmill *jirgs*, one frightened girl *skellochs*
and another *frunches*, a seagull *skreels*, a raven *gloags* (seemingly an
invented word), thunder *bullers* and *dunders*, the wind *wheeples, wheemers,
yammers* and *rowts*. Physical actions of many kinds are suggested by
words of which the sound would convey an appropriate sensory impression even to readers hearing them for the first time: some are familiar
(for example *dunch* "strike, bump into", *snowk* "sniff, like a dog"), others
so rare as to suggest nonce concoctions (e.g. *climp*, for which Soutar's
gloss is "to gather up hurriedly"). Words with frequentative suffixes are
notably abundant: *blatter* (beat violently), *fimmer* (move rapidly and
gracefully, as in a dance), *fitter* (patter, move restlessly), *hotter* (swarm,
mill around), *lopper* (lap, ripple, used of water), *styter* (stagger), *whitter*
("move with lightness and velocity" – Soutar); *driddle* (dawdle, saunter),
howdle (move with a rocking motion), *spurtle* (sprawl, struggle), *sprottle*
(scramble), *wamphle* (flap, flutter). The presence in Scots of a large number of words of this class gives Soutar scope for some linguistic inventiveness: he augments the word *flisk* (dart about) to *flisker*, both to intensify

its meaning and to contribute to a sound-pattern: "fliskerin and flitterin", referring to a wagtail; transfers the meaning of *reemle* from a tremulous noise to a wavering light ("The reemlin licht afore me Gaed up. . ."), and gives an odd suggestion of a double meaning in

> . . .yon wowffin tyke
> That yammers through the scudderin wüd
>
> > (*The Wind*)

by glossing *scudder* as "shudder", a very rare use of the word but one which applies readily to the *wood*, and leaving its much more common sense of "sweep along in gusts" to apply covertly to the *wind*. Often the context in which a movement-word is used provides a further clue, for the uninitiated, to its meaning:

> It was a gey puir laddie
> Wha howdl'd awa hame.
>
> > (*The Cutty*),

> Watty wi' a jeely-bap,
> Whan breengin frae the door,
> Be a stane was trippit up
> And sprattl'd in the stour.
>
> > (*The Jeely-Bap*).

The effect of Soutar's choice of Scots words is to impart to the bairn-rhymes an intense sensory vividness. By the intimate union of sound and sense in the words, noises and actions are evoked with startling immediacy: an effect which, being impressive to a mature reader, would be far more so to a child, whose response to the poems would be wholly spontaneous and not mediated by habits of critical analysis. Soutar in his diary entry for 24 March 1932 wrote:

> I'm afraid these bairn-rhymes which I write from time to time must appear rather formidable for a child – yet what can one do? Even grown-ups in Scotland are children so far as their native tongue is concerned. All of us must wade through the vocabulary if we are to regain our lost heritage.

"Formidable" they may be in respect of the abundance of Scots words – that is, be it noted, from the perspective of a monolingual English-speaker. In other respects they are admirably suited to their intended readership: clear and straightforward in their content, and instantly "catchy" in their format. Despite Soutar's misgivings, the belief expressed in his frequently-quoted observation that "if the Doric is to come back alive, it will come first on a cock-horse" is one which his bairnrhymes are expressly, and most effectively, designed to further.

Soutar's lyrical poetry makes more restricted use of words from this particular register; and, indeed, an unusual density of Scots lexis is not a characteristic of this section of his oeuvre. In *The Auld Tree (For Hugh McDiarmid)*, his experimental use of an unending procession of heavily Scots lines in the service of a somewhat contrived vision is, in the end, wearing rather than inspiring. His distinctive skill is more readily visible in poems where unusual or exceptionally potent Scots words are used sparingly and judiciously, often as the climactic focus of a verse or an entire poem:

> As the sma', wilder'd fleur,
> *Flanterin* wi' licht.
>> (*Summer Song*),

> ... and the hungry beast
> That *runches* round the rocks.
>> (*The Waukrife E'e*),

> I hae nae word for a *jilly-jad*
> Wha can naither tak nor gie.
>> (*The Riddle*),

> But the fowk maun *funder* the auld house,
> An' bigg up anither.
>> (*The Auld House*).

Reminiscences of traditional poetry, particularly the ballads, appear in abundance: some of his most individual and most beautiful lyrics, including such familiar anthology pieces as *The Tryst*, *The Auld House*, *Sang* ("Whaur yon broken brig hings ower...") and *Birthday* ("There were three men o' Scotland...") make extensive use of repetition of words and lines in typical ballad style. In such poems Soutar's method, and its results in evoking an atmosphere of mystery, suggest comparison not with MacDiarmid but with Marion Angus.

MacDiarmid's overt presence in Soutar's poems, in fact, is often as an object of criticism. In *Apotheosis*, if the flagrantly pseudo-MacDiarmid imagery is not quite sufficient to prove a parodic intention, the appearance of *yowdendrift*, *watergaw* and *blethers* rhyming with *gowden feathers*, the bathetic "... an' winna shift" immediately following "liggs in the lift", and the gusts of laughter in the last section, show fairly clearly that what we have here is a mockery of the MacDiarmid vein of poetic fancy. *The Thistle Looks at a Drunk Man*, though making extensive and clever use of humorous words and rhymes, achieves its satiric effect by more specific and well-directed barbs; being pointedly written in the most traditionally Scots of verse forms, opening, Henryson-like, with the poet taking up a book on a stormy winter's night:

> On sic a nicht intae the neuk
> I got deep plankit wi' a buik;
> Peitry I thocht it by the look
> O' lines askewie:
> A' wrocht by ane, wi' scribbler's yeuk,
> They ca' Wee Hughie,

– which, however, in this case immediately sends him to sleep; and ridiculing MacDiarmid's preference for foreign over native models:

> "Wi' booze o' a' guffs he wud droon
> That honest Doric, as a loon,
> He throve on in a bonnie Toun
> Whaur fowk still speak
> Nae hash o' German, Slav, Walloon
> An' bastard Greek.

This suggests a preference for a literary Scots more firmly rooted in some actual spoken form; and it is observable that the "notes on pronunciation" with which Soutar introduced his poems refer, in some particulars, to his native Perthshire dialect: "*eu*, in heuk, neuk, etc.: pronounced as *u* in English cure" – "*ü*, in müne, stüde (stood), etc.: no exact equivalent in English: nearest is probably the sounding of the *e* in definite article (the) when unemphatic". On the other hand, he upheld the value of dictionaries as a resource for poets to exploit:

> To lump us [poets] all together as so many Jamieson raiders or Doric resurrectionists is a calumny. In speaking for myself I speak, I am sure, in great measure for MacDiarmid; and if the dictionary is ever at hand it is not a happy hunting ground but rather a country which our fathers possessed and into which we return to find what we have lost but yet retain

as a memory in our blood. Our return is not primarily an exploration but a recognition.[1]

The imminent appearance of the first fascicle of the *Scottish National Dictionary*, published in 1931, prompted a searching conjecture:

> Have we gathered all these once-living words into a mortuary, or is it a literary orphanage waiting for the authors, who are foster-fathers?[2]

And in an epigram he suggests that the Scots vocabulary is the main thing to survive of what was once a living national culture:

> Puir Grant[3] maun aften tak a thocht
> O' Jamieson; an' wish he'd wrocht
> Lang syne whan Scotland's hinds an' lords
> Were yet as halesome as her words.

Notwithstanding Soutar's willingness to use dictionaries as a resource, the Scots of his poetry suggests a native tongue, tastefully and sparingly augmented with rare words but conveying the vivacity of what was still an active community speech. Some remarkable illustrations of the power of his Scots can be seen in his last published group of poems, *Theme and Variation*, a set of translations from an assortment of poems from various countries (but always made from English versions). In *Star Swarm*, onomatopoeic rhythmic patterns (the leaping rhythms of

> Up and atour the Grampian snaw
> Gaed sterns; and owre the sauty links;
> And owre the rocks that runch'd the sea...;

the sudden halting effect of two adjacent stressed syllables in *wa's murl'd* and *thochts breeng'd*,) and an abundance of Scots verbs suggesting rapid or violent action (*breeng'd* (a word which suggests an uncontrolled, headlong rush); *runch* (grind, crush), *murl* (crumble), *smirl* (sneer), *flanter* (waver, tremble), *brash* (batter), *glunsh* (scowl), *crine* (wither, fade)) result in a poem far excelling its pallid English model.[4] Even more successful,

---

1. Diary entry for 31 January 1936, quoted in *Chapman* 53, Summer 1988, p.16, in a selection of extracts from his journals omitted from Scott's *Diaries of a Dying Man*.

2. 30 March 1930: *ibid.*, p.10.

3. William Grant, first editor of the *Scottish National Dictionary*.

4. For Soutar's models, renderings of Russian poems taken from *Soviet Literature: an Anthology*, eds. George Reavey and Marc Slovin, Wishart (London) 1933, see the appendix to W. R. Aitken, ed., *Poems in Scots and English by William Soutar*, Edinburgh (Oliver and Boyd) 1961.

both in itself and in comparison to its original, is *Poem* (based on a rendering of Essenin's *Tavern Moscow*), in which the colourless original line "My hovel will crumble without me" gives the intense visual clarity and emotive force of

> The fower thackit wa's I was born in
> Are stanes on a brae,

and a masterly choice of Scots words contributes to the evocation of the combined squalor and vibrant life of the city's underworld: the water *slooms* (creeps), the moon *breels* (rolls rapidly) and the speaker *lowches* (slouches – "goes with his head weighed down"); the streets are not "contorted" as in the original but *yowtherin*, an unusual and striking word meaning "stinking", and *stramash* and *sculdudry* (uproar, whoring) precisely convey the tavern atmosphere in an alliterative trio with *sin*.

The remarkable "readability" of Soutar's Scots poetry – a product of, in the first instance, the grace and fluency with which he manipulates traditional verse forms and rhyme patterns – has ensured his reputation as one of the most attractive and most accessible of the Renaissance poets. The fact that he has achieved this while writing in a Scots showing all the lexical richness of an ancestral folk-speech is a measure not only of his individual poetic skill, but of the enduring appeal which the mother tongue still has for Scottish readers.

9
Flood-Tide in the Lowlands:
Douglas Young, Sydney Goodsir Smith,
Robert Garioch, Tom Scott

In 1943, MacDiarmid contributed an introduction to the first volume in a series collectively entitled *Poetry Scotland*. Speaking of the Scottish Renaissance as an accomplished fact, he defined its purpose as: "...to revive those elements which had been more and more lost in the process of assimilation to English standards ... internationalism; wide-ranging linguistic and scholarly interests; an intense concern with the crucial problems, needs and potentialities of Scotland; and, along with that, a thorough knowledge of Scottish history, psychology, and the whole of the country from Maidenkirk to John o' Groats", as well as a concern for the revival and literary regeneration of "the Scots Lallans language" and – this was one of the earliest statements of what became a central element in his patriotic vision – "the need to restore Gaelic as the national language of Scotland [.]" He proceeded to discuss the linkage between cultural and political nationalism in Scotland, attributing the emergence of the SNP (at that stage only one of several small political groups with similar aims) to the new activity in the literary and intellectual spheres, but arguing, as he could have done at any time between then and now, that "the underground strength of the forces generated in this revived Nationalism was not adequately reflected in the sphere of practical politics". The poet whose work MacDiarmid was introducing, Douglas Young, was praised by the master for his political activism as Chairman of the SNP,[1] in giving voice to the demand for independent Scottish control of Scotland's armed forces and their contribution to the

1. A position which he held for only a few days before being imprisoned for refusing conscription. *Auntran Blads* was published while its author was in jail.

war effort, as well as for his extensive linguistic scholarship, commitment to Gaelic, international outlook and profound knowledge of Scotland and its culture.

By any standards, Young's *Auntran Blads*,[1] despite its small size and deceptively modest title, is both an impressive collection of poetry and a powerful underwriting of the ideals of the Renaissance. Opening, after an introductory poem in praise of Jamieson's *Dictionary*, with thirteen Scots translations from the Gaelic of Sorley MacLean[2] and one from George Campbell Hay, it proceeds to a selection of original poems in both Scots and English including several on Greek themes, a group of Scots translations from earlier Scottish and Irish Gaelic poetry, from Homer, Sappho, Catullus and Dante, and from French, German, Russian, Lithuanian and Chinese poems, and ends with a polyglot assortment of short pieces including two translations from Burns into Greek. And the almost ostentatiously cosmopolitan nature of the collection is counterpointed with an occasional subtle illustration of Young's Scottish nationalism: *Sabbath i the Mearns*, opening as a lyrical poem of scenic description, proceeds to draw a disconcerting contrast between the "mensefu fermer-chiels" and the heroes of Scotland's past – "They werena aye like thon, this auld Albannach race"; the elegy *For Alasdair* asks of the addressee's death in combat "Suld this be Scotland's pride, or shame?"; and in a short war poem in which Scots words are carefully chosen and placed for effect, the despairing conclusion is stated in language of elemental simplicity –

> In England's hour o need
> He quit his greitan bride,
> wi youthfu virr and pride
> gaed aff and focht and dee'd.
>
> Sick wi despair and grame
> tuim day follows day.
> Aa we do or say
> canna bring him hame.

1. *Poetry Scotland* Series 1, Glasgow (MacLellan) 1943.
2. Here these will be mentioned only as Scots poems; but for discussion of their relationship to the originals, see the present writer's "Three translations by Douglas Young" in C. Macafee and I. MacLeod, eds. *The Nuttis Schell: Essays on the Scots Language presented to A. J. Aitken*, Aberdeen: A. U. P. , 1987, 195–210, and "Douglas Young and Sorley MacLean" in D. S. Thomson, ed., *Gaelic and Scots in Harmony*, Glasgow: Glasgow University, 1990, 136–48.

– the second word of the poem is envenomed by the fact that the title is *For a Scotsman Slain*. Young's other collection of poetry, *A Braird o Thristles*,[1] published four years later as part of the same series, contains a similar mixture (except that the proportion of original Scots poems is much higher). Slim as they are, too, the two volumes are notable specimens of the typesetter's art, the poems standing out on the page in large and bold print (italics throughout, in the earlier book) and *A Braird o Thristles* being embellished with intricate and in some cases brilliantly-conceived Celtic knotwork designs by George Bain. Young's poetic contribution to the Scottish Renaissance was envisaged and presented in an impressive form.

Young's flamboyant personality and remarkable range of interests and accomplishments made him for many years a lively presence in Scottish letters and Scottish academe; and though his Scots poetry forms only a small part of his life's work it is of an importance that belies its unimposing bulk. In *Auntran Blads* and *A Braird o Thristles*, a boldly enterprising approach to the Scots language is applied in the service of a poetic vision combining tradition and innovation, nationalism and cosmopolitanism, as deliberately and as convincingly as the Renaissance ideals required. The Latin title of the first poem *Thesaurus Palaeo-Scoticus* is a symbol both of Young's own classical erudition (and by extension, the traditional Scottish pride in learning) and his determination to make explicit the roots of his own poetic language in the "ancient Scots" of Jamieson's *Dictionary*. Opening his poem in the simplest of registers, appropriate for a childhood recollection – "I mind when I was a bairnie hou ma mither / brocht out ae day a kist ..." – he proceeds to adorn this with rare and striking words from a highly-charged semantic field: *skinklin, gowdies, fallals, orleges*. All of these are from Jamieson: his definition for *skinkle* "sparkle" is the sense used by Young, though other meanings are attested; he alone testifies to the sense of "jewels" for *gowdies*, and in fact the usage is inauthentic; his definition "gaudy and superfluous parts of attire; superficial ornaments" for *fallals* is not supported by any evidence; and all his instances of *orlege* are from Gavin Douglas: Young is unlikely to have met the word in speech or recent literature. In the second stanza,

1. *Poetry Scotland* Series 12, Glasgow (MacLellan) 1947.

Douglas Young, Sydney Goodsir Smith, Robert Garioch, Tom Scott

a sudden cluster of Scots words in the couplet

> auld douce or ramstam, lown or virrfu words,
> for musardry o thocht or grame o dirds ...

includes the fairly familiar *douce, lown* and *dirds*, a grammatical transformation (*ramstam* as adjective instead of adverb) and a morphological augmentation (*virrfu*) of Young's own devising, a poetic word last used by Soutar, *grame*, and a Jamieson-derived mediaevalism (which remained one of Young's favourite words), *musardry*: this miniature bouquet at the outset of his book is a memorable testimony to Young's fascination with the Scots vocabulary and eagerness to experiment with it. If Soutar had fears that Scots dictionaries could be mere linguistic "mortuaries", Young clearly had none: this beautiful poem is not only a fine tribute to Jamieson's *Dictionary* but a proclamation of its status as a living source of inspiration: "Frae Jamieson's muckle buik the words *tak wing*".

The appropriateness of this claim is convincingly demonstrated by Young's highly individual poetic language. Words for which Jamieson is almost certainly his source appear in abundance; and it is noteworthy that Young shows a far more decided preference than MacDiarmid for words with an archaic ring. His "Jamiesonisms" include *bassanat* (helmet), *bestial* (cattle), *blasounrie* (charge on a shield), *blee* (complexion), *braal* (fragment), *braikit* (speckled), *brub* (check, restrain), *chaudron* (cauldron), *cowzie* (boisterous), *crangle* (twist), *doolzie* (frolicsome), *doungang* (sunset), *dullyart* ("of a dirty dull colour"), *flesche* (fleece), *forvay* (wander), *fruct* (fruit), *gesserant* (another of his favourite words: historically a noun meaning plate armour, Young – though he can hardly have been ignorant of its original meaning – invariably uses it with Jamieson's erroneous definition as "sparkling" or "brilliant white"), *gumphion* (funeral banner), *jenepere* (juniper), *orpheling* (orphan), *renay* (deny), *savendie* ("understanding, sagacity, experience"), *savendle* (stable, secure),[1] *slamber* (delicate), *slud* (calm interval), *sweek* ("the art of doing any thing properly") and *vivually* (used by Young to mean "vividly", though Jamieson's definition is "in life").

---

1. One of Young's worse lapses of judgement was to use those two unrelated words successively in *The Kirkyaird by the Sea* (a venturesome but unconvincing attempt at a Scots version of Valéry's *Le Cimetière Marin*):
...time skinkles, and the dream is savendie.
Savendle thesaur, Pallas' simple shrine...

Young's clear intention, though not always carried out successfully, has been to integrate old and contemporary Scots vocabulary in a consistent poetic language. In *Auntran Blads,* recondite words are used to varying degrees depending (at least sometimes) on the themes of the poems. The elegy *For Alasdair* contains none, a plain and sparse register being integral to its effect; by contrast, in the second verse of *Gealach Ùr: A Communist Sicht o the New Mune,* a translation of a bold if unsubtle propaganda-poem by Sorley MacLean, the suggestions of the military pageantry of a past age in *gumphion, blasounrie* and *ensenyie* (a pseudo-Middle Scots spelling of "ensign") evoke a picture altogether inappropriate to a vision of the Bolshevik revolution. Much more satisfactory is his version of *Dain do Eimhir LV,* in which Scots words appear in a concentration sufficiently emphatic to constitute a defiance of the poem's own reference to "a deean leid" (a description which, of course, could apply to Scots as well as to Gaelic, and could be countered on behalf of, and in, either language):

> I dinna ken the sense o ma trauchlan,
> pittan thochts in a deean leid,
> nou that the hale whuredom o Europe
> lowps up in a brulyie o sturt and dreid.
>
> Och, but a million o years is gien us,
> a wee bittock o the waesome space,
> the commonty's tholemudness and smeddum,
> and the rare ferly o a bonnie face.

His most careful and consistent evocation of the Scots of an earlier period – indeed, one of the finest vindications in modern Scots literature of the technique of writing in a quasi-mediaeval language – is *Ae time that I our flownrie life appraisit,* from Dante. Here, words which are archaic in the simple sense that they have by now vanished, or almost vanished, from common speech, such as *bruit* (noise), *forvay* (wander), *grame* (fury), *owerhail* (subdue), *waement* (lament), are juxtaposed with, on the one hand, words from the familiar Scots vocabulary (*chiel, dowie, dumbfoundert, ferly, glaikit, mirk, steek*), and on the other, words which at first sight have nothing Scots about them, belonging rather to an "educated" register of Standard English (*appraise, duration, firmament, fantasy, faculty, ponder, phantom*), several of which appear in a quasi-mediaeval spelling (*appraisit, duratioun, phantasies, facultie, phantouns*). The implications of

Young's practice here are more far-reaching than might be recognised at first sight. Words of Latin or French origin such as those belong to all speech-forms derived from Old English: that is, they have exactly the same "right" to appear in a Scots as in an English text. The long-term social developments by which Scots has come to be associated with lack of formal education and its range of literary uses restricted accordingly, however, have caused this fact to become obscured. Young is taking the courageous step of attempting to re-integrate words from an educated register into Scots, and to break their false identification as "English" in the exclusive sense. This aim is of course facilitated by the device of writing the entire poem with quasi-mediaeval spellings, because in Middle Scots such words were simply a normal part of the language; however, Young also adopts the same practice in poems which do not evoke a historic setting and in which the departures from conventional orthography are not mediaevalisms but simply Young's own individual habits:

Thon toom desartit eternitie
and their weirdit perpetuitie

> (*Dain do Eimhir XXVIII: The Ghaists*),

I fashna masel for the grand revolution
that'll redd up the puirtith o the human race,
nou I've seen the pictur o aa nobilitie
wrocht out i the glister o a bonnie face.

> (*Dain do Eimhir LIII*),

Aiblins the universalitie
and unco mathematicalitie
o Astronomie's naebut kenners' pretentiousness.

> (*Speculation*).

Besides reclaiming for Scots this whole area of its vocabulary, Young augmented the language by the still more innovative method of devising new words, a practice which he adopted more freely than any of his predecessors since the Middle Scots period. (He referred in a pamphlet to "words I make up for myself from Scots and kindred roots by old Scots principles, such as my words '*Ice-flumes*' for glaciers.[1]) Derivations from existing words (*sainless* from *sain*, hence "incurable"; *trullerie* from *trull*,

---

1. '*Plastic Scots' and the Scottish Literary Tradition*, Glasgow (W. McLellan) 1946. This is the text of an address given to the Dunedin Society in Glasgow.

a Jamieson word for "foolish person", hence "foolishness"; *untwynable* from *twyne*, hence "inseparable"; *thraipfu* from *thraip* "boast", hence "renowned"); calques (*owerset* "translate" and *yearhunder* "century" from the German *übersetzen* and *Jahrhundert*); compounds of a form notably common in Scots (*dounharl* "drag down", *upfraith* "send up in froth") and loosely-linked compounds of noun with noun-modifier (*glamarie-licht* "magic light", *ferly-potency* "magic-power", *water-flads* "water-slabs", *fuddrie-leams* "lightning-flashes", *swaw-pouther* "wave-powder", i.e. blown spray, and – one which deliberately out-MacDiarmids MacDiarmid – *howedumbdeidsunsheen*).

In *A Braird o Thristles*, Young's language shows both greater elaboration and more consistent success than in the earlier volume. The plainest register of Scots can be used for its hard-hitting emotive power:

> Drains faaen in, parks fuggit and moch,
> wuids clortit wi fozy stumps o birk and sauch.
>
> *(Hielant Colloguy)*,

or for passages of lyrical beauty:

> the reek gangs straucht i the luift, that's lither and gray,
> wi an auntran gair o gowd i the North by the Tay.
> The whyte muin owre Drumcarro, the Lomond shawan
> purpie i the West, and a lane whaup caaan.
>
> *(Sainless)*

By contrast, a register drawing on a more recondite vocabulary can evoke an imposing and exotic setting:

> ...a frozen sea, crustit wi rigid spume,
> owredichtit whiles wi sherp and skinklan pouther
>   frae a licht yowden-drift o snaw or hail,
> clortit by avalanche debris, gaigit deep
>   wi oorie reoch crevasses...
>
> *(Ice-Flumes Owergie their Lades)*,

or add what is surely a deliberately mystifying tone to a poem which, uncharacteristically for Young, calls for a purely imaginative response rather than making an intellectually comprehensible statement:

1. This, like several of the compounds in this list, appears in *The Kirkyaird by the Sea*, where the original has simply *eaux*. Presumably he means "waves".

Douglas Young, Sydney Goodsir Smith, Robert Garioch, Tom Scott

There's a steer amang the shadaws
    thrawn by a lowean thocht,
dern weeferty-wafferty shadaws
    flichteriff and aflocht.
                        (Reconciliation).

A further innovation in Young's poetry, and one which at first sight makes his Scots *appear* to be more unlike that of his predecessors than it actually is, is his spelling practices. Several of the orthographic features which shortly afterwards were enshrined in the Scots Style Sheet, such as the digraph *aa* (previously unknown in Scots of any period), the consistent use of *ou* instead of the anglicism *oo* for the sound of [u] and *ow* for [ʌu], and the abandonment of the apostrophe where Scots has lost (or never had) a sound which English retains, are conspicuous features of Young's writing. These are easy to justify on linguistic grounds: other practices which have no such support but nonetheless serve Young's purpose of making his Scots look more distinct from written English, and thus emphasise its status as an autonomous language, are the use of *y* instead of *i* in words such as *whyte*, *byde*; the preference for *-ie* over *-y* in unstressed final syllables (whatever their morphological status), and – an interesting but unrealistic resuscitation of a Middle Scots feature long extinct in most (though not all) forms of spoken Scots – the distinction between the present participle in *-an* and the verbal noun in *-in*.[1] Young, appropriately for the language scholar and polyglot he was, applied himself more consciously than any of his predecessors to the task of separating the spelling of Scots from that of English, instead of being content to use English spelling conventions with *ad hoc* and more or less adequate modifications; and though his achievement is very far from amounting to the establishment of a fully-developed Scots orthography, it at least was a first step in that direction.

The publication of Young's poems contributed to the controversy, increasingly lively and vociferous, on the practices of the Renaissance poets, an editorial in *The Glasgow Herald* (November 28 1946) pronoun-

1. Scots retained this distinction much longer than English: in Middle Scots the endings were written *-and* and *-ing* respectively. In some dialects of the far North, speakers can still be heard to distinguish them as [ɪn] or [ən] for the participle and [in] for the verbal noun. Surprisingly, Scots poets for many years followed Young in conscientiously indicating the distinction in their writings; though it is a safe bet that none of them used it in actual speech.

cing it impossible to believe that "the writings of Mr Douglas Young and his companions . . . bears other than the remotest relation to any form of Scots current today". Unfortunately for his case, the writer's quoted example was *Last Lauch*, certainly one of Young's least obscure poems – as Young was quick to point out.[1] He proceeded to justify the synthetic Scots of his and his confrères' poetry by a series of arguments which (it is depressing to realise) have still, fifty years later, not been universally understood: (a) modern poets in other languages (he cites Blok, Rilke, Eliot and Valéry) write poetry which is linguistically difficult; (b) poetry is never written in the language of popular speech, and dictionaries may be used as licitly as earlier literary texts as sources of expressive language; (c) Scots poets may take words from all dialects "especially as the dialects have only emerged since the disintegration of King's Lallans after 1560" – historically an error, but a clear implication that his intention is to reconstruct a Scots with the status of a national language such as it once had; (d) the motive behind the poets' attempt to dissociate Scots literature from English is not mere negative Anglophobia but a desire to restore the national culture to a position of independence from which it can proceed to re-establish links with other cultures.

The eagerness of poets to join in the debates on their linguistic, literary and political practices was also manifested by Sydney Goodsir Smith, a poet who combined Young's exuberantly innovative handling of Scots with a much wider emotional and imaginative range, and an equal dedication to the Scottish Renaissance ideals. In a short article[2] he decried, with perfect justice, the "dogmatic abuse" often directed at recent Scots poetry by unsympathetic critics, and their conspicuous failure to discuss the literary merit of the verse instead of the principle of writing in synthetic Scots. To counter the charge that the new literary Scots was excessively remote from actual speech, he produced a short list of words – *antrin* (occasional), *smittel* (infectious), *waukrife* (wakeful), *begrutten* (tear-stained), *wancanny* (unlucky) – which, he claimed (no doubt from experience) could readily be heard in the Canongate: a dubious proceeding, it must be admitted, for it would be equally easy to produce from Smith's

---

1. In *Plastic Scots, op. cit.*
2. "In defence of 'Lallans'", in *Scots Review*, May 1948, p.23.

poetry a list of Scots words of which this could certainly *not* be main-tained. In a home-thrust at the end of the article he suggested that the hostility to Scots poetry manifested by academic critics stemmed from a fear that the movement posed a threat to the discipline of "Eng.Lit." and the anglicisation of Scottish culture which that represented: a charge which he later developed with greater elaboration and greater force in an international academic journal.[1] The most frequently-quoted poem in his first anthology, *Skail Wind* (1941),[2] had memorably asserted the absurdity of criticising any poetry for its lack of resemblance to common speech –

> We've come intil a gey queer time
> Whan scrievin Scots is near a crime.
> "There's no one speaks like that", they fleer,
> – But wha the deil spoke like King Lear?

– and had also re-stated a tenet often expressed by MacDiarmid, that English had become devitalised and no longer adequate for poetry –

> But the Suddron's nou a sick man's leid,
> Alang the flattest plains it stots;
> Tae reach the hills his fantice needs
> This bard maun tak the wings o Scots.
>
> *(Epistle to John Guthrie)*

(*Fantice*, brought in unobtrusively, is a mediaevalism used in a modern sense: he evidently means "fancy, imagination"; but the sense which the word generally has in Middle Scots is "illusion".)

The fact is often mentioned that Smith was born in New Zealand (though of Scottish parents) and educated in England, and was not a native speaker of Scots. This is interesting, but hardly paradoxical: his well-known (indeed notorious) fondness for convivial company – the theme of drink recurs with a cheerfully defiant regularity in his poetry – gave him every opportunity to become acquainted with the full rich-ness of the spoken language; and his extensive and enthusiastic study of Scottish literature, particularly of the mediaeval period, provided a mine of raw material to be worked by his lively verbal imagination. In Smith's

1. "Trahison des Clercs: the Anti-Scots Lobby in Scottish Letters", in *Studies in Scottish Literature* 2:2, 1964, 71–86.
2. Also in *Collected Poems 1941–1975*, London (Calder and Boyars) 1975.

treatment of Scots a remarkable sequence of development and progress is unmistakeable. The poems in *Skail Wind* clearly demonstrate his eagerness for experimentation, but the main impression conveyed by the collection as a whole is that of a prentice poet's attempts to find both his medium and his feet. A style suggesting hyper-inflated T. S. Eliot, used in some of the English poems, emerges with an equal lack of success in Scots:

> Yir een maun watch the slaughtrous stramash, booted doom
> Fae sleep wheer aa ligs broun as the snug deep howe o the womb
> And oorie truth returns to ache lik snaw i the teeth
> And naethin but crottled despair beneath.
>
> *(Lament in the Second Winter of War)*;

and no more convincing are the pseudo-Hopkinsian flourishes which also make an occasional appearance:

> Ah, swoop heich, my splendid poet-deevil, pierce thae dowie gloffs that
> fear your sleepless sun,
> Bear i thon swift rapier beak the arrogance, my dark, my gallus
> independent yin,
>
> *(Merlin Bird)*.

For his vocabulary, Smith in these early poems swoops with neither discipline nor discrimination among all registers of Scots and English: a headlong poetic energy is unmistakeably suggested, and a power to convey and arouse emotions of great intensity (the fervid optimism of *The Quickening* or *The Dark Days are By* surely gave readers' spirits a momentary lift in 1941); but so is a grave lack of artistic orderliness. Such lines as the following must have been, frankly, a gift to critics sceptical of the Renaissance movement:

> Ill tomorrow dees in a dreich cauld womb tae be a stillborn spectre
> Gastrous as lupus loupin near, so split yir luscious grins
> Fat carpers pinned tae thowless yesterdays, and you my poet chiel wi
> doffed locks and een,
> Sich een that see owre faur aheid leching the glaistig's glaumerie,
> Maun ye recant, renounce love yer sweet daft ferlie –
> For aa yir dervish beauty reads is row o noughts, poor gull?
>
> *(Ode to Hector Berlioz, 1803 – 1869)*

A satisfactory poem cannot be wrought by throwing together an unsorted and disorganised collection of images, however interesting each

one may be individually; and very much less can a language be constructed by simply ransacking a treasure-horde of words and displaying
the loot in a chaotic jumble. In this early collection, it is when Smith
employs more traditional metres, simpler and more direct statements,
and a lexis drawn consistently from vernacular Scots, that he achieves
success. *Kinnoul Hill*, the best of a set of "Four Songs", is a potently evocative poem in ballad metre, evoking a chill and desolate scene much
more convincingly than the unstructured verse and unsystematically
recherché vocabulary of other poems in this collection:

> O black's the ice on Kinnoul Brae,
>   Dark scaurs lik wa's o doom,
> But nane sae mirk as this dumb wae
>   That maks aa Perth a tomb.

A bounding anapaestic metre conveys an exultant mood in *The Dark Days
are By* –

> O the glory's uprising, my luve, my luve,
> Ye can hear Scotlan's hert pulsin fierce wi the Spring,
> They'll not *[sic]* silence this music again, my luve,
>   Howeer they ding!

– and the combination of the same rhythm with a colloquial, slangy
vocabulary contributes to a tone of bitter mockery in *The Steeple Bar,
Perth*:

> O I'm getting a wee thing fou, my luve,
>   An donnert an like tae fleer –
> For, jeez, it's dreich tae get pissed, my luve,
>   Wi nane o my looed yins here.

And on rare occasions, a precisely-judged and steadily-maintained bal-
ance of expressive vocabulary and emotive imagery hints at the presence
of the poet Smith was soon to become:

> My swan, O sailing gull, my white winged childe,
> I touch yir burd-saft breists, thae honey hills, wi trummlin hans, an kiss
> Yir een, thae gleids, dark burns in spate, that licht this mirk I thole,
> O white as the poodry snaw that fa's the nicht ootby
> Is the ferlie o my gowden childe whaes loo has feift my saul
>   (*My Gowden Childe o the Snaw*).

Even in his second collection, *The Wanderer* (1943), there are signs that the propensity for wild and whirling words is now being brought under stricter control. The poems in ballad metre, as before, are among the best: the emotive (and fortuitously alliterative) Scots words *gastrous, gowl, gurlie* are dramatically deployed in the opening stanza of *The Ballad of Peter Morrison*; *The Rossignel* (a possibly erroneous Middle Scots spelling) draws on the same register to evoke gloomy weather and harsh landscapes: "The yatteran burns, the rairan swaw"; and in *Ma Moujik Lass* one of his stock poetic gambits, an instantaneous and fiercely ironic transition from lofty ideals to squalid reality, is underlined by skilful vowel-patterning:

Ma hert is lowpan ower the trees
  An fleein wi the wund –
Ma lips 're weet wi barley bree,
  Ma hurdies hug the grund.

It is in *The Deevil's Waltz* (1946), however, that Smith emerges as both a poet of unchallengeable stature and one of the great synthesisers of Scots. A deliberate recalling of the mediaeval Makars is visible, in the wide range of verse forms, occasional use of refrains, specific recollections of individual poets or poems ("Fredome is ane nobil thing" is quoted in *The Pricks*; *Timor mortis non conturbat me* serves as refrain in the appropriately-named *In Time o Deepest Wanhope*) and archaisms – real and invented – of vocabulary (*stuperie, demonrie, langerie, granderie, harborie*). As in Young's collections, one of the outstanding features of *The Deevil's Waltz* is the poet's success in evoking a contemporary Scottish vision – that of an angry radical nationalist in a Scotland enduring the bleakest and most desperate years of the War – against the background of the nation's history and that of the entire European culture of which Scotland is an integral part. The well-known *Largo* makes the diminution of the town's fishing fleet to a single drifter an emblem for the willing, deluded surrender of independence and self-sufficiency of a class: the Scots of this poem owes nothing to literary or scholarly sources except perhaps the word *crammasie*, which with its suggestion of opulence and splendour underlines the dwarfing of the solitary boat:

Ae black drifter lane
Riggs the crammasie daw.

The sequence *Armageddon in Albyn* places the carnage of the present war in the context of Scotland's own long fight for freedom: *El Alamein* combines imagery of stark potency with verbal references to the War of Independence –

> Yon burnan daw
> Than dumb-deid blacker,
> Whiter than snaw
> Will the bricht banes glitter;
> That this was for Alba
> Maun we mak siccar![1]

– and *The War in Fife*, after employing common Scots words to depict the desolate scene with chilling sensory realism:

> Gurlie an gray the snell Fife shore,
> Frae the peat-green sea the cauld haar drives ...

and associate the grimness of the weather with social demoralisation, drives to the bitter conclusion:

> Twa hunner years o Union's bled
> The veins mair white nor ony war.

Here too, one unusual word is placed to highlight a central element in the poem's message: the Union is "the lang *stouthrife*", an old legal term for violent robbery. The image of "a cauld haar that comes on Fife" is likewise associated with Scotland's political impotence in *The Arbroath Declaration, April 6th, 1320*. Celebrated Scottish freedom fighters – Wallace, Rob Roy MacGregor, Thomas Muir, John Maclean – are evoked in many poems: in *Agin Black Spats*, with *Prometheus* one of the most stirring calls for resistance to tyranny in the collection, the list is extended to include figures from other countries representing either active struggle against oppression or tragic subjection to it:

> Gregor was taen; Pearse was shot
> I' the cauld dawn frae prison;
> Wallace they hackit an hung on yetts;
> The guillotine got Danton;

1. Until a few years ago with the incredible abandonment of even a pretence of teaching Scottish history in schools, this phrase recalled by a mental reflex the traditional exchange following Robert Bruce's murder of his rival in the Franciscan Kirk of Dumfries: *Bruce:* "I dout I hae slain the Comyn!" *Kirkpatrick:* "Ye dout? I'll mak siccar!" Indeed, Smith's use here of an expression generally recalled as a joke, albeit in a context of bloodshed and warfare, is an audacious poetic stroke.

Marlowe got a drunkart's knife;
Maistlike a swayan rope
Tuik Frankie Villon's life;
Wi wershlie deean hope
O' libertie Pushkin lies
Gagged by royal spies;
While Byron dwynit in a bog
An Rabbie's leid gies text to clods
That prate o freedom
An practise feedom.

Chopin, Beethoven and Tchaikovsky are celebrated as heroic symbols of freedom: the last in one of the most haunting poems in the collection, *October 1941*, with its nightmarishly commingled imagery of tank battles, rain-soaked trees, swirling leaves and flowing blood, evoked again by the power of the Scots vocabulary:

Trees greit their tears o bluid, they mell wi the bluid o men,
By a daft God's weirdless breith the fey leaves blawn aa widdershin
In the screich o whup or shell the grummlan wunds o daith ...

It is probably not accidental, in view of his passionate identification with the cause of freedom and justice and his fury and horror at the devastation of the War, that the poem in this collection in which his Scots is densest and most recondite, as if to emphasise his own defiance, is *Ma Brither*, his translation of a Polish poem by Stefan Brukiewicz: *smouchteran grieshoch, gash wi stang an skaith, a coronach wreistit til targats, grundan doun the deif stour crinched / The rankreengin skreighan machines.* (*Rankreengin* is a unique word: Jamieson gives *rankringing* "wild, coarse, lawless".)

The chaos surounding him is epitomised in the title poem of the collection, one of the most Dunbar-like poems in Smith's oeuvre. The mediaeval makar's dual propensities for virulent satire and wild, macabre humour are combined in a fantastic imaginative *tour de force*, in which the rapid, stamping rhythm established in the opening lines,

Rin an rout, rin an rout,
Mahoun gars us birl about,

and maintained with unflagging energy throughout, hurls the reader through a contemporary dance of death with (as in the most obvious analogues *Fasternis Even in Hell* and *Tam o' Shanter*) Mahoun at its centre: the Devil of Dunbar and Burns takes on a terrifying new life in a succession of images culminating – for fear, it is tempting to think, that a reader might dismiss the figure as quasi-mediaeval grotesquerie – in one of the most hateful symbols of the Nazi regime:

> O rin an rout, we birl about
> Tae the rhythm o the Deil's *jack-boot*.

Scots vocabulary in this poem is skilfully integrated with the rhymes, grammatical patterns and sensory imagery, the crowning touch being the invented compound in the simile describing Mahoun in the last verse *black as auld widdie-fruit*: *widdie* means "gallows".

In his post-war volumes, Smith turned to love as the principal theme in his poetry, and by evoking it in a variety of moods and of lyrical forms developed his medium still further. If a single poem were to be chosen as the outstanding representative of this period, it would be the magnificent fantasy *King and Queen o the Fowr Airts*, another quasi-mediaeval poem replete with images of wealth and splendour (*gowd, emerants, siller*), wild flights of fancy ("Schir Wattie sclimmed his steeple's tap ...")[1] and far-ranging references to exotic and imposing places and figures (Tara Haas, Cathay, "Tamburlaine was a shilpiskate / Ozymandias a parvenu..."). (*Shilpiskate* is an inspired concoction from *shilp* "weakling" and *skate* "idiot".) Assuredly nothing could demonstrate the triumph of the Scottish Renaissance more clearly than a comparison between this poem, by any standards one of the great love-lyrics of Europe, with the loves of rustic Jocks and Jennies celebrated in Kailyard poetry!

Love is the theme of his masterpiece, the sequence *Under the Eildon Tree*, in which erudition, imagination, emotional intensity and a sustained linguistic inventiveness unsurpassed in modern Scottish literature combine in a coruscating, crepitating fireworks display of literary virtuosity. Love stories from classical mythology, early Celtic legend, Arthurian tradition and actual history (Antony and Cleopatra, Burns and Highland Mary) are either referred to in passing or given a full poetic exposition. Verbal references to the Bible, Chaucer, Marlowe, Shakespeare, Milton, Burns, Tennyson, MacDiarmid, and no doubt others, are woven into the verse: sometimes quoted with a directly appropriate reference to their

1. Referring to Princes Street's landmark Scott Monument, a white marble statue of Sir Walter Scott surmounted by an extravagantly ornate tower.

original context (*"Quhar art thou gane, my luf Euridices!"*) or used with unaltered sense as counters in a poetic argument ("A divinitie doth hedge a king / But our aureolie is surelie frae the pit...."); but in other instances parodied ("O, let there be nae girnin at the Bar!"), used ironically ("Fou as a puggie I, the bardic ee / In a fine frenzy rollan") or even set against each other in mutually destructive juxtaposition ("'Fredome / Is ane nobil thing...!' / Exile, chains and slaverie!" – this example from the poem *Hieland Mary*, where Burns himself is the persona). After a quiet and gracefully-cadenced opening in which an invented quasi-mediaeval lexeme delicately foreshadows the linguistic creativity to follow –

> Bards hae sung o' lesser luves
>> Than I o' thee,
> O, my great follie and my granderie ...

– and a second section where a convention of love-poetry so long out-worn that even Shakespeare treated it parodically[1] is dramatically revivi-fied by new and bold similes –

> For aa their whiteness is as pitch aside your snaw,
> Their hair but towe aside the raven wing,
> Their een as flints til your bricht emerants,
> Their mous as brick aside your lips o' gean...
> Their breists auld bitches' dugs til your white domes
>> O' hinnie-dew ...

– the effect of a dizzying emotional roller-coaster is evoked in a variety of registers ranging from the pellucid simplicity of

> A wee boat wi a broun sail
> Left the pier juist at our feet
> And sailed awa intil the sunset
> Silentlie, the water like a keekin-gless...

to the ponderous obscurity of

> Albeid the precipitate o our twa luves commelled
> Lowsit a combustioun whas Vesuvian spate
>> Outran itsel
> And thriftless waurit aa its heaped-up thesauries
> Doundingan ten Pompeiis o the saul
> Til bourach, skau, distraction o the sense
>> – And braggandie ...

1. In Sonnet 130.

– a passage containing, as well as learned words not exclusive to Scots (*precipitate, combustioun*), a mediaevalism (*thesaurie*), a Jamiesonism (*skau* "ruin, destruction"), compounds made up from existing morphemes (*commell* "combine", *dounding* "demolish"), and an outright invention (*braggandie*); and proceeds for the remainder of the poem (*Thus Spak Antony*) with many more words from all those classes; and from the sensual beauty of

> And the like wind that took her fause man aff
> Streamed throu her sable hair outblawn
> Schere-black as Ethiope nicht, wild her raven glorie
> Streamed i' the wind, the speed-flung mane
> O' a mear o Arabie hinnyan i' the race
> Owre siller sand – bluid cast til the wrack for libertie!
> The unpent cloud o' midnicht streamed in the dry simoon
> Sheenan like jet in sol's orsplendant nune...
>
> (*Dido*)

– *simoon* is an error, or a rhyme-forced variation, for *simoom*, a strong, burning wind of the North African deserts; *orsplendant* is another of Smith's concoctions, with the etymologically self-explanatory sense of "shining like gold" – to the blunt vulgarity of

> A cauld, scummie, hauf-drunk cup o' tea
>   At my bed-side ...
> Wi ase on the sheets, ase on the cod,
> And crumbs o toast under my bum ...
>
> (*Slugabed*).

And abrupt switches from one register to another demonstrate the versatility of Smith's medium as well as his literary audacity: often such transitions take place from one line to the next ("her lire as white as Dian's chastitie / In yon fyle, fousome, clarty slum..."). Lexical flights of fancy include words borrowed from, or constructed so as to suggest, the aureate register of mediaeval poetry (*scelartrie* "wickedness", *mapamound* "globe of the world", *schawaldour* (glossed by Smith as "wood ranger", though used in historic texts to refer to Border reivers), *nominomancie* "invocation of names for magical purposes" – presumably) and archaic but self-explanatory words and concoctions on the same models (*traitorie, fulerie, bravadie, pultrous, lemanous, velvous*). Jamieson provides *ramskeerie* "reckless, irresponsible" and *rambaleuch* "tempestuous"; and an idiosyn-

131

cracy concocted by Thomas Carlyle, *gigmanitie* (from *gigman* "one who keeps a gig", hence, a narrowly respectable "bourgeois") is drafted into service. Smith rings changes on existing onomatopes to produce *flegmageerie* "whim, daydream", *flichtmafletherie* "frippery, trifle" and *flichteriefleeterie* "flitting here and there". In this poem-sequence, the Scots tongue is revealed in all its richness as a literary language developed over centuries, with a vocabulary and range of styles and registers not only already immense but capable of expanding and proliferating at the will of an inventive writer. To denigrate Smith's medium as artificial would betray a truly amazing failure to appreciate the nature and value of literary creativity: *Under the Eildon Tree* offers to a reader not only the intellectual pleasure of responding to the challenge of tracing his full meaning via his sources and references as well as his unfamiliar words themselves, but also an emotionally and imaginatively stimulating experience rarely encountered in recent literature.

Smith in his later poetry continued to demonstrate the qualities which had enabled him to produce this masterpiece, though never again fully attaining to its heights: a development in *Gowdspink in Reekie* (1974), as in his earlier prose work *A Carotid Cornucopius*, is the use of wholly idiosyncratic lexical concoctions on the Joycean model: *cansoteratiouns, verbobesitie, perembrodrouthie, magnumunimondulous*. Perhaps fortunately, few other Scots writers have been persuaded to attempt this trick: nonetheless, Smith is again, on one level at least, simply demonstrating the capacity of Scots for experimentation along the most radical lines.

The second place, on overall merit, among Scotland's twentieth-century makars has often been claimed for Smith. Incontestably, he is one of the most ambitious and venturesome in his attempts to push the literary development of the language to and beyond its limits. However, if one of the Renaissance makars were to be selected as having attained to the greatest degree (indeed, sadly, *any* degree) of popularity, as distinct from renown, among the general poetry-reading public, it would almost certainly be Robert Garioch.[1] By contrast with Smith, Scots was his mother tongue; and in his poetry he draws on the still-rich resources of

---

1. Cf. the comment by Charles King in *Twelve Modern Scottish Poets*, London (University of London Press) 1971, p. 80: "There is no more enjoyable a poet writing in Scotland today".

a living community language. As he expressed it, "My language is my native local Scots, plus words and expressions of any other date and provenance, from speech, dictionaries and books".[1] Yet Garioch's reputation for the fluency, geniality and accessibility of his work is assuredly not due to any restriction in his language to the familiar reaches of the contemporary vernacular. A glance at the glossary to his *Complete Poetical Works*[2] shows that his vocabulary is drawn from a variety of styles, periods and registers as diverse as that of any of his contemporaries. There are, of course, an abundance of common-core Scots words: words with which any speaker of a well-preserved local dialect or reader of "mainstream" Scots literature is sure to be familiar: *ashet, begowk, causey, douce, ettle, fusionless, glaur, haver, ingle, jouk. . ...* As a special class within this register, there is a selection, smaller than in some other Renaissance poets, of the highly language-specific group of polysyllabic, emotive, precisely-focused and untranslatable words which are among the most distinctive characteristics of Scots: *camsteerie, clanjamphrie, disjaskit, gurliewhirkies* (this one is a dubious Jamiesonism), *jurmummil, peelie-wallie, whigma-leeries.* Drawing on a different criterion – this class and the first two are by no means mutually exclusive – there is a group of words of which (as will be shown) Garioch makes special use: words which, because of their conspicuous presence in familiar works of literature, will inescapably and by reflex action arouse echoes of specific literary contexts. The assignment of words to this group is in the nature of things subjective, but all readers with even a preliminary knowledge of Scottish literature would surely agree that the following are among its members: *agley, caller, cranreuch, forfairn, hanlawhile, hazel-raw, lily-leven, spleuchan.* Contrasting with these classes, all of which suggest the Scots of long-established written and spoken usage, there are many words with the unmistakable abrasive tone of contemporary demotic speech: *bevvy, confab, (gae their) dinger, fleean* (drunk), *keelie, nyaff, plookie, rammy, scoot, tumphie.* There are a few recent additions to the literary Scots vocabulary such as *ayebidan*; and some of what appear to be Garioch's own concoctions: the more or less jocular *bairn-fank* (playpen) and *siller-howkan* (money-earning), and

1. Duncan Glen, 'Editorial: Poetry or 'Scot.Lit'?", *Akros* 11:33 (1977), 3–12; quoted in Tulloch, *op. cit.*, p.53.

2. Edited by Robin Fulton, Edinburgh (MacDonald) 1983.

the ludicrous *potigaries-luckenbooths* (chemist shops). And finally – at first blush an unexpected observation of a poet so emphatically of his own time – there is a strikingly large number of words taken from Middle Scots, often from specific poems: these include not only "content" words, such as *amene, bistayd, celsitud, cowclink, dispitous, dowfart, habitakle, mansuetud, namekouth, orfeverie* and *seignory*, but adverbs such as *alsweill* and *nocht-for-thy*, and words for which a mediaeval spelling is used even though they have survived to our own day, in Scots, English or both, in altered orthographical form: *gudwyf, hap-schakellit, untheikit*.

To some extent, Garioch follows his mediaeval models in associating the register of his Scots with the subject-matter of his individual poems. As a clear example, use of quasi-mediaeval language is characteristic of his translations from classical literatures. An extreme example is *Dithyramb*, from Pindar, with its mediaevalisms of spelling (*schynand, benignitye, prymrois*) and grammar (participles in *-and*, noun plurals in *-is*, *bene* for "are": this last is a nice touch of verisimilitude, as this form in Middle Scots was an Anglicism, used rarely and only in order to contribute to the exotic and elevated tone of the most dignified courtly or religious poetry), and its preponderance of Latin-derived aureate terms (*habitakle, bontie, celsitud, mansuetud*): here, Garioch has produced a clever piece of pastiche Middle Scots for its own sake. In *The Traiveler*, from the Old English poem generally called *The Wanderer*, the language is much less conspicuously archaic; but here too the status of the poem as a translation from an early work is suggested by a sprinkling of old-fashioned spellings (*falow, gentil, warldis*) and words (*frane, felloun*), and by compounds which are actually literal or near-literal calques on the Old English: *middle-yird* (from *middangeard*), *yird-traiveler* (from *eardstapa*), *treisor-handsel* (from *sinc-ege*). A more varied and perhaps more subtle example is his masterly *Anatomy of Winter* from Hesiod. Here the diction suggests not the most exalted style which Middle Scots afforded, but rather its vernacular register, as exploited in – to cite the most obvious comparison and one from which Garioch emerges with real credit – Gavin Douglas's "Winter" Prologue. Only once or twice – in the word *genetrice* or the reference to the sun's *saitt celestial* – does the language acquire an aureate touch: Garioch's dual strategy has been to pay homage to the classical origin of the poem by the use of archaisms, and to convey its impression of winter's discomforts by a selection of words with sharply-focused physical referents and memorable sound-patterns, of which the pervasive alliteration is the most obvious: *Boreas . . . brulyies the braid sea an gars it blawp, it garrs the bestial grue, luittard loons that limp on three legs,*

> The haar soukit in steam frae ever-bounteous stremis
> is blawn heich abuin the yird by blaisters of wund.
> At dirknin it whiles draws to rain; while the blast's deray
> is ruggan at thwankan cluddis thruschit by Thracian Boreas.

Luittard (bowed) is a rare word from one of Dunbar's invective poems; *thwankan* is another of the doubtfully-authentic words attested by Jamieson and nobody else.

On the other hand, there is no assuming that Garioch *always* combines archaic language with antique subject-matter. George Buchanan, though obviously no Pindar or Hesiod in respect of chronological seniority, would certainly seem as a historical figure to be apposite for treatment in a linguistic form approximating to the Scots of his own time (as in the remarkable evocation of the language of James VI's court poetry which Garioch uses to translate Thomas Duff's *On the Daith of the Noble Wicht Maister Montgomerie, the Poet and Sodger*). But in *The Humanist's Trauchles in Paris* Garioch's linguistic precedents are Fergusson and Burns rather than Dunbar and Douglas. (Who else would have thought of the marvellously subtle literary trick of including in a couple of verses on the theme of the poverty and deprivation suffered by the great poets of ancient times the phrase *hous or hald* and the rhyme *yowes – knowes*?) The poem abounds in Scots words; and as in the work of those master satirists, the language is employed for its unique aptitude for discourse in a reductive, mocking, contemptuous vein. Much of the vocabulary is from the semantic field appropriate to flyting or satire: *dortie, mirkie, crabbit, mauchless, fusionless*. Classical references are present as in the eighteenth-century poets; but when Phoebus appears in the first stanza, his dignity is immediately whummled by the very down-to-earth triplet *blaw and bumm and blatter*; and when he re-asserts himself in the next verse under his other name we see him *begowkan* a *callant* frae his *faither's byre*. As a still more deft put-down the name Calliope (in stanza 5) has to be given an illiterate mispronunciation "Cally Opy" for the line to scan. The verse form, a sort of extended Habbie, invites the poet to make conspicuous play with rhymes; and this he does, positively revelling in the opportunities to make expressive Scots words reinforce their own effect by appearing in rhyming clusters. We find rhyming pairs or triads of which all members are conspicuously Scots: *harns - starns, tocher - slocher, fecht - wecht - stecht, grumphies - tumphies - sumphies, shauchles - bauchles - trauchles*; and also instances where an innocent word acquires sinister or ludicrous overtones by being made to rhyme with a much more potent one: *muses - gruzes, ranks - flanks - stanks. Garioch's Repone til George Buchanan* is similar in tone, and in its linguistic register.

Another example, this time a wholly serious one without the irony or humour of the "Buchanan" pair, of a poem in something like traditional literary Scots is *The Bog*. Here, along with a vocabulary and grammar that are strongly Scots, the formality of the treatment is emphasised by the regular and classical metre and stanza form and the frequency of alliteration and other sound-patterning. In the opening line "The lyft is lourd abuin the hechs an howes", the tone is set by the two alliterative word-pairings, which impart a ballad-like quality to the language. Sound-linkage often serves to throw semantically forceful words into relief: *feart. . . fusionless . . . forfochen, clatchin in thae never-endin clarts, pech an plouter, while bummlan boomers threaten broken banes*. Lexically the Scots is dense, but conspicuously there are few rare or archaic words (archaisms in this poem are very sparse and virtually restricted to spelling and morphology: *lyft, skinklan*): if a few of the spellings are idiosyncratic (*joater, skar*); hardly a word would be unfamiliar to a reader with a basic knowledge of literary or spoken Scots. The patterning of the lexical sets, however, is interesting. At first, the dreary, monotonous squalor of the landscape is emphasised by a preponderance of words suggesting entities, actions or qualities that are unimpressive or downright unpleasant: *puddock, coup, foazie, plouter, nesh, traipse, scarts, pech, hirple*: almost every Scots word in the first four verses, in fact, is of this type. A dramatic change occurs in the next stanza with a selection of words suggesting brightness or hardness, or actions associated with these qualities. Shortly afterwards the language becomes permeated with tricks involving German references: an appalling pun *Fuhrer - furore*, an alliterative pattern *heich in their Heinkels*, a rhyme of *F-moll* with *Usher Hall* in a climax verse which brings into shocking juxtaposition the sublimity of Beethoven, the comfortably, perhaps complacently, familiar Edinburgh landmark and the hideous tone of the sirens, all against the background of the dismal bog.

Garioch's Scots, then, can carry strong suggestions of the language of the Makars, or can suggest a virtuoso handling of that of the Vernacular Revival. It can also, at times, be grounded in neither fifteenth- nor eighteenth-century usage but very emphatically in his own day. Some of his Edinburgh sonnets – in humorous defiance of the exalted associations of this verse form – show his language at its most contemporary and most demotic: he achieves the remarkable feat of making poetry in an unchallengeably traditional format out of a register of Scots which is generally considered neither poetic, traditional, nor even respectable. The title *I was fair beat* hardly suggests a poem in Burnsian Scots; and the sonnet so designated indeed contains expressions like *a hie-brou clan, ye maun be in the swim, it fairly wad hae sent ye daft*. The deliberate juxtaposition of this register with references to the "cognoscenti" and their favoured artforms (culminating in the rhyme of *Debussy* with *randy pussy*) is characteristic of Garioch's use of Scots for satirical humour. The same slangy tone is conspicuous in *I'm Neutral* (*a kinna foreign cratur, shut your gob, I caa'd him ower*); and in *Heard in the Cougate* the realism of his language becomes positively merciless, with the semi-coherent speech of a drunken Edinburgher being represented by nonce phonetic spellings (*Ah ddae-ken whu' the pplace is comin tae*) and a selection of inarticulate noises. Garioch's skill in reproducing the cadences of contemporary vernacular speech is a major contribution to the remarkable success of one of the most impressive sections of his oeuvre, his translations from Giuseppe Belli, where as a counterpart to the dialect of the original he has adopted a register as firmly rooted in twentieth-century Edinburgh as Belli's is in nineteenth-century Rome.[1]

A fundamental point which emerges from a reading of Garioch's Scots poetry is that this is a poet for whom Scots, in all its richness, was both a spoken and a literary language. He was as familiar with the full range of

1. See further Riccardo Durante, "The Paradox of Distance: Belli Translated into English and Scots". in *New Comparison* 8, Autumn 1989, pp. 36 – 44; and J. D. McClure, "Is Translation Naturalisation? Some Test-cases from Scots", in *Publications du Centre Universitaire de Luxembourg: English Studies III*, eds. J. J. Simon and A. Sinner, Luxembourg 1991, pp. 193 – 213.

Scottish literature as he was with Scots as an ancestral spoken language, and capable of combining influences from all reaches of spoken and literary Scots into a poetic medium of enormous diversity. Yet even when his poetic language is most suggestive of the words, idioms and audible cadences of Scots as actually spoken, it remains a carefully-constructed literary artifact: he does not *reproduce* the material of actual speech any more than he copies the language of his great poetic predecessors, but re-shapes and interweaves them both for poetic effects of great subtlety.

One such effect is the unexpected irruption of features which momentarily depart from the linguistic register dominant in a particular poem. Indeed, if the persona of a poem is suggested by the choice of words,[1] a sudden brief intrusion of a word or phrase from a register other than the dominant one often adds to, or radically alters with humorous or ironic effect, our impression of the speaker. In the sonnet *Queer Ongauns*, a colloquial register is momentarily interrupted by the word *formatioun*, spelt as in Middle Scots and pronounced with four syllables. *Scottish Scene* is obviously in a form of Scots appropriate to argument at a fairly unsubtle and unsophisticated level, with its emphasis on highly realistic insults (...*wad gie ye the bats*) and nagging, heckling apostrophes (*ye ken the solution yersel*); but this too is undercut by an occasional glimpse of a more refined intellectuality on the part of the speaker than most of the monologue suggests: the word *antithetical* in the first and last lines; the sense of suddenly stepping back and commenting on his own words in *the glib third person tells*; the self-conscious artistry implied by *my clever abuse*. All this renders the speaker inexcusable by hinting that he is bright enough to know better than to assume the tone of self-righteousness and bigotry of which the poem is such a ferocious parody. Conversely, *The Hierodules*, appropriately for a translation from a classical Greek poem, is as archaic and literary as anything in Garioch's oeuvre, with polysyllabic Latinate words in rhyming position (*persuasioun - oblatioun - dedicatioun; sacrifie - ecstasie*), mediaevalisms of spelling and vocabulary in many cases directly reminiscent of familiar passages from Middle Scots poetry (*the beryall firmament, gentill and amene, sterne - superne*), and an abundance of classical

---

1. As Garioch argues in an important article in *The Scots Observer*, 18 Feb. 1933; reprinted in *Lallans* 18, Whitsunday 1982, pp. 5 – 8.

names. But what is the very undignified and dysphemistic word *hures* doing in this context ("Aphrodite's sacrate hures", no less); and why does he undercut the florid aureation with two obvious Burns-isms *fidgin fain* and *unco-guid* – why if not to provide a sudden, jarring deflation of the mood by letting us hear unexpectedly the voice of the most scathing satirist of all pretension, and most exuberant celebrator of *real* life's pleasures, in all Scottish literature?

Another application of Garioch's wide-ranging knowledge of spoken and literary Scots is his habit of incorporating direct references to earlier poetry, such as that just cited: a device so noticeable in his work as to be almost a part of his stock-in-trade. Not only does the "canny hen" of the eponymous poem get "fu and unco happy", but a few lines later, and still in the hen-battery context, we are reminded "A! Fredome is a noble thing!". *To Robert Fergusson* contains clear reminiscences of Fergusson and of Ramsay and Burns as well: these have a ready appropriateness, adding extra highlights to the picture of Fergusson's literary and physical environment which the poem conveys, and also emphasising Garioch's own kinship with the eighteenth-century poetic scene (since it is, after all, he who is articulating the Ramsay-Fergusson-Burns-inspired language). But the conspicuous reference to "wee white roses" in the last stanza then forces on the reader a sudden leap forward from the eighteenth century to MacDiarmid's "little white rose of Scotland", with all that that implies. The early poem *"That is Stade in Perplexite"* –

Scraping an encrustit stane
   wi some carved letters, lichent-owre,
   an archaeologist, ye glower;
sae lichtly, lichtly mak it plain.

Is it in verse? Lang-pairtit chimes
   tune in thegither; twa by twa
   ye lowse them frae their hazel-raw,
maikan lang-disparplit rhymes.

To set the thing in time and space
   is nou yer care; by estimates
   ye bracket it about wi dates;
ye geynear hae it in its place.

Gowden, aye new, in aureate leid,
   buirdly, unset, a sang is raisit
   that wad be dumb, ye are abaysit,
but for yer succoure and remede.

– contains obvious allusions to MacDiarmid's *The Eemis-Stane*; but its title is a quoted line from the oldest Scots poem known to have survived. The contextual references of the title and the other quotation from the old poem (*succour and remede*), when brought into contact with the MacDiarmid allusions, themselves casting a strange illumination on the surface meaning of the poem, result in a network of interlinked resonances of extraordinary complexity.

Intertextual references of this kind are not unrelated in principle, or in effect, to mixing of registers: it could even be argued that they are a special case of the same procedure. By deliberately causing the voices of other poets – each, of course, with his own characteristic Scots idiolect, arising from his temporal and cultural setting as well as his individual genius – to echo through his poetry, Garioch reminds us constantly of the sheer complexity which the distinctive social and literary development of Scots has imposed on the very act of writing in it.

Garioch's Scots is a multi-faceted medium. The disconcerting, even disorienting effect of some of his most characteristic work is precisely because of this: colloquial and literary, archaic and contemporary, traditional and experimental forms of Scots are all perfectly legitimate media, regularly and often most effectively exploited for poetic expression; but in Garioch's work they are brought into superficially incongruous juxtaposition, so that the assumptions and expectations aroused by any given form are almost bound to be shortly overturned by the sudden intrusion of another. Yet the impression is firmly conveyed of a master manipulator, playing with superlative skill on the complex and subtle instrument that is the Scots tongue. Because the nature and status of Scots are uncertain and ambiguous, a valid strategy would be to create a poetic medium of internal consistency. The measure of Garioch's skill, and of his claim to a place among the giants of twentieth-century Scottish letters, is his success in the much more challenging task of making the co-existence of conflicting and even incompatible developments in the language a positive source of strength.

The unique popular appeal of Garioch was never approached by Tom Scott, whose general critical recognition as one of the most outstanding poets of the Renaissance has been strangely slow in arriving. The reasons for Scott's relative neglect are not obvious from his poetry: his knowledge of the Scots tongue and facility in its poetic use are as impressive as those of any of his contemporaries, and much of his work shows a loftiness of poetic vision, a fervour of social, political and ethical conviction, and a ruthlessness of expression, matching or exceeding theirs – even Grieve hardly surpasses Scott in the ferocity of his social satire. In all this, and in his forthrightly stated Scottish nationalism, he typifies the ideals and the practices of the Renaissance. His extensive erudition (as with Smith, Biblical, historical and mythological references are part of his poetic stock-in-trade) and characteristic boldness in his choice of poetic forms and genres (he favoured long, discursive poems) should have been recognised as confirming and furthering the confidence and high ambition with which poets were now adopting Scots as their medium; and though his poetic persona is undeniably somewhat forbidding, lacking the geniality and humour of a Garioch to lighten his far-reaching, portentous and often pugnacious statements, this should hardly have proved an insurmountable challenge to critical appreciation. Be that as it may, the regrettable fact is that until recently[1] Tom Scott as a poet received nothing like the recognition accorded to Garioch or Smith – though his incisive and combative voice as a critic was impossible to ignore.

Unlike the other poets discussed in this chapter, Scott was already an experienced English-writing poet before adopting Scots as his medium; but the Scots voice of many of his poems suggests not an assumed poetic register but the mother-tongue of a community, not only affording the poet a fluent and expressive means of conveying his own thoughts but embodying that community's culture and code of values. In contrast to this, Scott also has recourse to a register derived from the language of the Makars: a period spent in studying mediaeval poets such as Dante and Villon, both of whom provided him with material for distinguished translations, proved a seminal source of poetic inspiration. *The Paschal Candill,*

---

1. A growing amount of critical attention in recent years led to the publication of his *Collected Shorter Poems* by Chapman and Agenda in 1993.

"modelled on the style and orthography of the great Renaissance Makars",[1] is his most sustained effort in this register; though even here the quasi-mediaeval language is used sparingly and for considered effect. The opening section, in an unusual stanza form something like an abbreviated version of that used in Milton's *Ode on the Morning of Christ's Nativity* (and later employed by Scott, with greater regularity than in this poem, for his outstanding translation of the Old English *The Dream of the Rood*), insistently uses rhyming words with the Middle Scots participle ending *-and* (*nearand, couerand, louerand*, and so on: the *-ing* of the verbal noun is kept distinct), and a conspicuous quotation from Dunbar in the phrase *the candill matutine*. (Here the phrase appears to refer to actual candle light, but in Dunbar it means the sun – the point of comparison betwen sun and candle being not only brightness but holiness, from the use of candles in ceremonies of worship – and this suggestion adds a potent overtone to Scott's use of the phrase.) Shortly afterwards, in *purpour scugs* ("purple shadows") the use of the mediaevalism *purpour* (instead of the more recent Scots *purpie*) is much more significant than might at first appear: this is not a mere colour word but has overtones of opulence, splendour and royalty, giving the phrase almost the force of an oxymoron and leading to the thought expressed in the fifth stanza (with its obvious reminiscence of St John I. v.):

> The mirk aye couried round
> As gif frae licht alane it teuk its meaning,
> As silence duis frae sound
> Or ocean frae the land
> And leid-lore frae the Word in the Beginning.

Dante appears as well as Dunbar, with the reference to "mid-life's forest" and later "Love / That moves the sun / And the ither starns." A hearkening back to the past far more fundamental than spellings or quotations from mediaeval poetic masters, however, is the subject-matter of the poem itself: a meditation on a sequence of central passsages and episodes in the Bible, culminating in the Lord's Prayer, prefaced by a description of a ceremony "In a kirk on Easter e'en". Orthodox Christian theology as observed through traditional ritual, expressed in language of power and

---

1. From the Author's Introduction to the *Collected Shorter Poems*.

dignity, is startling in a poem written in 1954.

The resources of Scots – its vocabulary, or its range of contrasting registers – are, predictably, often employed to further the argument of the poem. The image of Christ burdened with the Cross is evoked in realistic Scots including one of the forcefully physical words which nothing in English could fully match:

> But doun throu Jerusalem's stourie wynds
> See the ae true Traiveller comes
> *Staicherand* under a terebinth beam. . .

A few lines containing quotations from or reminiscences of Dominical utterances (*mony mansions*, *bidden guests*) are followed by a variation on the stanza form of the opening in a pointedly colloquial register:

> Ony eenin, ony day,
> Gif ye dander doun this wey,
> Ye'll find the chippie open at sax o'clock
> The milk-bars doun the street
> Whaur whures parade their beat
> Are full o brimmand cups, and gey tuim talk.

However, though the orthography of the opening section maintains the impression of an archaic language, the sparse Scots vocabulary contains no obvious mediaevalisms; and as the poem progresses, sections occur in which only an *-it* ending or a Scots form like *til* or *nicht* keeps the language within the bounds of Scots at all. Tom Scott's distinctive technique in this poem, in fact, inheres not in his choice of Scots words *per se* – only a small proportion of the vocabulary of the poem consists of words unique to Scots, and of these only a very few (*howt* "knoll", *mauver* "sway to and fro", *yim* "guard") are either archaic or unusual in any other respect – but in its idiosyncratic verse form (sequences of short, irregular and unrhymed lines interspersed with passages in regular metre, the five-line stanza of the opening section appearing at intervals like a metrical leitmotif), the use of different voices, sometimes marked by a change of metre, in the manner of *The Waste Land*,[1] and the rapid switches of the viewpoint from the Biblical world to that of contemporary Scotland and from exalted mystical meditations –

1. Eliot was for a time a poetic mentor of Scott's: by encouraging him to translate Villon into Scots he played a key part in directing him to the use of Scots as his principal medium.

There on that halie ground
My body seemed as needless as my reason –
   That skeleton of the mind
   Made live by lowand wind
Rouned in my ear its proud and clever treason.

– to evocations of the evils of the world as it is –

Pollutit by factorie,
Foundrie, coal-mine, sewage,
Lang desertit by its owners
Trout and saumon
Siller otter
The stink on hot days hell-reek, gut-rot,
Hame nou anerlie o rats and flees,
Man-made corruption.

– underlining a central point not only in this poem but in the message of Scott's entire oeuvre:

... the failure o twa thousant year
To teach what we're here to learn.

The audacity, both poetic and moral, of Scott's endeavour in this poem can hardly be overstated: what he offers is nothing less than an extended meditation on the theological and ethical teachings of Christianity and their message for the living world, written in a largely traditional language but a wholly contemporary poetic style. Though smaller in scale than *A Drunk Man Looks at the Thistle* or *Under the Eildon Tree*, *The Paschal Candill* holds a place alongside them as one of the most ambitious, and most impressive, achievements of the Scottish Renaissance.

This sequence, with the emphatic mediaeval overlay on its language, stands apart (if only in this respect) from the rest of Scott's work. In his other poems, his Scots can be seen roughly as varying among three broadly distinguishable registers: a highly realistic Scots firmly anchored in the vernacular of generations of peasants and artisans, a more ornate and obviously poetic language characterised by frequent use of rhymes and other sound-patterns and a more literary vocabulary, and a "thin" Scots in which distinctive phonological and lexical features appear rarely and often to underline a particular point.

The first of these is well illustrated in his *Brand the Builder* sequence.

The opening lines of the *Prologue*, with their easy cadences suggesting speech rather than the regular rhythms of verse and natural-sounding use of familiar Scots words, set the tone for what is to follow:

Come the sea road up frae the mooth o Eden
The white swaw girnan aye at the bents
Or ower the herring-ribs o sand roars up,
Channers at yon extravagance o links
Whaur its gulls, whaups and peeweeps channer ...

Sparing use of alliteration delicately embroiders the verse: appropriately, a line evoking bird song is the most highly decorated in this section: "Whaur the sang o spink mells wi merle and mavis". When the description of St Andrews scenes gives place to angry thoughts of "Scotland's Shame", the rhythm becomes more firm:

O whit a wound is there for aa to see
Whaur stood aa Scotland's culture shrined in stane:
For wi it's gane oor leids, oor croon, oor state,
Oor parliament, oor sauls, aa betrayed
For a puckle English gowd in a few pooches.
Oor sons enslaved ti Babylon-on-Thames.

– and Scots words add their emotive force to the descriptions: *"jauggy ruins"*, *"murlie bits o touers"*. A reference to MacDiarmid, the name by now being assumed to be perfectly familiar, leads to a passage in which technical terms from the building trade, whether common English (*scabble*, chisel stone into shape) or Scots (*shawddie*, a roughly-dressed stone), feature in a meditative passage on the erosion of the Castle. Another instance of the lofty reach of Scott's poetic vision is that throughout the prologue, aspects of the visible St Andrews scene serve as counters in a discourse on the ancient poetic theme of mutability and eternity, including, Shakespeare-like, a claim that his own lines will defy the destructive effects of time.

As the sequence continues, forceful Scots words depict a character –

A muckle, bleck an hairy savage ...
Like some callant oot on the gilravage
Eftir queyns – a skeery deil
Bleezan fou ye'd think, insteid o a cheil
Wi twa-three business premises.

                    (*Broun the Butcher*)

– or a scene:

> When scrawnie craws flap in the shell-green licht
> Towards yon bane-bare rickle o trees
> That heeze
> Up on the knowe abuin the toun ...
>
> *(Brand the Builder).*

The dense Scots of most of the poems in this sequence (the exception is *Professor Goast*, where the portrait of this cultural quisling is appropriately introduced in English) suggests the vocabulary, idioms and cadences of an ancestral language, as unyielding as the rocky St Andrews coast: the mother tongue of a race of men (and women, such as Elsie Brand) bred to a harsh life in a bleak environment and surmounting its challenges with unfailing resilience. In *Brand the Builder*, the regularity of the end-rhymes suggests on one level the eternity of sea and rock (at three points in the poem a couplet of the form

> Doun by the sea
> Murns the white swaw ower the wrack ayebidanlie

appears, all referring to the sea) and on another the routine of Brand's daily darg; contrasting with this, the irregular variations of line length suggests the rugged scenery of St Andrews' rocky shore, narrow cobble-stoned streets and ancient ruins. A different metrical effect is attained in *Brand Soliloquises* and its counterpart *Elsie Brand – Nae Penelope Her*, where the steady sequence of five- (or occasionally four-) beat lines with no fixed syllable count moves in harmony with the sequence of the speakers' meditations. In the later poems *Epistle to Robert Fergusson on High* and the two *Epistles to David Morrison*, a Scots with a more modern, colloquial ring is used to add a tone of sarcastic humour to the scathing social and cultural commentaries; this effect being enhanced by rhymes which alternate with cheerful perversity between the banal –

> The slorpin whusk you did in clubs
> We dae nou in howffs caaed pubs ...
>
> *(Epistle to Robert Fergusson on High)*,

> Some o aa this I ance set doun
> In an earlier poem, 'The Mankind Toun,' ...
>
> *(Second Epistle to David Morrison)*

– the strained or perverse –

And tho I've shared a pub wi Dylan
I've also roistered wi Frank Villon ...

> *(Second Epistle to David Morrison)*,

The haunt aye o spink and linnet
As it wes when, a bairn, ye paiddlet in it ...

> *(Epistle to Robert Fergusson on High)*

– and the venomously pointed:

And as Captain Heath and his bullies ruthlesslie
Betray us intil the fascist EEC ...

> *(Epistle to David Morrison)*,

Fashion-mongers, doodling poeticules,
Concrete-mixers, and ither poetry-blin fules ...

> *(Epistle to David Morrison)*.

(The oddity of the rhymes in these poems is clearly a deliberate effect, as Scott can use sustained rhyme patterns with complete unobtrusive fluency when he chooses: a notable example is *Fergus*, his poetic summary of Scottish history, in which a regular sequence of functional rhymes is maintained through seventeen stanzas; and a more elaborate one is *A Dream o the Rude*, where the disyllabic rhymes contribute to the dignified procession-like pace of the verse.)

Scott's more lyrical vein is heard in poems like *The Bride* and some of his classical translations, where words with the ring of mediaeval aureation like *purpour, eterne, superne, malorous, athil, compengons* (a modernised spelling of a rare Middle Scots form) are arranged in sometimes conspicuous but always carefully controlled sound patterning: the insistence on the vowel [i], with its combination of low sonority and high inherent pitch, subtly conveys both a hushed tone and an intensely anticipative mood in the following stanza from *The Tryst* (his translation from St John of the Cross):

Sauf frae speiran leerie
I gaed oot by the secret stair, unseemin
(O ferlie ploy and eerie!)
Sauf frae ill-willie deemin,
While aye my feres were deep in sleep or dreamin.

And in extended passages from *At The Shrine o the Unkent Sodger* the Scots features of the language become very sparse: abstract, philosophic terms found in English are deemed (as we have seen, with perfect justification) to be equally appropriate to Scots, and a Scots word is often made to stand out against a background of words common to Scots and English for effect:

> The same passions, dreams baith guid and ill,
> *Torkit* his mind and body...

> Gane as the wind lifts a *sparple* o sand
> Frae atween the Sphinx's sleepan stane paws ...

> Or fools exposed on extravagant mountain-sides
> Or deep in the earth's *inthairmit* passages ...

(*inthairmit* being a concoction from *thairms* "bowels").

Scott in later life resumed English for his medium: surprisingly, in his *Collected Shorter Poems*, a characteristically forceful work *La Condition Humaine*, originally published in Scots, appears in an English version. His Scots corpus, however, is on any showing one of the outstanding achievements of modern Scottish poetry: the impressive range of knowledge informing his work, the ambition of his themes (a poet who attempts to cover the entire gamut of successes and failures of human history in a single poem, as in *The Ship*, must claim our respect for his enterprise alone), the ferocity of a Dante (one of Scott's heroes, as repeated references make clear) with which he excoriates the evils of the human world, and the technical skill exhibited in his manipulation of all registers of Scots, earn him a place among Scotland's finest poets. An important poem, *The Real Muse*, states his belief that poetic inspiration is to be sought in the harsh facts of daily life –

> The tang o saut oil in the harbour air,
> The reek o stale ammonia on the stair ...

– and he assuredly puts this into practice; but he is equally capable of exalted flights of visionary imagination. And to a greater extent than any other major Renaissance poet except – doubtfully – MacDiarmid, he brings to his work the fiery social radicalism of Red Clydeside: a feature which was to remain constant in Renaissance poetry for some time to come.

10
Flood-Tide in the North-East:
Alexander Scott and Alastair Mackie

As in the eighteenth century Enlightenment period, Edinburgh was (certainly in its own estimation) the principal centre of Scotland's literary activity in the mid-twentieth century; but, again as in the earlier period, contributions from other regions were by no means lacking. Two poets of comparable stature to those discussed in the previous chapter, Alexander Scott and Alastair Mackie, were Aberdonians by birth and upbringing, and though their language is that of national and not regional poets, being based on the regenerated Scots of the post-MacDiarmid school rather than the pristine Doric of Charles Murray, the dialect of their native North-East leaves more than an occasional trace in the poetic language of both men.

Alexander Scott's poetry consists of a large and varied corpus published in several collections over a lifetime, and includes work in both Scots and English.[1] His Scots voice is highly distinctive, even among the group of strongly individual idiolects of the mid-century Makars; and one of its qualities is a subtle but pervasive North-Eastern flavour imparted by such rhymes as *clean - ane, bluid - reid, seen us - taen us*, the use of *nae* instead of the more general *no* for the negative adverb (*he's nae amused*), and local words such as *dreel* (furrow), *flirn* (twist the mouth), *dubs* (mud), *snurl* (twist, tangle), *tyauve* (hard, protracted labour), *deist* (dash down violently), *nott* (needed), and – a common example – *quine* (the invariable Doric word for "girl"). Another is an extraordinary exuberance in onomatopoeia and other forms of sound patterning: more than any other Renaissance poet, Scott seems positively to rejoice in the consonan-

1. Much of this chapter is derived from the author's article "The poetic language of Alexander Scott", in *Northern Visions: the Literary Identity of Northern Scotland in the Twentieth Century*, ed. David Hewitt, East Linton (Tuckwell Press) 1995.

tal clusters in which Scots words abound. Impressionistically (to ascertain this scientifically would require a major linguistic investigation) words beginning with sequences of two or three consonants seem to appear with greater than statistical frequency in Scott's poetry (a random search through his glossaries would produce, as a small selection, *bluffert, brashy, clinty, creishy, flichter, glister, grumlie, plowter, sclim, scraich, scran, skyrie, sklinter, sprauchle, strauchle* and *trinkle*); and his skill in manipulating the sounds into intricate patterns entitles him to rank among the greatest technical virtuosi in all Scottish literature. Scott's vocabulary draws on several of the characteristic areas in which the language is notably rich: we find an abundance of onomatopes for noises, for example *clapper* (rattle), *drant* (drone monotonously), *gurl* (howl, often used of wind), *rowt* (bellow, used of cattle), *skraich* (scream), *yammer* (whine), *yowt* (roar); of words suggesting violent action, for example *breenge* (charge headlong), *clour* (a blow, or to deliver one), *clyte* (fall heavily), *ding* and *dunt* (beat), *sklaff* (slap – another local word), *yark* (jerk); and of insults, for example *bletherskite* (one who talks nonsense), *hallarackit* (boisterous, unrestrained), *randie* (promiscuous), *ramstam* (rash, headstrong), *scrimpit* (miserly), *shilpit* (feeble), *thowless* (listless, lacking in energy). And to an even greater extent than Soutar, Scott shows a fondness for the words in – *le* and – *er*, suggestive of repetitious and often clumsy and ineffectual action: *bauchle* (shamble), *brangle* (struggle), *fankle* (entangle), *hirple* (limp), *hurkle* (sit, or walk, in a crouched position), *sprauchle* (clamber), *strauchle* (struggle); *belter* (batter), *flaffer* and *flauchter* (flutter), *flicher* (palpitate), *hubber* (stutter), *hudder* (crowd together in a disorderly fashion), *hyter* (stumble), *kelter* (undulate like seaweed in water), *plowter* and *squatter* (flounder in mud or water), *swaiver* (sway, stagger), *swither* (hesitate, or a state of confusion).

Scott's technical virtuosity is readily illustrated from his longest and most elaborate poem, *Heart of Stone*, his tribute to his native city. This poem was written for a television broadcast, pictures of Aberdeen scenes and landmarks appearing in synchrony with a reading of their poetic evocation, and the steady rhythm of the stress-timed lines suggests – indeed, positively demands – a speaking voice. If the prosody is that of native North-Eastern speech, however, the sound-patterning could have been achieved only by a craftsman of the first order. That the poem is highly alliterative is obvious from the opening lines:

> The sea-maw spires in the stane-gray luft,
> Owre sworlan swaws o the stane-gray sea,
> Flaffers her wings – a flash o faem-white feathers –
> And warsles awa i the wake o the trauchled trawler
> That hirples hame hauf-drooned wi the weicht o herrin.

Alliteration, however, is only the beginning. There is alliteration on consonant clusters (*flaughtered fleets, skimmerin scaud, stanced wi stalliard stane, to clour his clypie baa wi nane to claik*); there are interweaving patterns of alliteration on different sounds (*naukit sand whaur nets for saumon . . ., esparto gress that greened in Spain, een blunted on grumlie blads o granite*), there are tricks played with the component sounds of a cluster (*a cantier ploy nor ony poetry clavers, the trauchle the toun's freedom for ilka fermer, scrannin crumbs in the cracks o the thrang causeys*); vowels as well as consonants enter into patterns of assonance (*crans clanjamfrie, breem bield, glower at's gowan*) and reverse rhyme (*trauchled trawler, thrang thrapple, wallockin waters*): in fact there is every trick of sound patterning in the book; and many lines in which several appear at once:

> their cleedin steel, their steekin reid-het rivets . . .
> skyrie wi mauts and skinklan bricht wi beers . . .
> whan seipan swaws are graveyaird gray on the sand . . .

And yet in all this incredibly dense and intricate embroidery of sounds there is scarcely a word of which the meaning is not perfectly appropriate to its context; and very few which could not have been heard, at least well into living memory, in the mouths of North-Eastern speakers. Lexemes such as *flaffer* (flutter), *skyrie* (bright), *skimmer* (shimmer), *steerach* (disturb) and *cleek* (muck-hoe) could probably still be heard in the North-East hinterland; and any contemporary Aberdonian would know the meaning of *sharger* (youngest child in a family or weakest animal in a litter), *hyter* (trip or stumble), *scutter* (work aimlessly and ineffectually) and *seipan* (soaking). Regional pronunciations, too, are represented by spellings such as *wyde* (wade) and *spad* (spade).

The same qualities of a densely Scots vocabulary with a conspicuous local colouring, a pervasive stress-based rhythm and a high concentration of elaborate sound-pattering make of Scott's poetic idiolect a singularly appropriate medium for his translations from Anglo-Saxon poetry: three

Old English poems, *The Wanderer*, *The Seafarer* and *Deor*, appear in Scott's corpus as *The Gangrel*, *Seaman's Sang* and *Makar's Lament*; and a fragment of *The Battle of Maldon* is rendered as *Sang for a Flodden*. Without attempting an exact reproduction of the rhythmic or alliterative patterns of the originals, Scott employs his own distinctive handling of vocabulary and prosody to evoke the bleak, austere mood of the Anglo-Saxon elegies. The opening line of *Seaman's Sang* is quiet and restrained – "Anent mysel I'll tell ye truly – but immediately afterwards in "Hou stravaigin the seas in trauchlesome days" the irregular rhythm with its repeated choriambic pattern ("-*vaigin the* seas – *trauchlesome days*") and partial alliteration of a three-consonant cluster with a two-consonant one ("**stra**-vaigin – **trauchlesome**") contributes to the sense of strain and discord conveyed by the carefully-chosen words. Partial alliteration is again used, combined with assonance, later in the poem to produce the memorably plangent phrase "the lane stravaiger scraichs". Soon afterwards, the menace of the stormy seas is intensified by the virtual personification of "the coorse girn o the swaws": here the homeliness of the words (*coorse* in particular is ubiquitous in the local speech) suggests the seaman's weary familiarity with the dangers and hardships of his life. Twice the opportunity is taken of using the North-Eastern pronunciation of *chain*, "chyne", for a pointed assonance with *ice*; and the emotive Aberdeenshire word *tyauve*, exactly suited to the mood of the poem, appears at a pivotal point in its sequence of thought. In *The Gangrel*, likewise, lexical, prosodic and phonetic effects are combined with unfailing skill: the intricate sound-patterning in

> there's livan nou
> nae feir that I daur o my hert's ferlies
> richt clearly tell,

the union of alliteration, vowel-harmony and hammer-beat stresses in

> The nicht gaes black and blaws frae the north
> an onding o ice to connach aa,

and the judicious use of words from the local dialect such as

> Whan dule and sleep hae *snurled* thegither
> to wap about his puirtith and his wae

which with its overtones of confusion and disorder ironically undercuts the suggestion of comfort in the next line, and

> Sae the Makar o men made *mools* o the warld:

the usual North-East word for "earth", but with suggestions of death and graveyards. In *Makar's Lament*, where Scott has performed the interesting experiment of naturalising as well as translating the poem by finding Scottish equivalents for the heroes and villains of Germanic tradition in the orginal, the same verbal ingenuity is shown in such lines as "Argyll, throu gurlie winters, grippit his neive..." with its grating patterns of *g*, *r* and *gr*, the excruciating internal rhyme, almost a pun, in "he stampit his *heel on* the *Hielands*", and the memorable rendering of the refrain (with a slight elaboration on the original line, which means simply "That passed away; so may this") as "Thon dule has dwynit awa, as this maun dae." Unfortunately, Scott's rendering of a pair of equally famous lines from *The Battle of Maldon*, often seen as epitomising the ethos of the heroic age, in *Sang for a Flodden*[1] is weakened by the presence of a word used to excess in modern Scots writing:

> Thocht maun be the harder, hert the keener,
> *smeddum* the mair, for aa that oor micht is dwynan.

Even when no sustained pattern of sounds or specially important rhythmic effect is in evidence, Scots words are employed in Scott's poetry with unusual frequency: his poetry is a treasure-hoard of Scots lexemes; and, notably, with fewer archaic, obscure or purely literary words than in many of his contemporaries. In the dignified elegy *Daith Sang for an Auld Man Young*, Scots words are used to capture a telling visual or auditory detail:

> The mools frae the minister's neive
> Gae dirl on the aiken kist ...

> The flouers wir hands hae laid tae deck his lair
> Hae aa their petals weet and lourd wi rain ...

to reinforce a simile or metaphor:

> the mochy reeks o eild ...

1. The latter part of this translation was later published in revised form under the title *MacDiarmid in the Shield-Ring*. (See the introduction to *The Collected Poems of Alexander Scott*, ed. David S. Robb, Edinburgh (Mercat Press) 1994.)

> ... the open grave
> That girns, a gash i the yirth ...
> ... thon luve o life the years hae hid
> Frae ither bodachs' herts wi haars o grey ...

or simply to contribute their energy to an arresting turn of phrase:

> Speldert wi sunlicht, smairged wi snaw ...

> A starn o gledness sclentit in his ee,
> Mair bricht for aa the weather's stang and nip ...

> It's us maun dree the brash o wind and weet
> Whas blatter cudna mak him bou his heid ...

Apart from an occasional word suggestive of modern inventiveness such as *bonnieheid* or *hardieheid*, or a poetic archaism like *lyre* (complexion), the Scots of this elegy is firmly based on what was until Scott's generation familiar speech. Some of the most moving stanzas of the poem, in fact, demonstrate clearly the adequacy and appropriateness of an almost unadorned Scots for expressions of deep emotion:

> And aye his lauchter – och, his lauch was young!
> Nae hauflin callant, kissan his first quine,
> Cud soun sic gledness frae his throat and tongue
> As he whas lassies aa were kissed langsyne
> But minded yet the sangs his hert had sung
> And kent the lips o life ower sweet tae tine.

By contrast, Scott at other times intensifies the concentration of unusual and powerful Scots words to a degree which shows unmistakably that a daunting obscurity of lexis is intended precisely as a contributory factor to the desired poetic effect. A good example is *Haar in Princes Street*, in which an asymmetrical (but regularly repeated) verse pattern, a series of long and rhythmical lines that almost demand to be sung rather than spoken ("Its gangrels tint i the haar that fankles the future" – "They swaiver and flirn i the freeth like straes i the sea..." – "Alane, and lawlie aye to be lanesome sae"), a pervasive alliteration in which the contrasting phonaesthetic effects of different consonants is skilfully exploited, and a preponderance of words like *rauchens, hudder, gastrous, smochter, swaiver, swither, blufferts*, combine to evoke an actual Edinburgh scene with intense clarity and to invest it with an almost overpowering imaginative force. And it is perhaps a measure of Scott's confidence in the recovery of a full literary and artistic integrity for the Scots language that he is not above using the vocabulary itself as a source of humorous effects, as in *Top of the Pops*:

Lowpers, gowpers,
Duntily dowpers.

Skirlers, dirlers,
Bumpily birlers.

Yowlers, growlers,
Sappily sowlers.

Ravers, clavers,
Hotchily havers ...

(and so on for another five-and-a-half verses.)

An ability to make poetic capital out of the mass entertainment scene is another idiosyncrasy of Alexander Scott: whereas many of his Renaissance confrères emphasise the antiquity and cosmopolitanism of Scotland's literary culture, Scott as well as this is concerned to associate the language firmly with the contemporary world by using it for poems, albeit satirical ones, on such things as films and pop music. Titles like *Kong was King, To Mourn Jayne Mansfield, Big Beat, A Gey Flash Gordon* or *Prehistoric Playmate* accurately suggest this scathingly humorous side of his poetic vision; a wholly serious poem with a similar inspiration is *Grace Ungraced*, where images of the funeral ceremony of Grace Kelly, her glamorous performance in a classic film, and the vicious terrorist war in Lebanon are evoked in descriptive language and interwoven to produce a ruthless exposure of the bitterly ironic contrast of art and reality. The effect of this theme on his language is interesting: words and expressions suggestive of pop jargon and voguish slang appear in entertaining juxtaposition with traditional literary Scots:

Thon Zarkov the beardie weirdie,
A brain-box wi Balkan accent
To hap his Yankee hert,
and Dale the brainless blondie
wi big roun een
and boobs as bigsy ...

(A Gey Flash Gordon)

or, a more elaborate and extravagant example,

A bonnie bucko, gifted (by God?) til tumphies,
Stounds like a stirk, and back they grain like grumphies;

A spanky spade lats lowse as heich a yammer
As tines aa sense (langsyne he tint aa grammar) . . .

(Big Beat).

In *Dear Deid Dancer* this mixing of registers is taken to an extreme in one
of the most riotous poems in modern Scottish literature, with demotic
and slang expressions together with words from the more undignified
reaches of traditional Scots being "sent up" together in a truly glorious
cascade of crazy rhymes:

A rinawa Rolls-Royce flivver
That drounit her getts i the river . . .

They buckled their sarks wi their booin,
But back she gaed boke at their gruein . . .

She fand she was freindless and fremmit
Wi scarcely a sark til her semmit . . .

Gat bleerit, gat bladdit, gat blotto,
Gat smorit to deid in an auto . . .

The prevailing mood of Scott's poetry is that of a defiant and ruthlessly
honest response to the harshness and tragedy of life: though humour is
often present, it usually has a fierce and bitter ring. In the service of this
austere poetic vision, he applies an astonishing fluency and versatility in a
linguistic medium which includes the most uncompromising ranges of
the Scots vocabulary: the impression is often given that this poet, having
brilliantly surmounted the challenge of writing in a difficult medium, is
presenting the results as a challenge in the same vein to his readers. His
voice is one of the strongest and most distinctive among the Renaissance
makars.

Like all his contemporaries, Scott was keenly aware of participating
actively in a new and thrilling development in Scotland's poetic history,
of which the outcome was as yet uncertain. The poem *Rescue* uses a picturesque image to present the struggle of

. . . eident makars, answeran true
MacDiarmid's cry for musardrie

to revive the drowned Scottish muse; and *The Gallus Makar* is a joyous celebration of MacDiarmid's achievement. (Scott, though to a somewhat lesser extent than Garioch or Smith, often uses words which deliberately recall the works of his predecessors; the recurrence of *cramassie* in this poem being an example.) *Fable*, though a general moral application is obvious at a first reading, acquires a specifically nationalist overtone when it is recalled that the leopard, vanquished by the eagle in the poem, is the animal which appears in the crest of the kings of England. Those poems were written in the mid and late 1940s: much later, *Mak it New* expresses his confidence that a new generation of Scots poets will

> ...daur the dark wi lowean rose o rhyme,
> And mock the mools in ilka mairch and time.

The poetic voice of Scott's fellow citizen, Alastair Mackie, could hardly present a more striking contrast. Both employ the Scots tongue with outstanding skill; but whereas Scott's medium is that of a flamboyant virtuoso, using words for their music as much as for their meaning and weaving intricate patterns out of the rhythmic and segmental components of the spoken tongue, Mackie conveys his poetic vision with equal force in a realistic, down-to-earth Scots based on the mother tongue of generations of Aberdonians. Mackie, as many of his poems make clear, was as strong as any of his fellow Makars in his commitment to the preservation of the language and his belief in its importance as a mark of national identity; but Scots for him required neither any augmentation by literary or obsolete words nor surface embroidery of elaborate sound patterning: the language remembered from his childhood was an adequate medium for his poetic statements. Such lines as

> A barren strand, a skaith, a man bydan at dayligaun
> Wi's hert in targats, onwytan a bard's retour ...
>
> (Smith, from Tristram),

> Dern weeferty-wafferty shaddaws
> flichteriff and aflocht ...
>
> (Young, from Reconciliation)

or

> They swaiver and flirn i the freeth like straes i the sea
> An airtless swither ...
>
> (Scott, from Haar in Princes Street)

are not to be found in Mackie's poetry: his characteristic voice is rather to be heard in

> It's the cauldest grue in the universe
> yon skelloch.
> It never waukens the deid.
>> (*Pieta*),

> His beard was a touzled divot,
> lyart ess and darkness.
>> (*Orpheus*),

> fae the pirn-taed bogle, slater grey,
> Fae the beardit witch wi the claw-hemmer neb ...
>> (*Rodden Tree*).

Mackie's vision is no more circumscribed than that of any other Renaissance poet: as one illustration of this, he is among the most accomplished translators in modern Scots literature, re-creating in Scots the works of French, Italian, German and Russian poets; and references not only to the stock currency of Graeco-Roman mythology but to European poets and their works occur throughout his corpus. Wide-ranging literary erudition is a characteristic of the modern Makars, but one of the individual aspects of Mackie's achievement is in showing that Scots does not require any special adornment to demonstrate this.

The introduction to his late collection *Back-Green Odyssey and Other Poems* includes a statement of his indebtedness to MacDiarmid: "I cam oot o ane o the pooches o his jaiket as did aa the makars o worth that used Scots as the medium for their work. Yon man was a kinna Christ o the Scots tongue, a maister-mason o unco skill that biggit a Chinese wa o poetry eneuch for two three literatures". Several of his early poems bear the unmistakeable stamp of this inspiration: *Sea-Scunner*, in its verse form and its use of physically repugnant imagery –

> The sea's a fule ashet
> the lyft canna scoor...

– proclaims itself the offspring of *In the Pantry*, and *The Shepherd* evokes the night of the Incarnation with an imaginative force recalling the cosmic visions of MacDiarmid's early poems:

> The bale-fire dwines to a spark
> in the lowe that lowps abune,

and the Ploo is rugged asunder
and aa the starns gang roon.

And aa the lyft and aa the yirth
is yokit till a sang
while like a blindrift in the air
birls an unco thrang.

– though the fact that the poem closes on a note of fear rather than exultation –

Yon licht that rived the mid-nicht 'oors
will gar me grue for lang.

– shows Mackie's own characteristic mood.

MacDiarmid's influence is less strong than this in the individual voice which Mackie quickly developed; and elsewhere in his work, as with Soutar, the master-poet is addressed in a doubting and critical tone. A sonnet entitled *To Hugh MacDiarmid Whiles* invokes Bosch's nightmarish painting of the temptation of St Anthony, applying a fine trio of Scots verbs of movement to its monstrous figures: "Ramstam they slidder, swash and flisk"; and proceeds to a sceptical depiction of the results of MacDiarmid's labours and a querying of their value. "Your mell's dreich / dunt doun in the Scots stane-pit" with its asymmetrical thumps and alliteration on [d] depicts hard, dreary effort, likely to produce "a coorse thrawn soond ... a staney skreich". Scots as it had developed as a medium for himself and other poets is the subject of searching and troubled questioning in Mackie's poetry. His choice of title for his 1972 collection *Clytach* is itself a remarkably complex statement of his beliefs and intentions as poet. The word is defined in his glossary as "barbarous speech", the sense with which it is attested in North-East dialect, and with which MacDiarmid used it ironically in *A Drunk Man*:

He gied man speech but to the Scots gied nocht
Barrin' this clytach ...

Another definition of the word, however, also known in the North-East, is "a large mass of any liquid or semi-liquid substance";[1] and its use in the first poem in the collection, *Through the Deid-Chack*, is in a context in which it *could* refer to the accumulation of phlegm in the throat of a

1. Definition as in Gregor's *Dialect of Banffshire*.

man at the point of death. For a poet to describe his own work as "barbarous speech" is, on the face of it, odd (less so when it is recalled that Gavin Douglas described the Scots with which he produced the greatest single poem in the national literature as a "lewit barbour tung"); that he should associate it with the suggestion of impending death, and a particularly ugsome aspect of it, is even more so; but the many-layered irony of Mackie's voice is fully sufficient to accommodate both facts.

The poem itself shows the same interplay among possible meanings and possible emotional and imaginative responses. The opening line "I hiddle in the mids o a deid-ruckle" contains two words of which the English translations are "hide, take shelter" and "death-rattle"; but the syllable *-le* is so common in Scots words referring to clumsy or useless movement – *hirple, shauchle, wauchle, wammle, wamfle,* etc. – as to have acquired almost the force of a phonaestheme suggesting something silly and ludicrous: an overtone which adds a discordant and uneasy note to the macabre image. The last lines of the poem –

> Tho I hear the deid-chack
> I mak.

– are even more potently ambiguous: the face-value meaning is "Though I hear the click of the death-watch beetle [an omen of impending death], I write poetry"; but "I mak" *could* be read not as a principal clause but as a qualifier of *deid chack*: "though I hear the death-portending sound [which] I make". The being of which the death-rattle is heard is not specifically identified, but what else could it be but the Scots language? "It says 'Aye' / jist / and nae mair": "Aye" is one word, not originally Scots but now surviving principally in the mouths of Scots speakers, which *does* survive: in any street in Scotland "Aye" can be heard daily, if no other Scots word can be. And it is the "yes-man" mentality inculcated in Scotland's political culture since the Union which has led the nation and its languages to the brink of death. "...the auld body / aince a horizon / noo a pirlicue": once a fully-developed language of international status, now diminished to a mere fragment.[1] The two key-words in "Atween the breidth o that /

---

1. Mackie's definition of *pirlicue* as "space between thumb and middle finger when fully extended" is not attested in the *SND*, but "space between thumb and forefinger" is a definition given in Alexander Warrack's *Scots Dictionary*. The *Linguistic Atlas of Scotland* testifies to *pirlie* or *pirlie-winkie* being known in a few localities as the word for "little finger".

there's room eneuch / for neive poems / gowpens o auld-farrant wirds"
develop the image suggested in *pirlicue*: a fist (*neive*) is smaller in breadth
than a *pirlicue* but much more forceful, and a *gowpen* is a double handful.
Finally, the ambiguity of the last lines is peculiarly apposite to Mackie's
position: does he mean that he will write in defiance of the approaching
death of his medium, or that his own poetry *is* the last gasp of the Scots
tongue ("the deid-chack I mak") – or both?

The state of Scots and the task of Scots poets form a recurring theme in
Mackie's poetry. As *Clytach* opens with a defiant statement that Scots is,
even if at its last gasp, still not totally dead, so it ends with a suggestion
(*Probe*) that amid the "yird-braid clachan" (an exact Scots rendering of the
catch-phrase "global village") deaved with "Yes, si, oui, ja, da" [but not
"Aye"?], his "hame-made module" occasionally "dirls wi Lallans". Here
again, the implication is ambiguous: at first sight the speech is nothing
but "shakky trimmles", and the "clash o the toun" is a negligible component of the "yird-braid clachan"; but on the other hand it may be more
vital and closer to the listener's own life than the unending Babel of the
"muckle tongues". And the image of the "long-leggit spinner" is a symbol of quiet, unobtrusive tenacity: the deliberate plainness of the language, particularly the central lines

> My spinnleshanks grup
> their bit space on the yirth.

is a sign that we are seeing something deceptively frail but indomitable
and indestructible. If Mackie seems much more doubtful about Scots
than most of the Renaissance makars, his scepticism never amounts to
despair: on the contrary, his poetic querying of the viability of Scots itself
imparts a kind of heroism to his determined persistence in writing it –
and not only writing it but doing so well enough to provide a triumphant
rebuttal of his own expressed doubts. Another poem from the same collection, *Scots Pegasus*, contradicts the expected poetic associations of
"Pegasus" with a perversely brilliant collection of Scots words and
expressions with overtones of the grotesque, repellent and ridiculous:
mocking references to physical defects or ailments (*a humphy back and
cockle een, the belly thraw*), a forceful expression descriptive of ugliness or
unhealthiness (*yon etten and spewed look*), prosaic anatomical details

(*intimmers* "entrails", *rig-bane* "backbone", *spauld* "shoulder"), an unattractive simile (*spales* [splinters] *drap aff like sharn* [dung]), and words of which the contemptuous force is emphasised by placing them in cacophonous juxtaposition:

> He's fed on *bruck* [rubbish]
> *scranned* [scavenged] frae aa the airts –

an obvious allusion to the rare and recondite words, and foreign allusions, in much recent Scots poetry. Yet this decrepit and dilapidated "timmer naig" to which some Scots give "the hee-haw" – a call of derision, of course; but in Scots urban slang *hee-haw* also means "nothing" – seems not to be devoid of a glimmer of hope: if "naebody, dammt, kens the horseman's wird" there *is* a "wird" which could send Pegasus soaring aloft – if only it could be found.

In a much more elevated tone, *Weet Kin* presents the constantly frustrated hopes for the spirit and the language of Scotland through a beautifully-developed metaphor. (*Kin* is "kind" and the phrase is the vernacular form of "kind of wet" – in pronunciation *kin* is unstressed – and Mackie in his glossary calls it a "Scots understatement".) Opening with a rare but expressive North-East word *blyberin* (hard drinking), the impression of unrelenting rain is evoked in a memorably onomatopoeic line "in the seep and the wheesht o the rain". The ground "fu o worms and tap-reits" is a typical double-edged image: the dank, sodden earth is, nonetheless, alive, even if worms and roots (the pronunciation suggested by *reits* is North-Eastern) make little impression on the visible upper world. The bird song (MacDiarmid's *whuram* comes in pointedly here) is echoed in a series of words chosen, unusually for Mackie, primarily for a sound pattern: "sweeled, swaaled, melled, belled": this sudden peal of bells seems to transcend the dismal imagery and plodding rhythms of the poem up to then. Yet the emphasis on the fragility of the hope – "twa three craigs contered aa that smirr" – is further insisted on in what follows: the repetition of *jist*, placed on its first appearance at the end of its clause in a realistic rendering of idiomatic vernacular speech: "a wey oot o the coorse weet / jist" conveys almost pathetically the lowliness of what was aimed at; and the glimpse of the light for "jist a thocht" is brutally extinguished by the iambic hammer-blows of the last line:

afore the brodheids hemmert doun the nicht.

Alexander Scott's poem *Rescue*, similar in theme, likewise ends on an ominous note, but with nothing like the fatalism of *Weet Kin*. And yet, the "blue bore" *did* break, the horizon *was* seen, and night, in the course of things, is followed by dawn. Perhaps the best of all Mackie's poetic arguments on his use of Scots is *Châteaux en Ecosse*: the title, of course, being a parody of the old phrase *châteaux en Espagne* meaning "castles in the air". The four sections each begin with a line from what is evidently an old nursery-jingle:

Lauchin at the puffin-lowe,
Fit saa ye there?
Aa the widden-dremers
Biggin castles i the air,

recalled as a memory of the speaker's granny (whose Aberdeen voice is sugested by *fit saa* . . .). The body of each section reads like a meditation, the free verse lines running like prose; with Scots words evoking the central image of fire (*ingle* "hearth", *gleed* "glowing fire", *aizles* "red-hot embers", *bleeze* "blaze", *lowe* "flame" and at last *cauld ess* "cold ashes") interwoven with reminiscences of the "auld wife" *hurklin* (sitting crouched) beside the fire and singing a song made of what even to the speaker, in his childhood, were "unkent words". The association of Scots with this dream-like evocation of a bygone age, the song even then being "an orphelin / that has langsyne tint the faimily o the tongue"; and of his own present endeavours to write Scots poetry with imaginary visions in the fire – a fire, at that, which has long ago died away to "cauld ess" – is a paradox *par excellence*: the poet is telling us that Scots is as dead as the ashes of a fire at which his grandmother sat, and yet himself using this dead language for poetry of extraordinary visual and emotional intensity.

In proclaiming his medium to be unusable while at the same time using it with superlative skill Mackie is exposing, in a strange and disturbing manner, a paradox at the heart of Scotland's linguistic identity: the enduring vitality of Scots as a spoken language, co-existing with the chronic refusal, or inability, of its speakers to recognise (much less assert or exploit) the amazing resources which it places at their disposal. And Mackie's demonstration of this, since he uses a form of Scots closer (at least in its vocabulary) to the remembered speech of an actual community than that of any of the other Makars, is more incontrovertible than that offered by Young or Smith. Mackie's Scots is lexically rich, and often abounding in words with a North-East ring, but rarely resorting to words not found (or never having been found) in popular speech. *Orpheus and Eurydice* evokes confused and anxious activity in darkness (*mirk* and *pit-mirk* recur, and *gloff* "variation in darkness" appears in the first line) by an abundance of words relating to bodily actions or sensations: *rax* (reach out), *swither* (hesitate), *claught* (seized), *showd* (sway – NE), *pech* (pant), *binner* (bump together – NE), *styter* (stumble), *dirl* (tremor). *Pietà*[1] uses a shockingly incongruous comparison for the image (familiar from many photographs of the Vietnam war) of the grief-crazed mother with her dead child:

> It micht hae been a mercat day
> an him for sale.
> Naebody stoppit tae niffer.

– the irony of the last line (*niffer* is "bargain") is unbearably poignant – and proceeds to emphasise the horror of the picture with deliberately homely vocabulary: *semmit* (vest) and *hippens* (diapers), *cleck* (lay an egg – a wearily ancient euphemism for "drop a bomb"), *on their hunkers in the stour, bubblin and greetin*. The stark despair of the final line "It niver waukens the deid" is underlined by the plainness of the language following a section where two words of high emotional intensity, *grue* (shudder) and *skelloch* (scream), are brought in in close juxtaposition; the idiomatic word-order of

> It's the cauldest grue in the universe
> yon skelloch

playing down, but only as a first impression, the power of *skelloch* (a local word: *She wasna aa come*, meaning she had lost her wits, is also a North-Eastern expression). One of his finest poems, *Leopardi on the Hill*,[2] con-

---

1. *Pietà* is the Italian word for "mercy" or "pity"; but in art *a* "pietà" is a representation of Mary with the dead body of Christ. The full import of the last line of the poem is lost unless this is understood.

2. Mackie wrote graceful and sensitive translations of several of Leopardi's poems. See, for discussion and references, the present author's "Alastair Mackie's translations from Leopardi", in Steven R. McKenna, ed., *Selected Essays on Scottish Language and Literature: a Festschrift in honour of Allan H. MacLaine*, New York (Edwin Mellon Press) 1992, 241–258.

veys the hushed, almost mystical impression of "undeemis spaces o the universe" by words suggesting faint, indeterminate sounds: *sough* (sigh), *flaff* (flutter, of wind), *reeshle* (rustle), *risp* (make a dry rasping sound, of leaves), *swoosh* (swish) – their vagueness and remoteness emphasised by contrast with

> the fairm-cairt clunkin, the far-aff bae o yowes,
> the owsen snocherin i the riggs ablow.

Mackie's use of this brilliantly expressive but thoroughly realistic Scots for poetry of enormous erudition, technical skill and imaginative power entitles him to a place among the giants of the Scots Renaissance. He has also a much stronger claim than Alexander Scott to be the North-East's principal representative in the movement: his language is rooted and anchored, throughout his oeuvre, in the speech once to be heard in the back streets and playgrounds portrayed in his sequence *In the Thirties*, and still surviving to an extent that would surprise many sceptics in the Aberdeenshire of today.

> We spoke o girds, scuds, quines, bleedy doctors...
> I'm richt gled the auld words still come back
> like migrant swallas, black shears o the gloamin.

Indeed they do; and if any poet other than the pure "Doric" company has a chance of ensuring that they continue to do so, it will surely be Alastair Mackie.

11

The Emergence of Glasgow:

Ian Hamilton Finlay, Tom Leonard, Stephen Mulrine

"The unsavoury and amorphous phenomenon of Glasgow", as Edwin Morgan called it with humorous irony,[1] is exasperatingly difficult to characterise or reduce to easy generalisations. Until the seventeenth century a small town centring on an ancient religious foundation, it suddenly burgeoned in the eighteenth as a principal centre for trade with the American colonies, and with the Industrial Revolution transformed itself, with startling rapidity, into one of the most important manufacturing cities in Europe; paying the price of its magnificent commercial and industrial success with appalling slums and the associated social ills of crime, drunkenness and bad health. In almost grotesque contrast, a robust and cheerful camaraderie, a culture of easy hospitality, an indomitable community spirit and a hearty civic pride became part of the city's communal identity: an identity expressed by music-hall songs in the vein of

> I belong tae Glasgow,
> Glasgow on the Clyde.
> There's no anither hauf sae guid
> In a' the warld sae wide.
> For be ye rich or be ye puir,
> Or be ye up or doon,
> Ye'll always find a welcome
> In dear auld Glasgow toon!

Glasgow's sudden development was accompanied by immigration on a massive scale, and rapid expansion of the boundaries of the city: an astonishing twenty-five-fold increase in the population is recorded between

1. "Glasgow Speech in Recent Scottish Literature", in *Scotland and the Lowland Tongue: Studies in the Language and Literature of Lowland Scotland in honour of David D. Murison*, ed. J. D. McClure, Aberdeen 1983, p.195.

166

1750 and 1900. Many of the incomers came from the rural areas of Scotland; refugees from the Highland Clearances and the Irish potato famine further accelerated the city's demographic explosion. Linguistically, the effect of this was the emergence of an urban patois differing in many respects from the original dialect of the area, in which the traditional vocabulary of agricultural life was superseded by a new and often inventive and colourful word-stock reflecting the habits and preoccupations of the urban proletariat.

The appearance of a distinctive Glasgow voice in Scots poetry was surprisingly belated. Fictional presentations of Glasgow life, ranging from the somewhat idealised, but well observed and entertainingly presented, scenes of childhood in J. J. Bell's *Wee Macgreegor* (1933) and its sequels to the harsh and brutal evocation of the city's gangs in A. McArthur and H. K. Long's *No Mean City* (1935), often made use of a Scots with at least some local touches for their dialogue, and poetry of widely varying quality was written about the city and its people from its first emergence as an important trading centre; but to the extent that a Glasgow literature existed, it was distinguished from the general mainstream of Scottish literature by little more than references to its geographical setting.

It was in the 1960s that the dialect (or rather, sociolect) of Glasgow's working class emerged, quite suddenly and dramatically, in a new and radical poetic movement. Edwin Morgan[1] has plausibly associated this development with the large-scale programme of slum clearance and rebuilding undertaken in the city during this period: a project, incidentally, which though conceived with the best of intentions had social results which were almost unequivocally disastrous. An often underrated influence on the transformation of Glasgow patois into a poetic medium is a typically idiosyncratic short sequence by Ian Hamilton Finlay, of which the intriguing title *Glasgow Beasts* instantly startles the reader by switching from English to a phonetically-spelt rendition of the dialect, complete with interjections: "An a Burd haw, an Inseks, an, aw, a Fush." This set of minimalist sketches is irresistibly humorous: the notion of a consistent laconic Glaswegian spoken by *something* which

1. *Glasgow Poets Past and Present: the Story of a City*, University of Waikato, New Zealand, 1992.

has in successive incarnations appeared as a fox, a mouse, a bed-bug and much besides is ludicrous enough in itself; and the comic rhymes, occurring sufficiently at random to catch the reader unawares, enhance the effect (*the shoogly caur – ma wee jaur*; *midgie – didjye* "did you"; *mair liker – the hiker*). Though the absence of punctuation, fragmentary lines and atomistic grammar convey an immediate impression of incoherence, the evocation of the sharp tones of the Glasgow voice is realistic: *haw, aw, heh heh* and such unstructured sounds recur throughout the sequence; the opening *see* ("see me") is a regular means of introducing a topic in West of Scotland vernacular; the truncated pronunciations suggested by *kep*[t], *foon*[d], *s e bess* "'s the best" are familiar even if the suggested rhyming of the last with *honess* is hardly credible; and fragments of coherent speech in the local idiom occasionally flicker forth: "so ah says / haw Sara / an she says whit / way ur ye staunin / aa bandy-leggit?" The vocabulary of this sequence is, arguably, not entirely that of urban demotic: *douce* and *sleekit* have the ring of a different register; but as a potent, if lightweight, cantrip in a thitherto poetically untried speech-form *Glasgow Beasts* not only earned itself an immediate and lasting popularity but opened up a new range of literary possibilities for the dialect. The poet who most effectively availed himself of them, and who has always maintained his place at the centre of the Glaswegian poetic movement, is Tom Leonard.

By 1969, when Leonard's first writings in a medium other than standard English were published as *Six Glasgow Poems*, the achievement of the Renaissance Makars had made of Scots a familiar and – by some readers at least – respected vehicle for modern poetry. Even readers accustomed both to Scots poetry and to "modernism", however, were startled at first by:

> heh jimmy
> yawright ih
> stull wayiz urryi
> ih
>
> heh jimmy
> ma right insane yirra pape
> ma right insane yirwanny uz jimmy

see it nyir eyes
wanny uz

heh

heh jimmy
lookslik wirgonny miss the gemm
gonny miss the GEMM jimmy
nearly three a cloke thinoo
dork init

good jobe theyve gote thi lights

(*The Good Thief*)

This remains Leonard's most famous poem and the one taken as epitomising his style: a style which, notwithstanding some attempted imita-
tions, is still unique. The enduring power of the poem to puzzle,
intrigue and shock its readers is visible on several levels. First, the almost
opaque spelling, a quasi-phonetic transcription of the short, disjointed
phrases, pronounced with a high degree of ellipsis of unstressed syllables,
characteristic of uneducated Glasgow speech: *yawright* "are you all
right?", *ma right insane* "am I right in saying . . .", *yirwanny uz* "you're
one of us". Next, the phonological distinctness of the dialect from either
traditional Scots or Scottish standard English: neither *gaun tae* nor *going
to* but *gonny*, neither *aa richt* nor *all right* but *awright*, neither *yin* (or *ane*) *o*
nor *one of* but *wanny*, neither *is it no* nor *isn't it* but *init*; and the rapier-like
accuracy with which the writing evokes the cadences of the Glasgow
basilect, punctuated by the appelatory particle *heh*, the question marker
ih and the all-purpose vocative *jimmy*. Next again, the plethora of clichés
and banalities, woefully realistic as a representation of actual speech but
wholly unlike the sparkling imaginative richness of Scots poetry until
then: *still wayiz* ("still with us", i.e. still alive), *wanny uz,*[1] *ma right insane*
("Am I right in saying . . ." is a sadly overused phrase from televison quiz
shows), *see it nyir eyes*. And finally, the truly shattering realisation –
which readers are liable to experience some time after their initial

1. Cf. Roddy McMillan's play *The Bevellers*, where the young apprentice, driven by the bul-
lying of his workmates to leave the job after his first day, is dismissed by the most vicious of his
tormentors with "Fuck him. He's no wan o us." (Edinburgh (Southside) 1974, p. 69.)

acquaintance with the poem, and which (as Leonard observed[1]) some of them miss altogether – of the significance of the poem's title: the persona is that of one of the thieves crucified along with Christ.[2] A link, hinted at by the reference to "the gemm" but not overtly mentioned, is that Parkhead, Celtic's football ground and the scene of annual tussles at which violent brawls used to occur with deadly regularity, is nicknamed "Paradise" (*today shalt thou be with me in Paradise*) – and according to an ancient Church tradition, the death of Christ occurred at three p.m., the hour of an afternoon kick-off. The monstrous translocation of the Crucifixion to contemporary Glasgow is, on one level, a searing comment on the city's reputation for sectarian violence.

The same technique is employed in the other poems in the collection, though none reaches this level of audacity. Spellings which at first seem barely intelligible turn out, if read phonetically, to be sardonically precise representations of the local pronunciation (*gonabootlika*... "going about like a..."), slang and idiomatic expressions occur (*dayniz nut* "doing his nut", i.e. in a transport of fury); titles add extra dimensions to the meanings of poems (a piece referring to the dismissal of the Rangers manager Scot Symon – *jis gee im thi fuckin heave* – after his team failed to win a European trophy is called *Simple Simon*). The last of the six, *Good Style*, is ironically self-referential:

> helluva hard tay read theez init
> stull
> if yi canny unnirston thim jiss clear aff then
> gawn
> get tay fuck ootma road
>
> ahmaz goodiz the lota yiz so ah um
> ah no whit ahm dayn
> tellnyi
> jiss try enny a yir fly patir wi me
> stick the bootnyi good style
> so ah wull

This poem is "modern" in the specific sense that there seems to be no

1. *Twelve More Modern Scottish Poets*, eds. C. King and Iain Crichton Smith, London (Hodder and Stoughton) 1986, p. 166.
2. Luke 23, xxxix - xliii.

possibility of a single, simple interpretation. Why, for example, such spellings as *theez, enny, unnirston, patir*? *Enny* perhaps emphasises that the form used is not the Scots *ony* (though this would have been perfectly realistic in Glasgow patois); but what function is served by the other three, for which the phonetic "face-value" is exactly the same as the standard English *these* and *patter* and the standard Scots *unnerstaun*? The use of eye-dialect of this kind is a well-recognised literary device normally used to imply that the supposed speaker is illiterate: but if, as appears to be the case, the persona here is that of the poet himself, how should this be interpreted? The character suggested by the words is that of an ignorant lout reacting with brutish aggressiveness to any fancied hint that his interlocutor is talking down to him (*Jiss try enny a yir fly patir wi me . . .*): a readily recognisable type in a Glasgow context, but are we to imagine, even as a fiction, that this is how Leonard is presenting himself, and by extension the class whose language he is using as his medium?

In some sense at least, later poems by Leonard suggest that an affirmative answer is actually called for: his work is a proclamation that the Glasgow working-class patois has appeared on the poetic scene with all its overtones of violence and brutality, and is no more to be trifled with than its speakers are in real life. The status of Glasgow demotic speech has always been, and remains, a vexed issue. A very common attitude – indeed, an orthodoxy – among teachers and school inspectors is that while the traditional rural dialects are worthy of at least nominal respect, the urban vernacular is merely "vulgar", "common", "slovenly" or "neither good English nor good Scots". Facts which sociolinguists and other language scholars can and often do cite, such as the grammatical self-consistency of the dialect, its innovative and expressive vocabulary, the merely contingent association of its distinctive pronunciation features with unattractive social conditions, the regularity and frequency with which urban sociolects develop in comparable circumstances elsewhere, make no impression on the deeply-ingrained, visceral dislike which the speech form commonly evokes among those who do not speak it. The result of this – a result which teachers have observed for decades without drawing the obvious conclusion regarding their assumptions and methods – is all too often a sullen defiance, expressed as a taciturn refusal to communicate, on the part of school pupils, and in adult life an attitude of hostility to speakers with "proper" accents. (*No Light* describes a vicious assault by a trio of thugs – "so a looksit wullie / an wullie looksit jimmy / an jimmy looksit me ..." – on a man who speaks "dead posh".) Countering this is a perverse pride in the sociolect as a mark of class solidarity. What Leonard is attempting is the promotion of this despised speech-form to a medium for literature: to make poetry out of inarticulacy (or monosyllabicity misconstrued as such), or out of a patois which by its nature, even by its existence, embodies an active rejection of the values which the education system is designed to instil.

The implications of this are nothing less than revolutionary: far more so than the revival of literary Scots by the Renaissance makars. Scots had formerly been a national language in the most comprehensive sense: the mission of MacDiarmid and his successors was to re-establish it as such. There neither was nor ever could be any question of the basilect of a city claiming this status: on the contrary, it is by definition and by its nature a class dialect, used in defiance of "establishment" attitudes. MacDiarmid's Scots could, at least in theory, become the language of gentlemen and scholars; Leonard's patois could never be anything but the speech of an underclass except by the kind of total destruction of an existing social order which was, perhaps, naively dreamed of in the early days of Marxist thought but of which actual experience has made humanity immeasurably sadder before making it wiser.

To that extent, Leonard's endeavours are profoundly subversive in that they call in question, rather than reinforcing, the achievement of the mainstream Renaissance poets. In view of the fact that Glasgow has been the industrial and economic powerhouse of modern Scotland, is it not at least a tenable position that the voice of Scotland is most truly heard in the speech of working-class Glaswegians rather than in the "synthetic Scots" of scholars and literati? Even if most of these have been native speakers of Scots, as they justly claim, is it not the case that their mother-tongue represents pre-industrial Scotland rather than the nation as it now is, and is therefore less capable of relating to contemporary life? Yet an affirmative answer to these questions, should it be offered, at once leads to a contradiction: this patois is that of a people without a voice, since it is in itself the mark not of literacy but of the rejection of literacy; and therefore how can it be used to express anything but an inarticulate protest? By the same token, can it even, logically, be written at all? Leonard's prose essay *Honest* expresses, albeit with ironic exaggeration, the irreconcilable confusions inherent in any attempt at this:

> But ifyi write down "doon" wan minit, nwrite doon "down" thi nixt, people say yir bein inconsistent. But ifyi sayti sumdy, "Whaira yi afti?" nthey say, "Whut?" nyou say, "Where are you off to?" they don't say, "That's no whutyi said thi furst time." They'll probably say sumhm like, "Doon the road!" anif you say, "What?" they usually say "Down the road!" thi second time – tho no always. Course, they never really say, "Doon thi road!" or "Down the road!" at all. Least, they never say it the way it's spelt. Coz it *izny* spelt, when they say it, is it?

More than any other contemporary Scottish poet, Leonard is preoccupied with language and attitudes to language. Many of his poems are on this theme, enforcing re-evaluation of conventional beliefs. *A Summer's Day* – the title, once again, adds a level of irony to the work, being a reference to Shakespeare's Sonnet 18 – evokes with almost painful familiarity the voice of a boy trying to express his feelings to a girl, ending with:

> ach a luvyi thahts
> thahts
> jist thi wey it iz like
> thahts ehm
> aw ther iz ti say

Natural shyness and awkwardness, a traditional Scottish reticence in expressing emotion, and the attitude, proper to the speaker's class, of rejecting any elaborate or practised use of language, combine to reduce him to silence: "thahts ehm / aw ther iz ti say". By contrast, *The Dropout* provides a sufficiently clear demonstration of the venom which the sociolect, clichés and banalities notwithstanding, has been developed to express. *Paroakial*, with caustic humour, sets two language systems against each other and demolishes them both: the supposed speaker dismisses Scottish writers as "aw theez sporran heads / tahty scoan vibes / thi haggis trip"; but undermines his credibility not only by the infantile silliness of his insults but by his attempts to express himself in phrases from American pop slang, vacuous in themselves and reduced to utter risibility through being pronounced in broad Glaswegian: *thahts no whurrits at / thahts no cool man . . . gitinty elektroniks man / really blow yir mine.*

The vowel in the last two lines *mawn / turn yirsel awn* (the pronunciation of *on* in Glasgow is generally represented by Leonard as *oan*) suggests that the speaker is adopting an obviously-faked American accent. The first three poems in *Unrelated Incidents* are linked by the common theme of language: the first with its reiteration of "its thi langwij a thi guhtr" ridicules the supposed speaker who is himself using this "language of the gutter"; the second queries a whole field of linguistic assumptions by raising (but not, of course discussing) "thi diffrince tween sound n object n symbol", the third exposes the fact (well established as such by socio-linguistic experiments) that the perceived authoritativeness of a speaker's utterances varies with the degree of prestige attached to his accent: "If I [a BBC announcer] talked about the truth like one of you scruff you wouldn't think it was true" is, at worst, an exaggeration of an attitude so deeply inculcated as to be almost unquestioned; but when written "if a toktaboot thi trooth lik wanna yoo scruff yi widny thingk it wuz troo", the statement, now being mentally heard as spoken with the accent of "scruff", becomes self-contradictory. And the attitudes of language scholars are no more exempt than those of the uninformed laity from Leonard's sarcasm: a linguist says "ah wish I could talk like you / ahv lost my accent", and the speaker of another poem dismisses the reflection "ma language is disgraceful ... even thi introduction tay thi Scottish National Dictionary tellt mi"[1] with "fuck thi lohta thim".

In the sequence *Ghostie Men*, the same voice becomes that of the urban underclass in protest against the socio-political system through poems which, while abounding in multi-layered ironies, contain an irreducible hard core of satire directed at – in sum – the fashionable attitudes of people equipped with knowledge which they fail to realise is irrelevant. Yet Leonard's Glaswegian is, from one point of view, the ultimate deconstructionist weapon, in that it automatically undercuts not only the victims of his poetic attacks but the supposed speakers of the poems, who inevitably emerge, notwithstanding the strength of their feelings as expressed in their words, as ignorant, unsophisticated, and therefore ultimately helpless.

1. "Owing to the influx of Irish and foreign immigrants in the industrial area near Glasgow the dialect has become hopelessly corrupt." *Intro.* 93.8.

Leonard's achievement has been to establish in modern Scottish writing a register which directly challenges literary Scots as much as it does English. An important fact first remarked on by Caroline Macafee[1] is that though his Glaswegian does not abound in Scots lexemes, it is in its orthography and – less obviously, and more interestingly – also its grammar more distinct from standard English than is literary Scots, in that it adopts phonetic spellings for words identical in Scots and in English instead of simply using the conventional spelling, and that it regularly represents the grammatical developments which characterise most forms of vernacular Scots but, because they do not conform to canonical English grammar, are stigmatised and (by unrecognised conditioning) often refused admission to literary Scots, such as indiscriminate use of historic past tense and past participle forms and loss of number concord between subject and verb. The political implications of Leonard's medium are also decidedly unlike those of MacDiarmid and his successors: Leonard is not concerned to use his language as a weapon in the cause of Scottish political and cultural independence. His field of concern is the class system within Scotland, rather than the country's international status; and while Scottish nationalism was overtly associated with radical socialism in the works of, most notably, MacDiarmid, Smith and Tom Scott, Leonard's voice was first raised in a period of disillusionment with the ideal of political nationalism arising from its failure, by the late 1960s, to have made any apparent headway.

Glasgow demotic speech rapidly achieved success in another literary genre, dialogue (and extended monologues) in prose fiction, in the hands of writers of the calibre of Alan Spence and James Kelman. In poetry too, several poets have followed Leonard in using it to give their work a distinctive voice, though none has confronted all its linguistic and philosophical implications with his relentless logic. Stephen Mulrine's corpus, sparse and uneven though it is, includes two or three poems which have become Glasgow icons. *Glasgow No. 7*, as Mulrine later acknowledged,[2] is

---

1. "Nationalism and the Scots Renaissance now", first published in *English World-Wide* 2:1 (1981), 29–38 and reprinted in M. Görlach, ed., *Focus on Scotland*, Varieties of English Around the World General Series 5, Amsterdam (Benjamins) 1985.

2. "Poetry in Glasgow dialect", in *Focus on: Scotland*, Varieties of English Around the World General Series 5, ed. Manfred Görlach, Amsterdam (Benjamins) 1985, p.231.

a collage of disjointed phrases remembered from childhood; but rendered memorable, and cumulatively amounting to an elegy both entertaining and touching, by the accurate recollection of the playground argot and the clever arrangement of it into rhyme:

> When we wur wee
> it was aw berr feet
> an who likes candy
> an nane o yir cheek
> an see us a lenny
> an dreepin aff dykes
> an kick-the-can
> an shots oan bikes
> wis rerr . . .

The vocabulary, to a much greater extent than Leonard's, is specific to the area, and most of the words and phrases are chosen with delightful aptness to recall memories good and bad: phrases used by adults to children (*nane o yir cheek, dae whit yir tellt*) and by children to each other (*see us a lenny* "give us [singular] a loan of . . .", *gaun yirsel* "go on yourself!" – a shout of encouragement); images of children's games (*kick-the-can, heid-the-baw*), pranks (*doggin it* "playing truant", *chickie-mellie* (trick of rattling a button on the window of a house to annoy the occupants within)) and mishaps (*melt ye wan* (bash you), *six o the belt*). A celebrated shibboleth of Glasgow pronunciation is emphasised by the rhyming of the five short lines *wis rerr, dje* (do you) *derr?, no ferr*, etc. *Nostalgie* is much more elaborate. Nonce spellings cause the authentic sound of the dialect to echo in the reader's ear: *caur, taur; therr, terr; thur, thull* (they're, they'll), *ooty* (out of), *fulla* (full of); several of the vocabulary items are general Scots (*howk* "dig", *glaur* "mud", *chuckies* "small stones") but others are specific to Glasgow demotic (*broo* "bureau", i.e. the Labour Exchange, *stchumer* "idiot", *lucky* "lucky find", *Clenny* "Cleansing Department"). The attitude of the speaker, and the invited attitude of the reader *to* the speaker, are disturbingly ambiguous: the "nostalgie" evoked by childhood memories of playing near and in a filthy canal is distinctly a *nostalgie de la boue*, yet the stretch of dreary urban motorway which has replaced the canal is evoked with almost equally unattractive realism; and the liveliness of the speaker's recollections contrasts pointedly with the lifelessness of the present scene. The speaker's status as a "non-runner", too, is conveyed by the banal rhymes, "easy-oasy" metre ("Bit Ah've seen the Canal easy-oasyin by...") and abundance of clichéd phrases ("jis shows ye", "thull gie ye the jile", "ach, nivver mind, son"). In *The Coming of the Wee Malkies*, Mulrine achieves the distinction of creating the archetypal celebration of Glasgow tenement life: the scene is evoked with references to architectural features like *the wash-hoose dyke, the sterrheid light, the loaby*; and the exuberant, indeed frenetic, activity of the unidentified "wee Malkies" is suggested by the sequence of verbs, many of them local (*dreep, blooter, chap, caw, tim*) predicated on *they*, and by the idiomatic phrases suggesting vigorous actions such as *tummle thur wulkies* (turn somersaults – general Scots); *pit the hems on* (wreck), *stick the heid on* (deliver a head-butt to the face – Glasgow sociolect). The anarchic force of the Malkies is pointedly contrasted with an orderly domestic setting represented by the overtones of *missis* (the addressee to whom the repeated question *whit'll ye dae* is delivered as a challenge) and the association of the woman so addressed with symbols of routine, reassuring solidity – though the fragility of this reassurance is implied by the insulting adjective in *yir sapsy* (soft, feeble) *weans*. This short poem, with its assured use of the dialect to evoke a scene of uproarious chaos, ranks as a defiant paean to the undisciplined vigour of tenement life.

Mulrine's Glasgow poetry, despite his accurate and fluent reproduction of the city's vernacular, remains limited not only by its small bulk but by its restricted intellectual horizons: unlike Leonard he does not examine the nature or the implications of his medium or use it to suggest philosophical questions. Several other poets have adopted phonetically-spelled Glaswegian, to the extent that it is now a fully-established register of written Scots: notable individual poems are *Lament for a Lost Dinner Ticket* by Margaret Hamilton, opening with the familiar introductory *see*:

> See ma mammy
> See ma dinner ticket ...

and proceeding with renderings of apocopations worthy of Leonard (*Nabigwoffldoon* – "and the big waa fell doun") and, by a wittily ironic reversal of the same device, a parody spelling of a "posh" voice asking a sadly self-revelatory question *Ees thees chaild eb slootly Non verbal?*; and, a much more elaborate and experimental example, *Wurd Cairns* by Maud Devine, in which a reminiscence of Garioch's much-quoted epigram –

> Thae twa-three chuckie-stanes
>   I lay on Scotland's cairn,
> Biggit by men o bigger banes
>   Afore I was a bairn ...
>
> (*Dedication*)

– is expanded into a partly "concrete" poem (with its pyramidal arrangement of the words on the page), combining a patchwork of highly imaginative metaphors with the resolute plainness of urban vernacular in what amounts to a meditation on the nature and the potential of the author's poetic medium:

> Yiz
> shid lissen
> Cairns huv echoes
> silent speak o ghaists
> staundin shadaless ower the cairn.

Urban demotic speech in Scotland is a medium with expressive resources often unrecognised, even unsuspected, by outsiders. Its initiation as a vehicle for poetry has added a new extension to Scots as a literary language; and if its implications have as yet been confronted to the full by only one poet, forthcoming developments may be awaited with interest.

12

The Doric Continues to Flourish:
John M. Caie, Flora Garry, David Ogston,
Raymond Falconer, Sheena Blackhall

As the Scots tongue has developed and diversified, one factor has remained consistent: the voice of the North-East. The tradition established by Mary Symon and Charles Murray has not only endured but flourished; and there is no question that the local populace evince both a proprietary interest in and a warm affection for their "Doric" poets which they deny to Alexander Scott or Alastair Mackie. Throughout the century, a succession of gifted poets have used the local dialect to commemorate aspects of the way of life, effectively keeping pace both with material and social changes and with developments in poetic fashion. The cumulative result has been to develop in the North-East what is qualitatively and quantitatively the strongest regional dialect literature in mainland Scotland, a fact not unrelated to the notably greater degree of support given to the dialects in primary and secondary education than elsewhere in the country.

Among the most individual and most accomplished of Murray's immediate successors is John M. Caie, a man of farming stock whose life's work was on the Board of Agriculture. Appropriately, farming life is a dominant theme of his poetry; but there is no idealisation of that life in the elegiac and often gloomy and fatalistic meditations which his characters conduct in a rich, authentic and skilfully-turned Doric. The first of his two collections of poems is called *The Kindly North*;[1] but it includes poems like *Lowsin' Time* and *Tire an' Fa' Tee Again*, ironically humorous treatments of the toils of farm life; *Sair Wark's Nae Easy*, a relentless account of the varying tasks, but unvarying hardship, brought by the revolving

1. Aberdeen: D. Wyllie & Son, 1934. The title phrase is taken from the poem *Rivers o' Hame*.

179

seasons; *Donal'*, a sad monologue in which an old man speaks affectionately to his closest surviving companion, an equally decrepit pony;[1] *Fat's the Eese*, a bitter retrospective meditation on a luckless life; and *The Auld Ploo'man*, the soliloquy of a weary, ageing man, bereft of both his son and his wife by the War, facing a cheerless future. Caie's delicate poetic touch is shown in the opening of the last-mentioned poem:

> It's a bonny-lyin' craftie, fine an' lythe ayont the hill,
>> An' the hoose, gin it were snoddit up, wad dee;
> Ma e'e was on't for lang, but things has a' gane vrang
>> An' the hoosie an' the craft are nae for me.

The characteristic Doric diminutive *craftie* (*craft* is "croft") conveys the speaker's fondness for the place; and there is a suggestion of the reticence said to be typical of the area[2] in the second line: *the hoose wad dee* is much higher praise than it appears to be. The metrical contrast between the continuous flow of the opening line and the strongly marked caesura, emphasised by the internal rhyme, in the third subtly underlines the change of mood: this pattern is repeated throughout the poem, but without the same emotional significance.

Features of the local dialect appear consistently: besides details of pronunciation (e.g. *twal'* rhyming with *caul'*, the initial fricative in *vrocht* and *vrang*, the metathesis in *wardle*), some interesting grammatical details are the ellipsis of the auxiliary verb in *I'd likit* (I would have liked) and *I wadna nott* (I wouldn't have needed), and the use of *be* – really an elided form of what is elsewhere written *bude*, pronounced [bid] in the North-East: a Scots development of *behoved* – to mean either "have to" (*I be tae steyter doon the brae ma lane*) or "had to" (*The war cam' on an' syne of coorse he be tae jine*). In keeping with the mood of quiet stoicism which the poem

1. To criticise this as sentimental would betray lamentable ignorance. *Lowsin' Time*, for much of which a ploughman is likewise represented as speaking to a horse, depicts with sympathy and sensitivity the intimate understanding of and affection for his horses developed by a man who works with them daily and whose own welfare is mutually dependent on theirs.

2. The Swiss dialectologist Eugen Dieth, whose *Grammar of the Buchan Dialect Vol.1* (Cambridge (Heffer) 1932), a landmark in Scottish philological studies, appeared two years before *The Kindly North*, remarks almost in tones of surprise on this characteristic of the North-Eastern populace: "Buchan speakers do not indulge in high-sounding, bombastic expressions: the utmost delight is conveyed by 'I'm rael gled tae see ye' or 'Man, it wes gran'." (p. xxi: quotations in phonetic transcription in original).

evokes, the vocabulary is plain and utilitarian: markedly dialectal words and strongly emotive terms are rare, though in the unobtrusive "a short-some wee bit *ted*", referring to his son, the speaker indulges in a local word of endearment, and once a flash of anger at the injustice of life momentarily breaks through his philosophic resignation:

> Still an' on, it's gey an sair tae be strippit, *flypit* [i.e. "flayed"], bare
> Efter trauchlin' i' the yird for fifty year.

In this poem Caie portrays, with an admirable lack of sentimentality, a figure who represents a central aspect of the North-East character: a man whose "wardle's a' in leems" (a regional word for pieces of broken china) but who simply continues, fortified by no conscious assumption of courage but simply by the unbreakable strength of his breed, to perform his tasks in a comfortless world. (It is observable, incidentally, that the Christian faith appears to play virtually no part in the lives of Caie's characters. The auld ploo'man mentions the Church only as the location of his wife's grave: "she's happit i' the mools ahin' the kirk"; and there is no trace of religious consolation in his "Ah, weel, fat maun be maun be, an' there's naething for't but thole." Only in the last verse of *Donal'* does a speaker make any overt statement of faith in the traditional teachings of the Kirk:

> A fearsome road's afore me, unco brae-set, dark an' caul',
>   An' weel-a-wat I'm jist a thochtie lame;
> Man, Donal', gin a shilt like you had only haen a saul,
>   I'd yokit ye – an' ye'd hae ta'en me Hame.

And this, a mere hint, gives little sense of cheer in its context.)

Caie's Doric conveys with remarkable success the impression of a mother-tongue, employed naturally by whatever persona he adopts for his various poems. His North-East characters reveal themselves and their responses to life's challenges by their idiosyncratic use of language. In strong contrast to the steady rhythms of *The Auld Ploo'man*, the impatience of "a spunky loon" is suggested in *The Halflin* by irregular clusters of jostling anapaests; and the forceful words, comically obtrusive alliteration ("The grieve, a glowerin', grummlin', gurly breet") and trisyllabic rhymes present his cocksure response to the unpleasant people and conditions on the farm where he finds himself working:

The orra beastie's cleekit, spavin't, aul,
  A blaffart o' win' wad ca the cratur totterin';
There's nae eneuch cauf i' my bed, an' the chaumer's caul',
  An' wi' rottens at nicht ye wad think the place was hotterin'.

In *Sair Wark's Nae Easy*, the frequent repetitions (*An' aye yoke, yoke – It's hingin' in, aye hingin' in – Syne birze an' scraap an' birze again – For hashin', hashin' throu*) convey the unsparing laboriousness of farm work, words and phrases referring to weariness and discomfort abound (*ye've fir't* [inflamed] *yer feet, pech an' swyte, trauchlin' aye an' tyaavin, ye're like tae drap*) and the diverse (but never easy and rarely agreeable) tasks evoke reactions well described by the native vocabulary: cutting peat is "a fusome, clorty business", stacking hay is "nesty, scuttery kin' o' wark." In *Broken,*[1] the bitter tirade of a farmer ruined by his failure to adapt to modern methods, a rhyme suitable for a humorous effect is used to emphasise the furiously ironic tone of the speaker:

An' horse! Warkin' wi' horse – muckle, clumsy an' camsteerie –
Instead o' a bonnie peetrol engine or an electric whigmaleerie!

Caie's work evinces not only a profound empathy with the people of the North-East but a strong affection for the region itself: many of the poems in which no particular character is adopted evoke its tranquil landscapes in the changing seasons; *Rivers o' Hame* combines evocation of the sound and motion of Scotland's watercourses –

There's some gyang birlin' tae the sea,
  Aye lauchin', bickerin', doon they stour,
An' some gyang quaitly daun'erin' by
  Or fyles are grumly, deep an' dour

– with graceful playing with their names, finishing in the North-East with "a sma' bit modest tinklin' burn"; *Hills* likewise weaves the toponyms into an expression of exuberant joy in the rugged landscape; and a remarkable tour de force, *The Enzie*, consists almost entirely of farm names arranged into rhymed verse, the cumulative effect of the lexically opaque (except to specialists) but phonaesthetically potent and distinctive words being a marvellous confirmation of the region's unique identity.

The writers of the introductions to Caie's two volumes, respectively Peter Giles and Sir Herbert Grierson, pay tribute to the accuracy and flu-

1. *'Twixt Hills and Sea*, Aberdeen (D. Wyllie & Son) 1939.

ency of his dialect; though Giles feels it incumbent on him to provide extended paraphrases of several poems as if in fear that Caie's readers may not understand them. In the history of Doric poetry, Caie's distinctive place is that, writing when changes both within and beyond the farming communities were tending inexorably towards the demise of the traditional ways of life, he provided an epitome and an epitaph for the not always kindly North in its authentic mother tongue.

The attraction of poetry in traditional styles and genres for North-East Doric writers has never shown signs of diminishing: to cite only a few of Caie's most accomplished contemporaries and successors, J. C. Milne, a teacher and educationist, has contributed several humorous evocations of the classroom to the annual curriculum of local schools, Peter Buchan has commemorated the life of the herring fishers in a small but vivid collection of poems and anecdotes, and two remarkable and locally much loved poetesses, Liliane Grant Rich and Flora Garry, have endowed the Doric repertoire with carefully-wrought and shrewdly observed lyrical pictures from the old North-East communities.[1] Flora Garry in particular, whose one small collection is a landmark in modern dialect literature, is uncompromising in her use of the pristine, unadulterated Doric, as a single example will show:

> Bit Mains is in a bog o swyte, his winkers fite wi styoo.
> He's stecht in's wivven draavers an sair hankit in's surtoo.
> He's burssen, fool an yokie, an crochlie i the queets.
> The vera feet o him's roassen an fair lowpin in his beets.
>
> Wi Mally lows't an stabl't noo, he hyters to the shore,
> Skytin upo' knablick steens an slidderin amo' waar.
> He's caain for a lippin peel, a lythe an sinny nyook,
> For he's dwebble an he's druchtit an he's mangin for his dook.
>
> *(Mains o Yawal's Dook)*

Of the rich store of Scots words in this short extract, *winkers* (eyelashes), *stecht* (stuffed), *hankit* (entangled), *yokie* (itchy), *queets* (ankles: the usual (non-regional) spelling is *cuits*), *lowp* (leap), *lowse* (free from work), *skyte*

---

1. J. C. Milne, *Poems*, Aberdeen University Press 1963; Peter Buchan, *Mount Pleasant and Other Poems*, Peterhead (Scrogie) 1961 and later editions, several poems reprinted in *Fit Like, Skipper?*, Aberdeen Journals 1985; Liliane Grant Rich, *The White Rose of Druminnor* and *Echo of Many Voices*, Aberdeen University Press 1969 and 1980; Flora Garry, *Bennygoak and Other Poems*, Aberdeen (Rainbow Books) 1974.

(slip), *slidder* (slide), *waar* (seaweed), *lythe* (peaceful), *neuk* (secluded place), *dwebble* (feeble) and *dook* (bathe) are general Scots, though some have local pronunciations; *styoo* (an idiosyncratic spelling for *stew*, blown dust), *surtoo* (jacket), *burssen* (breathless), *crochlie* (lame: a rare and possibly idiosyncratic derivation from *crochles*, a crippling disease of cattle), *hyter* (stumble), *knablick* (knobbly), *lippin* (brimming), *druchtit* (dehydrated) and *mangin* (longing) are characteristic of North-Eastern dialects. The use of *wivven* ("woven") to mean "knitted", *fool* ("foul") to mean simply "dirty" without an extreme or strongly pejorative sense, and *caa* ("call") to mean "search" are also local; and characteristic North-Eastern phonological features, besides those already cited,[1] include the diphthongisation of *swyte* [swʌit] and the development of the fricative from original [w] in *draavers*.

By contrast with her absolute refusal to dilute the strength of her dialect, Flora Garry shows a noteworthy variety of style and mood in her poems; and though the communities remembered from her childhood and youth form her principal subject and their folk-speech her medium, no more than Caie can she be charged with mere nostalgia. In *Spring on a Buchan Farm*, the sudden arrival of fine weather is evoked in language of startling intensity, an unusual concentration of repetitive sound patterns combining with powerful active and animate verbs:

> Syne, on a suddenty, the lift's rivven wide.
> Hivvenly licht poors doon an blins an droons
> The dozent, thowless wardle. Snaw-bree loups,
> Ice-tangles fae the eezins dreep, the Furth
> New quickent blinks an glinters i the sin.

(Of the vocabulary of this passage, only *ice-tangles* (icicles) is local, though the spellings *hivvenly* and *eezins* (for *easins*, eaves) are idiosyncratic.) This mood of rejoicing, however, is immediately displaced as the poem describes a return of winter; and onomatopoeic words suggesting noise or quick energetic action evoke the savagery of the natural world:

> The lammin yowie *yammers* fae the bucht,
> The rottan's pykit teeth *chudder* the barley seck,
> The *skweengin* hoolet *clooks* the moosie's wyme ...

Yammers (whines) and *clooks* (seizes) are general, *skweengin* is a local form

---

1. See Chapter 4.

of *scungin* (scrounging), and *chudder* (gnaw) is apparently a nonce formation. The truth of the penultimate line, "Treachery, a broken tryst, that's
a Buchan spring", is demonstrated in language of force and vigour.

Flora Garry's poetry can also suggest the passing, or imminent passing,
of the old ways of life. *Mains o Yawal's Dook* is on the surface a comical,
yet sympathetic, portrait of an old farmer enjoying a sea-bathe; but the
poem is said to be "based on Chapter 5 of *Johnny Gibb of Gushetneuk* by
William Alexander": the novel referred to is set in the period of the
Disruption, and the poem, by implication, therefore recalls an aspect of
life well over a century in the past. As a more certain example, the title
poem *Bennygoak* is the lament of the descendant of three generations of
farmers who now longs to quit the hard and monotonous labour of life
on the land; and a poem with the significant title *Figures Receding* draws
vivid pen-sketches of three representative characters ("A sma', reid-mow-
sert chiel, I min', wi a mad look in his e'e" – "A toozy, sinbrunt wife in a
tartan shawl" – "A big, fite-winkert man, slow, bashfu' amo' folk") and
ends with a firmly stated acceptance of the sad but inescapable fact that
the world to which they belonged is gone. An ambiguity of attitude, psy-
chologically very realistic, which raises Flora Garry's work above the
level of simple descriptions, is present in both those poems. *Bennygoak*
evokes the speaker's *scunner* – the Scots word, used in the poem, is more
fitting than any English word could be in the context – at the dreary toil
of farm life; but a strong and profound affection for the land itself is suggested by the use of local place names:

> I look far ower by Ythanside
> To Fyvie's laich, lythe lan's,
> To Auchterless an Bennachie
> An the mist-blue Grampians ...

and still more by the realism and beauty of the seasonal descriptions:

> Bit it's warst ava aboot Wutsunday
> Fin the nichts are quaet an clear,
> An the floo'erin' curran's by i the yard
> An the green corn's i the breer ...

That the speaker's unhappiness should be at its most intense when the
natural world seems most conducive to serenity and peace demands from
the reader a complex response: on a miniature scale, the contradictory

emotions felt towards the land by Chris Guthrie in *Sunset Song* are hinted at here. In *Figures Receding,* a subtle ambivalence emerges in the final stanza, which draws a contrast between learning and native wit:

> There's twa wyes o kennin.
> Hiz wi wir heids, wir rizzon, wir printit wird;
> Them wi their een, their finger-eyns, their midder wit,
> Ootlins noo in a warl they widna fit.
> Time canna rin back. They'll seen be oot o' min'.
> We winna see again folk o yon kin'.

The language of the "printit wird" and of the seats of learning which develop "rizzon" is of course English, and the growth of a world in which "midder wit" is no longer sufficient is associated with the rise to dominance of English and the decline of Scots; yet notwithstanding this and the fact that the speaker identifies herself (*hiz* – "us") with the new age, the language in which the death of the Doric-speaking world is announced is Doric.

The voice of a younger generation is heard in the poetry of David Ogston.[1] The poem *White Stone Country,* a phrase which is also the title of one of his collections of Doric prose tales, immediately emphasises the enduring integrity of the dialect by translating the English phrase:

> I gaed back for a steen,
> A fite steen ...

The following free-verse meditation on preserving the memory of the speaker's calf-ground is couched in a somewhat sparser Doric than that of Ogston's predecessors: the phonology is North-Eastern ([f] for [ʍ]: *fite, faan, faar*; sporadic diphthongisation of [i]: *seiven*; maximal raising of Middle Scots [ø]: *skweel, steed, eesed*; raising of [e] from original [aː] before [n]: *steen, eence*), but the vocabulary is mostly general Scots (*park* "field", *enrig* "land at the end of a furrow", *intimmers* "entrails"): only *bourach* "heap" has a definite Doric resonance. Since the persona is identified as having left the Doric-speaking community, this is not inappropriate; and the unstructured verse, conveying nothing of the assured fluency in the dialect of a Murray, a Caie or a Flora Garry, gives emphasis to the symbolic meaning of the lines:

1. Poems in *The Living Doric*, ed. Cuthbert Graham, Aberdeen (Rainbow Books) 1985, pp. 80–87.

> I climmed ower the palin
> An steed for a meenit, nae sure
> O my balance ...

This sense of moving uncertainly between two worlds is suggested elsewhere in Ogston's work. *My Father's Sark* relates the poet's present calling, the ministry, to the ancestral farming life which he abandoned in his youth, activities of the latter being transferred metaphorically to the former:

> ... plooin wi the Beuk,
> Sawin wi the Wird, hairstin wi daith ...

and the sark (shirt) of the title is a tangible link between the two phases of his life. The impossibility, to a man born and brought up to farming, of fully escaping the old life is well suggested by the immediacy of the descriptions:

> Nae yearnin for *caul clorty* grun
> An the *sotter* o a weet park
> O' sneddit swedes wytin for a cairt ...
> Nor the *pleiterin* an *soss*
> O' a fu' byre mornin an nicht,
> Nowt roarin in the travisses,
> Barras tae be rowed an *sharn*
> Up ower the beets ...

In this, words with strong overtones of physical unpleasantness abound: *sotter* (dirty unpleasant work) and *soss* (muddle, confusion) are from the Aberdeenshire dialect, *pleiter* (splash in water or mud) and *sharn* (dung) are local pronunciations of words more generally pronounced *plitter* or *plowter* and *shairn*; and the "freedom" of his new vocation is defined negatively with a passage full of words relating to work:

> ...I'm free tae yoke an louwse,
> Tae hash on or tae scutter
> At my ain lick. Naebody stauns
> At my shooder skirlin: Mak! Mak!

A longer passage of reminiscence later in the poem, however, suggests a more agreeable recollection of harvest work: laborious no doubt (five present participles, *powkin ... liftin ... drappin ... flingin ... biggin*, appear in three lines) but allowing for rests with

187

> ... the roon perkins
> an the stem yoamin fae a kettle,
> Pipes stappit wi Bogie...

(*perkins* (a kind of biscuit) is general, but *stem* is a local pronunciation of *steam*, *yoamin* (puffing out) is a North-Eastern word, and *Bogie* is a coarse tobacco named after a river in Aberdeenshire); and coming eventually to an end. The last line of the poem, where he describes himself as still sustained by "the thocht o clyack, sometime", uses the local word for the traditional rite of harvest-home, in which the last sheaf is decorated and ceremonially brought in to the barn and the farm household and workers join in a communal supper. Ogston's Doric is richer in this poem than in *White Stone Country*, including the local expression "fobbin (panting) like a fat kittlen" and the rare word *suskit* (threadbare); and though many readers seeing the simile

> ...the fite collar roon my throat
> Like *yowdendrift* that winna thaw

will think at once of MacDiarmid, the association would be wrong: the word is authentically North-Eastern, and more at home in Ogston's dialect than in that of the Border poet.

Despite his experimenting with free verse and his recurring theme of turning away from the life of the land, Ogston remains within the traditional bounds of Doric poetry: his move from farming to the ministry has, after all, been in itself a common course of life among young men of rural Scotland. The song-like *'Gowd an Yalla'* is an affirmation of love for the home ground in the vein of a hundred music-hall numbers, though with more vigour and a greater linguistic inventiveness than most. The imaginative *Man, Ye were Safe*, addressed to Christ, is both moving and thought-provoking beneath the surface impression of a cheerful and engagingly fluent rhyme, but it is in keeping with the Reformed Kirk tradition of assuming a tone of man-to-man familiarity with the Deity: this poem would surely have won the approval of one of the most admirable and most individual of North-Eastern writers, and representatives of Scottish Christianity – George MacDonald. A strongly contrasting voice is that of Raymond Falconer: a North-Eastern poet whose emphatic rejection both of familiar verse forms and of a fundamental assumption of the Doric tradition, namely that of the community, has perhaps hindered his full recognition and acceptance in his home territory.

Falconer's poetry[1] takes the form of carefully constructed sentences divided into short, irregular lines, sometimes with end-rhyme but more often without it; and the combination of this "modern" format with a Doric as rich in vocabulary and as consistent in grammar and phonology as that of many of his predecessors could certainly seem odd and forbidding to readers of traditional dialect poetry. Humour is not conspicuous in his work: his exploration of the grim and saddening aspects of life has a bleak realism that sometimes recalls Alastair Mackie; and several of his poems deal with characters in an isolation emphasised by the use of a plain vernacular register. The first poem in the set is called *William of Bogjurgan*, but the name never occurs again, and the poem takes the form of a series of questions by an undetermined *ah* [I] concerning a *he* whose identity with the eponymous man is never ascertained. On one level, this poem is an evocation of the harshness of a life spent "tyaavin wi coorse thrawn grun", telling with stark realism of slow and laborious tasks, bitter weather, and the physical effects of hard manual labour:

His back rackit wi work,
hauns bent roon wi the shape
o the grape shaft, the ploo
or the hyow.

(*Hyow* is the local dialect pronunciation of "hoe".) The "three craws ... Crawin crawin as he edged / his wy alang the dreel", breaking the silence with their discordant and menacing noise, are associated symbolically with the three forces of "Piety, toil an the men o siller" which imprison and blight the lives of men of the land. This is imaginative writing of a respectable order. The curious contrast between the use of a specific individual name for the title and the uncertainty of its reference within the poem, however, adds depth to the writing by raising almost existential questions: "Ah winder whit his face / wis like?" ... "Wis yon him ah sa ..." ... "Or wis yon him ah sa ..."; and the final section –

1. In *Four Scottish Poets*, Garron Publications, 1983, pp. 3–18. Falconer is absent from the many anthologies of North-Eastern poetry which enjoy steady and regular sales in local bookshops.

> Wis thon een o his bairns
> ah sa ahent the steadin last nicht ...
> Windrin aboot hersel and
> the stars
> and her faither.

– adds a further layer of uncertainty: what is the nature of the child's
"windrins" about her father? In the simplest terms, the poem appears to
be asking whether "William of Bogjurgan" has any existence apart from
the unending labours which he can be seen to perform: Tom Scott's line
"An this is aa the life he kens there is" is recalled, but whereas Brand is a
fully realised and dramatically presented individual, Bogjurgan's identity
remains mysterious, that of "a dark silhouette on the brae".

Carefully selected and highly-focused details likewise combine with
sparse and realistic language to evoke a mood of loneliness in *The Sair
Hert*. The boy, overwhelmed with grief at his mother's death, is set
against a background of "aul wid glaur / an rotten leaves" as mercilessly
indifferent as "the men wi his father, / lum hats, / stinkin o baccy rick, /
aye an drams." (*Rick* "reek" and later *sickin* "seeking" represent a characteristic local pronunciation.) The colloquial "the loon grat, / for aa he wis
worth" suggests a sympathetic observer, but the narrator is not present
in the action; and the boy's only human contact is with the grieve,

> roch an coorse
> wi his unfeelin grasp.

The Invalid is an internal monologue in which the speaker's sense impressions and recollections are suggested by distinctive Scots words: "bairns
traipsin (trudging) aff ti skweel", "ane *scushles* (shuffles – a local word) on
ahen the rest", "the kitchie deem *dachles* (dawdles, also predominantly
local) we er lad", "nithingness, *sweelin* (flowing) ower ma skin"; by contrast, *No Voice of Man*, a picture of a silent and deserted landscape,
eschews emotive words until a mood has been established by visual
images evoked with exquisite clarity, and makes no use of the Scots vocabulary in the stanza which breaks this mood:

> A voice taen ower
> by bleatin brutes.
> A memory trampit on
> by strangers,

wi laws and greed
impervious tae human
needs.

Falconer's language, in respect of its phonology, grammar and vocabulary, is essentially that of his Doric-writing predecessors; but two factors cause his work to differ profoundly from theirs: the absence of a strongly-identified persona even in the first-person poems, and the tenuousness of the linkage between the events of the poems and any imagined background. The lonely figures of Caie's poems have definite life histories and are seen against the picture of an entire social culture, thoroughly documented and assumed to form part of the living, or at least the imaginative, world of the reader; Falconer's "invalid", despite the intensity with which his (or her? – even this is indeterminate) sense impressions are evoked, has no such anchorage in space and time; and the speakers or characters of shorter poems such as *Storm* or *Sweer Deith*, despite the unfailing precision and appropriateness of the descriptive details, are almost without any definable identity. This is, of course, in no way unusual in poetry; but it is very unusual in a poetry as firmly rooted in the life of a community, and reflecting it as intimately, as that composed in the North-East dialect. Falconer has taken the radical step of causing the Doric to slip from its moorings in the busy communal lives of the ferm-touns and fishing villages; and the full effects of this have yet to be felt.

There is no question of either the success or the popularity of the most prolific and most adventurous exponent of Doric poetry active at the time of writing, Sheena Blackhall. Her first collection of poems, *The Cyard's Kist* (Rainbow Books, Aberdeen, 1984) establishes its Doric identity by its title: *cyard* represents the local pronunciation [kjard] of the Scots word for "tinker", elsewhere *caird*. And two poems on facing pages, *Mither Tongue* and *The Dominie*, fling down a ringing gauntlet at the oppressive social and educational attitudes from which the dialect has suffered. *Mither Tongue*, "written on hearing the Rev. Lamont's Service in Scots, Denburn Parish Church", opens with what at first seems a decidedly unsubtle line: "'Twis a gey stammygaster, a meenister spikkin' like yon –"; yet as the poem proceeds through the bitter recollection of how

> ... I sat ma lane
> In a cauld hard chair, at a fantoosh schule
> Recitin' the 'Puddock.' [a Doric poem by J. M. Caie]
> Abody snichered an' smirked as the wards fell deid
> At the only bairn o' the hale jing-bang, tae ken fit she read ...

to the speaker's admission that this memory still arouses in her "a pang o' shame" on uttering a Doric word, the hint of mockery is seen to be self-directed: the speaker's education has led her to the absurd and deplorable state of feeling shock at hearing a sermon in what is, for both her and the minister, the mother tongue. In *The Dominie*, her reaction to the teacher who described the Doric as "orra, coorse, ill-fared, / A peer relation o' the Southern spik" is

> The mannie's deid, or, if he's nae,
> By God! he should be!

Here – decades after J. C. Milne wrote the line "Faur's the bonnie dialect?"[1] – is a writer vigorously proclaiming, and demonstrating, that it is still very much alive, and anathematising those agents of cultural deracination whose attempts to kill it have been unsuccessful. Already in her first collection, Sheena Blackhall's lyrics are marked by an impressive variety of tone and mood, and an adroitness in selecting the appropriate word from the Scots or specifically North-Eastern vocabulary. The picture evoked may be romantic and nostalgic:

> The salmon swims tae the lochan's briest,
> The bees win hinney frae the muir,
> Sae 'tis wi me a tug at the hairt
> An it's sair, man, sair ...
>
> Tae stan at the mou o the quate hoose
> Whaur ilka room is teem,
> Hearin the step o a bairnie's fit
> Come lichtsome doon, in a dream.
>
> *(Homecoming)*

or immediate and realistic:

1. As I gaed doon by Memsie,
   I heard an aul' man speir,
   "Faur's the bonnie dialect
   That aince wis spoken here?"

From *Tempora Mutantur*, in *Poems*, ed. Nan Shepherd, Aberdeen University Press 1976, p.30.

Fowk squattit in doorwyes –
Shifty-eed, reid-biddy carls,
Watchin the seamen scalin aff the docks,
Scraunin the streets for a hard-faced quine,
Buyin an 'oor o warmth
Far the screichin seagulls dine.

(Johnny)

A definite progression is recognisable in her second volume, *The Spik o' the Lan'* (Rainbow Books, Aberdeen, 1986): here the scansion and rhyming, in the poems that employ them, are more assured, the images more vivid, the thoughts expressed with greater force. An unpleasant man is characterised using familiar but expressive similes and racing metre:

Dalriggin wis sleekit – he'd teeth like a meer's,
A snicher tae match them – a tongue like a shears,
That'd clip ye tae size – he'd the braidth o' yer claith,
Ye'd be thrimmles an thrummles afore ye drew braith.

(Dalriggin)

A tongue-tied lover expresses his frustration in lines both ludicrous and poignantly realistic:

That ony quine sud bring me doon,
I' faith – it's maist provokin,
I'm saft's a bap fin Belle's aroon,
She disna gie a docken!

(The Thwarted Suitor)

And by contrast, a few lines in *Breem Beddit* suggest the intensity of erotic passion with remarkable power. Many of the poems evoke some aspect of life on the land; but the vision is not earth-bound: a supernatural aura is imparted to the landscape in several poems, and *Pastoral* begins with a list of the pleasant aspects of farm life:

... reid-cheek't bairns, an hamely fare
O' reemin brose bowls, sickle an the seed ...

contrasts this with the "bane-weary, numb-neived, cauld" night labour of delivering a calf, and proceeds to a visionary passage:

Ootbye, the mune-struck hills are a stair.
Oh, gin I cud, I'd climb them
Up till the stars, that hing
A frostit furrow, in the air.

193

This collection too contains a poetic statement of Sheena Blackhall's thoughts on her native speech, *Doric's No Dodo*.[1] A contrast is forcefully drawn between academics (and probably she has some writers in mind too) concerned with *literary* Scots, which they attempt to preserve and develop artificially as if it were "a muckle weet haddie streekt oot on a slab", and the native speakers who have it as a living *spoken* language:

I've news for them –
Scots disna bide in a buik!
It's alive, an it's kickin,
Gin they wid bit look.

Sheena Blackhall is far from unique among North-East writers in suggesting that Scots as known to scholars and poets of the "synthetic" school is a far cry from their own vital and dynamic community speech, though she expresses the idea more exultantly than most. The references to spelling in the poem are clearly directed at the many individuals and (usually short-lived) committees who have undertaken to suggest possible standardisations for the spelling of Scots: an argument regularly brought against such endeavours is that a canonical spelling system would impair the freedom of those who wish to write in a local dialect.[2] The Doric, her claim is, needs no help from academics or language planners, since its enduring and flourishing life is assured by the enthusiastic delight in its expressive opulence felt by its native speakers.

In her prolific output of poems and short stories, Sheena Blackhall has continued to develop, and to confirm her status as one of the most gifted poets currently writing in Scotland – not only the North-East – in respect of her command of the language, her technical skill, and the range of her imagination. Her most recent collection of poems, *Lament for the Raj*, includes translations (some made from English versions) from Chinese and Spanish, as well as original poems in Doric, English and –

1. Cuthbert Graham, to whom this poem is dedicated, was a journalist, writer and editor of greatly respected memory, for many years a lively and vociferous figure giving enthusiastic support and encouragement to the dialect, literature and traditional culture of the North-East.

2. It would not, of course, any more than the standard English spelling which has existed for centuries prevented, say, Tennyson, Hardy or Kipling from writing in representations of non-standard dialects. At the time of writing a computer spellcheck for Scots, using a spelling system which has been devised after well-informed, prolonged and often heated debate, has just been produced: a development which should materially enhance the status of the language as well as encouraging more attempts at writing it.

an interesting new departure – Gaelic, the medium of a few short and simple, but highly charged, poems with Doric versions.[1] The title poem, in a metre wittily reminiscent of Kipling, recalls the stirring of her childhood imagination by Oriental nick-nacks brought home by relatives:

> Mither's Uncle Dougie, an faither's Cousin John
> O Aiberdeenshire fairmin stock, war eident an won on;
> Twa sahibs brocht up on sowens, cheengin kail for vindaloo,
> Spikkin Hindi melled wi Doric on the roads frae Katmandu ...

The vigour of the Scots vocabulary is exploited as skilfuly as ever, perhaps the best example being the poem *Wanted*:

> Soo-moued, ringle-eed Jock McBride
> Is socht bi polismen far an wide
> An identikit o his coorse physog
> 'S been sent frae Turra tae Auchenshog.
> His teeth are nesty's a nettle's nip
> His pow is huddry's a scaffy's skip
> His neb is brukken (a caber bowed)
> His lugs are thirled tae the clink o gowd.

The significance of Sheena Blackhall is not merely that she writes in an unmixed and uncompromising North-Eastern dialect. It is that she provides a conclusive refutation of any suggestion that a strongly local language, intimately associated with a highly distinctive material culture and embodying a long-standing literary tradition in which that culture is depicted in every detail, is necessarily unable to emancipate itself from its local origins. Her Doric poetry ranges widely in its subject matter, and her flights of sensual imagination and philosophical speculation demonstrate clearly that the North-Eastern dialect is (despite what its own speakers appear to pride themselves on believing) by no means as earthbound as has often been assumed.

There is a certain amount of irony in the fact that while controversy has always attended Scottish poets' use of Scots to proclaim the distinctiveness of their cultural identity from that of the rest of the United

1. GKB Enterprises, Aberdeen, 1995. Other collections are *Hame-drauchtit* (Rainbow Books, Aberdeen, 1987), *The Nor'East Neuk* (Charles Murray Memorial Trust, Aberdeen, 1989), *Fite Doo Black Crow* (Keith Murray Publications, Aberdeen 1989), *A Toosht o Whigmaleeries, Back o Bennachie, Druids, Drauchts, Drochles, A Kenspeckle Creel* (all from Hammerfield Publishing, Aberdeen: 1991, 1993, 1994 and 1995).

Kingdom, the poets of the North-East are unequivocal, and have the enthusiastic support of their public, in using their unique dialect to proclaim their distinctiveness from the rest of Scotland. [1] However, it is a matter for pride, and most certainly not for regret, that in a region of Scotland with a distinctive social history and a well-preserved local folk-speech the resulting sense of communal identity should be so proudly and determinedly maintained. North-East Doric is a form of Scots; and in its flourishing state as a poetic language we can recognise one of the most reliable sources of hope for the continuing life of the Scots tongue.

1. For discussion, see the present writer's "'Lallans' and 'Doric' in North-Eastern Scottish poetry", in *English World-Wide* 8:2, 1987, 215–34, and "The importance of local dialect in a regional literary tradition: Ayrshire and Aberdeenshire compared", in *Literature of Region and Nation* 1:2, 1988, 1–16.

13
The Next Generation:
Tom Hubbard, Harvey Holton, Kate Armstrong, Robert Crawford, W. N. Herbert, Alison Kermack

The Scots Renaissance is still in vigorous life. Collections by individual poets, general anthologies, literary magazines both regular and ephemeral, and occasional poems in newspapers testify to the fact that Scots as a language for modern experimental poetry is flourishing to a degree and an extent little short of amazing. (And, though this is not the concern of the present study, the field of poetry in Scots is only a section of a splendidly vital and energetic national literary scene comprising fiction and drama as well as poetry, to which English and Gaelic make equally interesting contributions.) An adequate discussion of the range and variety among the forms of Scots currently being used by younger poets would require a book in itself. The present chapter will not attempt this, but will examine the practices of half-a-dozen individual poets, chosen not necessarily because they are the best or most representative writers in the field, but because collectively they illustrate the astonishing variety of Scots as a poetic medium at the present day.

As an exemplar of what might be called the classical vein in Scots poetry, Tom Hubbard may be chosen: the keynote of his verse is a disciplined regularity, using traditional verse forms (the sonnet, ballad metre, rhyme royal, unrhymed iambic pentameter) and a Scots characterised by a rich vocabulary largely eschewing rare, archaic or idiosyncratic words, carefully constructed and balanced sentences, traditional figures of speech and ordered and logical sequences of thought. In accordance with the principles of the Renaissance, his vision (like his own experience: he has an impressive record of teaching and lecturing in many different countries) is cosmopolitan. Pompeii and Lidice, the

Danish composer Carl Nielsen and the South African freedom-fighter Simon Tubakwe, all provide inspiration for his poems; and titles such as *Raskolnikov*, *The Retour o Troilus* and *The Lane and Luveless Leddy Turandot* (the last a verse drama) demonstrate his wide-ranging literary inspiration.

The first of his *Sax Sonnets in Scots*,[1] his first published Scots poems, is visibly inspired by early Irish poetry. It is, in fact, an expansion and development of a song of creation assigned in Irish legend to the poet and judge Amairgen;[2] and Hubbard's title *The Makar* could be seen as referring to the vast magical powers wielded by poets in the ancient Celtic world – to which, of course, contemporary Scotland is linked by direct descent. From the powerful verbs in the first two lines –

> I am the win that *blousters* owre the sea,
> I am the swaw that *reenges* deep and far ...

– the vocabulary maintains a consistent register: the picturesque and evocative imagery is conveyed in words which, though not necessarily in common spoken use, are sufficiently familiar from earlier poetry to be immediately clear to a reader with any degree of experience. Vowel harmony and alliteration are present throughout; unobtrusively so except in the line "I am o grugous gyres the gurliest", where clearly the excessive emphasis on [g] is designed to emphasise the grotesque quality of the image. In contrast to the exotic beauty of this poem, the next in the series, *In a Kirkcaldy Warkin-Cless Airt* – *1962:1987*, uses plain and prosaic Scots words to evoke a harsh and dreary life: "... the scuil, the store, the clerty grun ..." – " ye wad howk / This roch an rowthie syle ..."; and the social barriers resulting from the contrasting speech of the working and the professional classes are mocked in the reductive language of "Yon buik-leired doctor goavin lik a gowk". The quiet and meditative tone of *Schellbronn* is conveyed by a dearth of noteworthy or distinctively Scots vocabulary items and the careful strategic placing of the few particularly emotive ones: *gloamin* forming a one-word sentence to open the poem, and *braisentlie* (a word from Hubbard's native Fife) in a vivid evocation of the colours of the darkening sky. (A couple of details in this

1. This and the other poems by Hubbard discussed here are in *Four Fife Poets: Fower Brigs ti a Kinrik*, Aberdeen University Press 1988, pp.93–125.

2. For a translation and discussion of the song, see *Celtic Heritage*, eds. Alwyn Rees and Brinley Rees, London (Thames and Hudson) 1961, pp. 98ff.

poem suggest that Hubbard's literary Scots is not quite a mother-tongue: *ane muivement* should, by Scots grammar, be *ae muivement*; and *dawn* rhymes with *gone* in Scottish-accented English but not in Fife Scots.)

Other poems by Hubbard show the same thoughtful choice of words: whether evoking a comical image:

> A wifie shoogles ti her yett, in bauchles.
> She disna rich'lie ken whaur she's gaun:
> The left bauchle's on the richt fuit,
> The richt bauchle's on the left fuit.
>
> (*Impressions du Matin*),

a violent one:

> There wis an awesome bouff,
> An inklin that the ruif wad faa, an yit
> It cam fae faur ablow: a crack, a cleavin,
> An a blaelik vapour gurgit ti the face ...
>
> (*The Daith o Simon Tubakwe*),

or a graceful and beautiful one:

> The rare Cresseid; she, whase flichterin hairt
> Felt delicate as ony timorsome mavie
> That liltit owre oor heids; she, whase quick muivement
> In guidin me ti a neuk, wis sib ti the con
> Wha derts athort the pad, then vainishes ...
>
> (*The Retour o Troilus*),

his sensory impressions are precisely observed, and the Scots vocabulary by which he conveys them is invariably appropriate and thoughtfully selected. *Pompeii*, a poem in nine rhyme-royal stanzas, shows the logical progression of argument which is another of his hallmarks: the opening line, "The leevin enter at the lang-deid yett", establishes a keynote of the poem, the interaction of present and past, life and death; and the sequence of thought, from the stillness of the ruined city with its once-flourishing life, the destructive force of the volcano now surpassed by that of modern weapons of war and the defiant symbol of enduring life in the mosaic of the faun "Dauncin as gin he were alive. Dance on!", is elegantly arranged and presented. Verbal repetition and balancing parallel phrases emphasise the imagined closeness of Pompeii to contemporary life: "This is a day unlike thon weirdit day. / Sic chiels as us, *we* ..." in stanza 3; "This is a day maist like thon weirdit day. / Sic chiels as us,

they . . ." in stanza 4; and the same purpose is served by the homely familiarity of the Scots words used of the vanished life of the city: ". . . they
tuik their dauner here, / Blethered, slockened a drouth . . .". The gentle,
quasi-Arcadian imagery of the lovers of the ancient time, "Their sang
taen up by foontains an by burds", is effectively shattered by the line on
the volcano which concludes the stanza: "Spewed furth the horrors o a
crimson hell" – though it is observable that Hubbard does not attempt
to find Scots words here, nor in the clever punchline at the corresponding
point of the next stanza, "The past's disaster is the future's crime."

Occasionally an ominous hint appears of an English underlay to
Hubbard's Scots: "at schuil" is not a Scots usage (it should be "at the
schuil"); and "they hae aareadies peyed / Their tickets" is uncomfortably
suggestive of a literal translation. *Nocht* for "not" in the fifth stanza is not
only an archaism, tolerable in a poem written entirely in quasi-archaic
language but not otherwise, but, unusually, a mistake: "Sall we traverse
thir doolie strachts, an *nocht* depairt [. . .] *un*cheenged?" is not the question he wishes to ask. Notwithstanding such occasional lapses, however,
Hubbard's medium in this poem and others is for the most part a careful
and consistent Scots, with a vocabulary judiciously combining familiar
common-core words, words with an old-fashioned and poetic ring (*The
Retour o Troilus* has *cauldrife* "cold", *cryne* "wither", *drow* "drizzle", *leman*
"beloved", *mishanter* "misfortune", *steidit* "founded", *timorsome* "fear-
ful", *umwhile* "former", *vieve* "lively"), and an occasional word from Fife.

By no stretch of the imagination could Hubbard be described as a poet
of passion. In *Speerit o the Leid* he uses the novel metaphor of a South
American Indian drink brewed from roots, for which the fermentation
is begun by spitting the chewed fibres into a jar, to illustrate his vision
of Scots as a language for

> . . . a synthesis
> o conscious an unconscious sel,
> o heichs an deeps, o facks an dreams,

but his Scots, despite its virtues, is not intoxicating. The melancholy ret-
rospections of his Troilus, though beautifully expressed –

> Whaur nou it's daurk, then glintit my leman's een,
> Whaur nou it's foustie, then fufft her body's scent,
> Whaur nou hing cobwabs, she cleikit me in her hair . . .

– are as far from the erotic dynamite of *Under the Eildon Tree* as his gentle-manly criticism of Cooncillor Swalgut in *Impressions du Matin*:

> A bing o flesh, he leers at a bing o siller,
> Glint o his ee cleiks at the glint o coin . . .

is from the incendiary radicalism of *At the Shrine o the Unkent Sodger*. Nonetheless, his disciplined and methodical poetry has its own merits; and indeed could be seen as a demonstration of a renewed self-sufficiency in the language, in that an almost neutral register of Scots can now be seen as capable of supporting a poetry of ambitious themes.

In strong contrast to the lucidity of Hubbard's language and style is the dense, highly imaginative and often obscure poetry of Harvey Holton, a Borderer by birth but now resident in Fife. Like Hubbard, Holton favours strictly-organised and traditional verse forms: a particularly intriguing and elaborate example is his sequence *In the Silent Licht o the Bluid*,[1] a cycle of twelve poems each of twelve lines, the second six in each verse rhyming with the first six but in reverse order, the last line of each being a repetition, often slightly varied, of the first and the last poem being a repetition of the first in its entirety, and the successive lines of the first poem being used in turn as the opening and closing lines of each poem in the series. To a much greater extent than Hubbard, however, he uses words not only as units in the exposition of a sequence of thought but for their phonaesthetic and sensory power as individual elements: his poetry is far more "modern" in that logical development is replaced by imaginative association. (The intense and disturbing combination of mystical vision and strongly physical imagery to evoke the vitality and the ruthlessness of the natural world in *In the Silent Licht o the Bluid* is more than slightly reminiscent of Dylan Thomas.)

Holton's poem-sequence *Finn*,[2] as its title at once shows, is a treatment of a figure from ancient Gaelic lore; and the association of the Celtic past with the contemporary cultural scene is emphasised by his use of titles which recall Yeats in *The Wind Among the Reeds*: *Finn Names the Beginnins an Thinks oan the Hunt* – *The Weather Braks an Hard Storms Come In* – *Finn Daurs the Weather an Sets tae Speir the Baist*. The poems

1. Ibid., pp. 73-8. Except *Finn*, Holton's poems cited here are all in this book.
2. In *The New Makars: the Mercat Anthology of Contemporary Poetry in Scots*, ed. Tom Hubbard, Edinburgh (Mercat Press) 1991, pp.131–5.

combine, to impressive effect, the rhythmic and grammatical patterns characteristic of Old English poetry with a powerful sense of intimacy between man and nature recalling Gaelic poetry of all periods. The metre of the opening is a free and flexible version of the four-beat alliterative line:

> Owre oceans o blossoman sea-bree oor brocht,
> Frae fire i the dawan tae the makan o mairches
> An the castan o cauldrons at binds us baith;

giving place in later sections to a highly compressed version of the same pattern, the four stresses being distributed among sometimes as few as five syllables:

> Owre broken bracken peeld pads
> craiklan quick; owre mairch muir
> taiglan tongue licht laps
> derk dubs ...

The densely-packed syntax and forceful rhythm of those sections convey a sense of abounding vigour. Realistic nature imagery ("owre bens o broon bracken ... amang weit allers an blawn leaves o birk...") collocates with words suggestive of physical effort and exertion (*pech, hechle, schauchle, craichle*); and in the "storm" section the force of the Scots vocabulary is deployed with skill and boldness:

> ... joukan jaggit breikan blasts.
> aingert airts breingean brak
> strikan sair the guid-like grund
> whiles whummelt oo wanner
> torn an trackless in gapean guillies
> o derknan an dreid.

Oo, used consistently for "we" in this sequence, is the only feature which reveals the language to be that of a Borderer; but it does so unmistakably.

In *Finn*, notwithstanding the grammatical compression and lexical density, the sequence of thought and the account of the narrated events is generally straightforward. This is far from true of *In the Silent Licht o the Bluid*, where ideas and images merge in strange and unpredictable sequences. The title, which is also the opening line, sets the tone by its odd and puzzling collocations, and such commingled impressions occur throughout, juxtaposed with images of intense clarity (*the Helm wunds whistle in up street an closey, the neb that twitches roond wuid an wheel rut, cauld crystals in the lift*). The dominant semantic fields of the sequence are living creatures, divided into predators (*hoolet, brock, tod*), victims (*doo, pheasant, geese*) and furtive, skulking things (*mowdie, worm*); organs (*bluid, neb, hert, harns, gut*); physical actions, especially involuntary ones (*flauchter, shak, twitchin an shiftin, shiver*); and above all visual and auditory impressions, either of intense sensations (*crammasy, scraich*) or of negative ones (*silent, quaitlike, blind, cauld*). *Derk* and *derkness* occur again and again, often with powerful and unexpected qualifiers (*orange derkness, clear derkness, saft derkness*). Phrases suggesting cosmic immensity (*the unkent airts o space an time, the tirn o the yird in the universe*) contrast with the small-scale, precisely-focused images.

The circular structure of the poem-sequence underlines its theme: the cycle of life and death, and of the life of organisms renewing itself by the death of others. The poems make free and fluent use of Scots words and Scots grammar, yet the imaginative force with which the theme is presented, which is potent by any standards, is not dependent on this fact. There are a number of Scots words which convey the physical or emotional force of an event more powerfully than any English word could (*gralloch, dwam, fuff, breinge, blinter*); but many of the Scots words – most of those listed in the previous paragraph, for instance – carry no special connotations. Furthermore, Holton freely incorporates words which are not Scots in the exclusive sense (*chronology, spectrum, navigator, quadrant*) and belong to a fairly specialised and scientific register: a mark of confidence, perhaps, in the maturity of his medium, which is now capable of simply adopting such words when appropriate rather than ostentatiously unearthing or constructing substitutes from the exclusive vocabulary of Scots.

Holton's Scots is a fully contemporary literary language, fit for poetic expression in a thoroughly modern idiom. His method varies: sparse, dignified tones with an unexpected reminiscence of an earlier age appear in his elegies to his grandfather and father-in-law:

> You whase grave lies bi poortith unmarkit,
> Progenitor o ma ee an verse,
> Allow me noo tae sing yer praises.
>   (*For the Grandfaither: Samuel MacDiarmid Young*).

And at the other extreme, in *Caledonian Pines* a dense embroidery of alliteration and internal rhymes accompanies a sequence of violent, commingled and disturbing images –

> Gien the wanderan drift o the thristles shift,
> The forfochen mainer o the bleck knifies favour,
> It's thrapples A'll slit an bluid A'll savour
> Tae be a retainer o the bardies guid gift

– to convey the defiant impression of the tormented but enduring trees:
"For ma kintra's pine sties fast whaur it wiz born." The Caledonian pine
here becomes a symbol with something approaching, if not reaching, the
power of MacDiarmid's teuch sauchs; and the broken, irregular rhythms
and unrefined force of the Scots sound-patterns form an integral part of
the effect.

A poet whose experimental approach to Scots inheres not in the use of
modernist techniques of thought and expression but in the delicate yet
venturesome use of rare and striking words is Kate Armstrong, the oldest
poet discussed in this chapter. Her experience of living and working in
various parts of Scotland is said to be the explanation for the appearance
of local words from widely separated areas of the country.[1] Be that as it
may, the device is applied in her poetry with a high degree of skill and
tact. The poem *Mary* provides an excellent illustration of this aspect of
her method. The words in the first verse could mostly be described as
common-core Scots. Though in no way recondite or obscure, they are
carefully selected: the opening phrase,

> The hoose door *shoogles*. She's iled it fer the *skirl*
> O the *girnin* hinge.

introduces three useful, expressive and still popular words, frequently
encountered in all dialects of Scots; and the hint of personification in
the latter is consistent with a noteworthy use throughout the poem of
words, particularly verbs, which suggest a life in inanimate objects: "the
wind *sings* tae the gress that *catches* the yett's *fingers*", "music sheets *scouk*
in the press", "the stour *hauds its braith.*" Only *howder* "move with a roll-
ing, uneven gait," which is found mostly in North-Eastern dialects, gives
any kind of regional flavour to the first verse; and the context ("she how-

---

1. In the biographical note in *The New Makars, op.cit.*, p.190.

ders wi a sey tae the wal"), combined with the phonaesthetic impression of the word, would make its meaning clear to any reader who had not encountered it. The first line of the second verse, however –

Orra sma fittie baists *fimmer* and *flirr*

– at once requires of the reader a response to the sound rather than the meaning of the words: *fimmer* has only one attestation in the *SND*,[1] its definition being "To move the feet swiftly but gracefully, to trip along in dancing or walking"; and *flirr* in the sense of "to stir, ruffle, fly out in a passion" only two, both from the North-East. Rare though they are, however, as onomatopes suggesting the movement of scuttling insects they are admirably precise. Similar instances occur in this poem where Kate Armstrong has used a word which, in isolation, would be unknown to many readers because of its restricted geographical distribution or infrequent use in literature, but used it in a context which not only reveals its meaning but demonstrates its phonaesthetic force with startling efficiency: "*Hornshottle* croftland" (a rarely-attested word from the Clyde area, defined in the *SND* as "in disorder or confusion" but conveying a strong visual impression of rugged, stony ground), "Whaups *cown*" ("weep, lament", a Gaelic-derived word from Northern dialects, not only *sounding* like a cry but, in a two-word sentence with *whaups* as its subject, having hardly any other conjectural meaning available to it).

Other poems show the same intriguing and delightful use of rare words in contexts which make it easy to deduce their meaning. "A *pleep* lets faa its cry in the mirk" (*Nicht*): that this is some kind of bird is obvious even to those for whom it is not their normal name for an oyster-catcher; "Thon *frimple-frample* watter ... is cried the River Tay" (*This is the Laund*): this is one of the Scots tongue's characteristic phonaesthemes, suggesting confused violence but also, in this context, perhaps evoking the visual image of the broken, swirling surface of a swiftly-flowing river.

In some of her other poems, Kate Armstrong (in the manner of Robert Garioch or Tom Leonard) examines the implications of using Scots as a language. *A Modern Use of English*, with its aggressively colloquial vocabu-

1. John MacTaggart's *The Scottish Gallovidian Encyclopedia* of 1824, a classic work on local language and culture. The word is also used, however, by Soutar.

lary and expression ("ye daft auld hizzy", "nae longer any bluidy guid, ken, teacher", "An Ah'm dead right") and clever puns ("Stremely's got an ex, sae ye ken it's frae the past") at first suggests merely a stubborn schoolchild's dogged refusal to learn anything at all; but "the ward ye need is dead, or maybe deid" hints at a defiant preference for the Scots form; and in the line "Absolutely, ken ma roots, away from the solutely" the word *roots* may suggest not only Latin roots but the roots of the folk culture, which include the native language. The final section, entirely in English, in which the voice changes to that of the teacher (thus retrospectively identifying the foregoing stanzas as a prepared classroom recitation) summarises the complacent insensitivity typically manifest among members of the teaching profession when confronted with the claims of their charges' native Scots. *Fer Martin Luther, William Lorimer and Jock Tamson*, a response to the publication of Lorimer's *New Testament in Scots* in 1983,[1] suggests an analogy between the pre-Reformation Church's insistence on Latin with that of modern educational authority on "speakin braw" and associates Luther's call for the availability of Scriptural texts in vernacular languages with Lorimer's magnificent translation – albeit the latter appeared four centuries too late to save Scots as a national language. The medium of this poem is neither the vernacular of *A Modern Use of English* nor the essentially traditional Scots of *Mary*, but an ironic combination of both, elliptic and somewhat elusive, exemplified by a line like "An whit was he cried? Ah mindna ava" in which the first half is accurately colloquial and the second (except for the spelling *Ah*) old-fashioned and literary. *Graffito*, of which the author writes, "I see the creators of graffiti as energetic, creative and literate in a subversive way",[2] demonstrates this anti-traditional and iconoclastic approach to language, parodying the voguish use of "Scot-" as a prefix with an irreverent list "Scotfegs, Scotherbs, Scoterse, Scotbog, Scotfag ..." and presenting the spraying of incomprehensible words (*Hentool, Tongsyabas*) on walls as a gesture of rebellion against "a coat o manky pebbledash" on "oor auld leid" – this "coat o manky pebbledash" is surely the English language; though the suggestion that resistance to it is effectively

---

1. See Kate Armstrong's note to the poem in *The New Makars, op. cit.*, pp.186 – 7.
2. *Ibid.*

expressed by graffiti is, one hopes, simply a poetic fantasy. Kate Armstrong's versatile and imaginative choice of topics is matched by an adventurous approach to the Scots tongue; and though her corpus is, so far at least, not extensive in scale, she is certainly a highly individual and attractive presence on the contemporary Scots poetic scene.

A much more violently iconoclastic use of Scots characterises the work of Robert Crawford. His contributions to *Sterts & Stobies*,[1] a joint production with W. N. Herbert, are notable for a discordant mélange of words from different dialects, sociolects and registers, and a cheerfully insolent use of vulgar and obscene words and expressions. *Cock o' the North*, the opening poem in the sequence, swipes at a vanishing type of negative-thinking Scot ("Big cocked-up Wallace, quit noo cryin / Yir monumental 'Naw!'") with a virulence that, in all honesty, had long ceased to be called for by 1985. His target is a superficial Scottishness based on outdated icons which has often passed as a compensation for a lack of active commitment to Scottish independence; and this is lambasted, cleverly if not very subtly, in a grotesque simile:

> – lik sheep's-heid broath
> A' spilt an fozie oan a tartan cloath
> O' chak-heid Scots!

Rude insults ("tae wet yir dreams" – "maister-baitin" – "caught in yir Y-fronts") and a Leonard-like use of spellings suggestive of low-prestige pronunciations (*Scoatlan* and other representations of the [o]: *poatit*, *broath*, etc.; *git*, *ya* for "you") contribute to the intended effect of shocking, or at least startling, the reader. (His insistence on the spelling *oo* in words like *noo*, instead of the *ou* preferred on valid historical grounds by most serious poets since the 1940s, may be an iconoclastic swipe in another direction, as if suggesting that the theories of historians are as irrelevant to the new Scotland as the fantasies of image-builders.) The technique is hardly sophisticated, but in this poem at least Crawford's somewhat callow vulgarity is balanced by an abrasive vigour and energy which raise it above the level of pub flyting. In the next poem in the collection, *Ghetto-Blastir*, similarly crass abusive language is combined with a smart and entertaining fluency in rhyme:

1. In *Sharawaggi*, Robert Crawford and W. N. Herbert, Edinburgh (Polygon) 1990, pp.11–24.

Wee naethins aye feathrin yir ain nests
O douce semis! Yir psychadelic tartan's
Shite tae oor white nichts an aw the guests
Oor laughtir's aftir. Sook yir fozie cartons
O guttir music; mak the Muse seik uttir-
lie wi yir gabbin, stabbin, sabbin
Ochones. Gang tae the Gents' an muttir.
Ladies tae! Bicoz we're grabbin ...

and in *Eftir the Vampires*, disagreeable images are reinforced with onomatopoeic lines:

That squaached wi a mumpy soon o fartin chaff ...

and words with double or multiple meanings (*mixt* "confused, disor-
dered, pale from illness"; *mumpy* "whisper-like, *but also* like chewing
without teeth"; *chaff* "chaff, but also rage, ill-humour, *also associated both
with loquacious talk and chewing*"; *jawin* "chattering, vituperating, pouring
out liquid" – the first two senses given for this word suggest English
slang rather than Scots dialect). *Miami/Siam* opens with an appalling
word-play: the emotive word *aivery* "eager, yearning" hardly needed
the concoction "Aye everywhaur [as inauthentic a form as ever appeared
in print] and averywhaur ..." to cast it into relief: and proceeds through
a mélange of clever sound effects (*dunnerin Ardnamurchan*), expressive
words (*oachenin* "night just before daybreak", *wheebertin* "whistling" –
not to mention *yowdendrift*!) and potent references ("... elefunts ower
yon lintwhite Alps" – "the airmies o heiven liltin 'Glore tae God'") to
an incomprehensible punchline; and in *Zickerty* the attempt to convey a
cosmic vision –

Skeigh abune the lift
Wi planets fur yir step-stanes...

– by means of a dense concentration of rare Scots words suggests a parody of early MacDiarmid: surely as retrograde a step as it was possible to
take in 1985. There is, of course, no argument against linguistic experimentation; and Crawford in unearthing *zickerty* (a children's counting-
out game), *nyabock* ("small, talkative person") or *saughran* ("lifeless, inac-
tive, sauntering" according to Jamieson; to which Crawford adds "taking
good care of oneself"), devising *nizzlin* ("direct exposure to a severe
storm") from – presumably – *nizzer*, a head-on storm, or to all appear-

ances concocting *scattermouch* ("an ill-conditioned rascal") is showing the kind and degree of creative imagination that in his predecessors and models often led to splendid poetic effects. On the debit side, the mixing of registers is notably discordant ("yir laverock's wing taks aff / An ups thro blinterin lippers o haur..."), the rhyming inexpert (*heivin* rhyming obtrusively with *leavin*, the conjunctive adverb *whaur* as a rhyme word), and a reader confronted with

> ... Sterns' scarrow lats yir gift
> Mak aureate nae scattermouch,
> But kythes the ewetrack oan ...

is entitled to respond – whit the deil's he bletherin about?

The poetic development of Sydney Goodsir Smith, as shown in a previous chapter, demonstrates very clearly that a young and enthusiastic poet whose early experiments with Scots produce chaotic results may proceed to the heights of poetic success; and there is no predicting what Crawford will achieve in the future. His fascination for playing with language is manifest, and his politically committed outlook is a powerful motivation for further poetic experiments (a pervasive theme in *Sterts & Stobies* is the sweeping away of the present effete Scotland by "yon new Scoatlan loupin tae yir street," though the nature of the "new Scoatlan" is not made clear; and one poem, *Semiconductors*, encapsulates a vision of a brilliant resurrection of Scotland by "a mirligoes o laser thro the livin leid"). In more recent writings he has continued to employ a lexically dense Scots in which rare and recondite words, and words used with idiosyncratic developments of or departures from their attested meaning, jostle with words familiar from a colloquial or vulgar register to give an effect at once invigorating and disconcerting. A trick unique to him of printing some poems with facing-page English prose translations (after the manner of many contemporary Gaelic poets) has complex implications. On the most obvious level, it underwrites the status of Scots and English as mutually foreign languages: for monolingual Anglophones, the suggestion is, even a glossary would not give access to a full understanding of Crawford's poetry. It also has the more unexpected effect of undercutting English as a medium for imaginative literary expression.

> Ah glaum lik a clood amang Munros, turnin the dwang
> O Scoatlan: gramlochness, thrawnness, granate plotcocks, savin-trees

Ar jist scaffie tae Goad, but it's noo we need
Yon pronyeand scuddin-stanes tae shak us free
An hair-butter a naishun. 'Proochie, baist, proochie!'
Ah'd scraich tae thi future – an nae tae a moartcloath
Fur haigs an snibbed haingles tae mak tairensie ower –

(The Herr-Knit Bunnet)

I grope in the dark like a cloud among high mountains, attempting the trial
of strength in trying to raise the heavy caber of Scotland: utter worldliness,
stubbornness, ingrained devils, abortionists' plants that kill the foetus in the
womb are just severe passing showers as far as God is concerned, but it's
now we need those piercing stones skimming the surface of the water to
shake us free and cleanse a nation of impurities. 'Approach, beast,
approach!' I'd cry out to the future – and not to a coffin-drape for tale-tell-
ing women and gelded louts to make evil fury over –

The Scots version is obscure by any standards: Crawford has clearly been
dictionary-dredging with vigour. *Glaum*, *scuddin-stanes* and *haingle* are
rare words but with a variety of attestations; *proochie* too is genuine,
being a call to cattle; *tairensie* is a Shetland word; the description of the
trial of strength known as *turning the dwang* (a *dwang* is a heavy iron lever)
is in Jamieson, and so too, uniquely, is the definition of *gramlochness*; *sav-
ing-tree* and *scaffy showers* are the subject of entries in MacTaggart's *A
Scottish Gallovidian Encyclopedia*, the former including the phrase "it is
said to kill the foetus in the womb" and the latter "showers which soon
blow by; 'a bad *scaff* o' a shower,' a pretty severe shower". To *hair butter*
is to extract hairs and other foreign material from butter by drawing a
serrated knife through it, but there was, until this poem, no compound
verb *to hair-butter* meaning "to extract impurities"; and *pronyeand* is an
inappropriate translocation of a Middle Scots present participle, with the
original spelling, meaning "poignant". (In Jamieson, its entry is on the
page facing that of *pruchie*.) On the other hand, if this passage is compared
with the English version, the combination of over-inflated rhetoric and
flaccid sentence-construction of the latter reveals, ironically, the futility
of trying to express the same idea in English: the semantic conciseness
and rhythmic control achieved by the use of richly-loaded Scots words
is essential if the thought is to be expressed with any degree of force.
Crawford's action might be seen as a bold gamble: a naive or lazy reader,
finding the Scots incomprehensible and the English unattractive, might

simply turn away; but a reader who did *not* turn away but took the trouble to decipher the Scots words and expressions would certainly be intrigued: sufficiently so, perhaps, to investigate further the resources of the Scots tongue. Crawford has an established reputation as a contemporary avant-garde figure in Scots poetry (and also, incidentally, as a scholar and critic); and it is a safe bet that the development of his career will repay attention.

An equally adventurous and equally radical handling of Scots is illustrated by Crawford's collaborator in *Sterts & Stobies* and other projects, W. N. Herbert. Born in Dundee, Herbert enjoys the distinction of being one of the very few poets to make a point of basing his medium on the dialect of that city: its most obvious shibboleth is the monophthongisation of [ae] to [ɛ] (*Eh, dreh, plehwid, hurehzuns* (i.e. horizons) and so on); and some of the very obscure words in which his poetry abounds are claimed as emanating from Dundee and its environs. The poem *The Gairfish*[1] has as its title a word which is, according to Jamieson, "the name given, in the vicinity of Dundee, to the Porpoise"; though the only attestation for the word in either Jamieson or the *SND* is the quotation from the *Statistical Account of Scotland* of 1795 which Herbert uses as the epigraph to his poem. *Polly-shee* "a pulley attached to a pole, from which a rope runs to a window, for hanging clothes to dry" is also claimed by Herbert as "peculiar to Dundee"; though this can be true, at the most, of the pronunciation *polly*, since similar words with *pulley* are attested elsewhere. References to the *Courier*, Dundee's local newspaper, and to the city's "Jute lairds", serve rather more convincingly to locate the poem.

The vocabulary of *The Gairfish* is, in fact, more reminiscent of the classic reference works than of the contemporary spoken dialect of Dundee or any other Scottish city; though it must be acknowledged that Herbert has applied his creative imagination to the words as he has found them. Jamieson provides the only, or almost the only, attestation for several: for one, *screnoch* "shrill cry", the form as he gives it is idiosyncratic (*scronach* has several attestations from the North-East); another, *plumashe*, is

---

1. First published in *Sharawaggi, op.cit.*.

211

cited specifically as an oddity: "corruption of *plumage*, a plume of feathers". Some words are used more or less with Jamieson's definitions, though sometimes with modified spellings: *slyte* "move easily or smoothly", *sejoinit* (Herbert gives the unhelpful gloss "disjuncted", for Jamieson's "separate, disjoin"), *offskep* "utmost boundary of a landscape", *pricker* "basking shark", *omne-gatherum* "a miscellaneous collection", *daith-dive* "putrid matter issuing from the body's orifices after death", *smore thow* "heavy fall of snow that threatens to smother". In other cases, the poet has modified the definitions given by the lexicographer: Herbert's gloss for *glammach* "a snapped-up morsel" suggests a conflation of Jamieson's definition for the verb, "to grab or snatch", and for the noun, "a mouthful"; *doggerlone* "wreck" until this poem was not attested outwith the phrase *gone to doggerlone* "gone to ruin"; his definition of *ogertfou* as "drunk with a sense of one's own good taste" is a decided elaboration (suggested by the last syllable?) of Jamieson's "affecting delicacy of taste"; *doister* is in Jamieson a noun meaning "a storm from the sea", in Herbert a verb meaning "thunder". Other words likewise suggest, from their rarity, an origin in specific reference works: *crancrum* "something difficult to understand" is in Watson, *dallow* "delve" in MacTaggart, *gleesh* "burn with a strong, clear flame" in Gregor. Besides these historical sources, Herbert has drawn on contemporary colloquial speech for *doss* "snooze", on what may be a local Dundee usage (it is unknown to the dictionaries) for *tabnabs* "teathings", and – for whatever reason – on an old-fashioned *American* dialect usage for *nary a . . .* "never a... ". Totally perverse mis-spellings such as *orran* for "or an" and *inna* for "in a", plain errors such as *onywan* and *ivrywhaur*, *foond* for the past tense of *find* (recte *fan(d)* or *fun(d)*) and *Giaconda* ("yir Giaconda's snicker"), and – a mannerism of which he avails himself again in later poetry – invented compounds such as *seeminsolid* and *waukindreme* complete the very peculiar mixture which is Herbert's medium in this poem.

In *The Gairfish*, Herbert has taken a late eighteenth-century quotation and used it as a peg on which to hang a witty and entertaining flight of poetic fancy, drawing on the biology and mythology of the dolphin and culminating in a vigorous battle-cry, uttered in the mame of radical Scottish poetry, against

... meenistirs & meenistirs' wives, auld leddies ivrywhaur,
Jutelairds' ghaists & thi faceliss face
that 'rins' wir deean facktries ...

The question which it invites, however, is whether the mixture of ingenuity and perversity – a fairly extreme degree of both – which characterises his language adds to the force of his message, or forms a distraction from it.

Fanciful use of obscure words marks Herbert's poetry to an even greater extent than Crawford's. Sometimes, as with MacDiarmid in *Sangschaw*, a poem appears to be devised as a showcase for one or a number of interesting words; though as the thought or image is not always of MacDiarmid-like clarity and potency the result is not always an unqualified success:

Yince auld mither Lirklips
Hoolocht owre thi land
Inna cauld sea's grouse an grue,
An doon thi sealblack deeps,
    Thi weelthrainit steps;

Nae camera cud recaa
Hoo dumbfounert aa 'ur weans
Did stare aboot lyk hotties, then,
Did thirsty raise
    A renaissance o sang!
                    (*The Renaissance of Song*)

Hoolocht, glossed by Herbert as "rolled like a rockslide", is a re-casting as a verb of a word which appears as a noun (meaning the roaring noise of a rock slide or avalanche) in MacTaggart's *Scottish Gallovidian Encyclopedia* and almost noplace else; *hotties* "those who have some message pinned to their backs of which they are unaware" is, seemingly, a term unique to Edinburgh High School, attested by Jamieson; *weelthrainit* "worn by constant use, like a familiar tune" is a clever conflation of two attested meanings of the word *thrain*, a rare Scots form of *threne*, lament: "a sad refrain, dirge, lamentation" and "to harp constantly on a theme". To that extent, the poem shows commendable linguistic ingenuity and can be expected to appeal to readers with an interst in rare Scots words and the opportunities they afford to creative writers. On the other hand, who is "auld mither Lirklips" (the meaning of her name presents no difficulty: *lirk* is a straightforward Scots word for "wrinkle"), what is the sea into which she descends, how does her action inspire a "renaissance o sang", why should a *camera* have any relevance? In *On the Cold Lido*, the first word *gaubertie-shells* "a hobgoblin supposed to combine loud roaring with barking like little dogs, and the sound of shells striking against each other" is a remarkable curiosity, and *ghaist-coal* "a piece of coal that burns white, retaining its shape" a very attractive expression; but a reader's predictable reaction is surely interest in the individual words rather than an imaginative response to the somewhat banal conceit which they mask rather than illuminate. *Scargivnet* "scrawny teenager", *cothaman* "surfeit", *gamphirt* "bespangled", *doggindales* "clouds of mist clinging to hillsides", *instoichert* "overpoweringly brought home" are among the other words with which Herbert treads the bounds of authenticity; and with *imparmiginaishun* "that aspect of the intellect which finds pleasure in the baroque or manneristic" or *huggurmagrilliund* "hunched up like a fat old woman" the responses of poetic appreciation and linguistic analysis must finally part company.

Elsewhere, Herbert's linguistic experiments lead to much more convincing results. In *2nd Doldrum (Elephants Graveyard)*, the syntactic oddity of *whaur doon yir pendies lurks it?*, together with the emotive force of *lurks* (which stands out by *not* being a Scots word) give a disturbing quality to the opening lines, vivid pictorial imagery and metaphors like *weldit tae wheelbarra ... soldert tae toil*, *deid buriit jaabanes o yir weans' hopes* effectively evoke a harsh, brutal, demoralising quality of life, and the quasi-Joycean compounds such as *eldscoorit*, *timedustchoakit*, *deidtrootdreh* ("dry as a dead trout") are evocative as well as ingenious. The reference to MacGonagall is potent: the somewhat perverse pride which Dundee's citizens still take in their eccentric townsman is here turned back on them with grim irony. And when Herbert abandons, or at least reduces, his dependence on obscure words and writes in an urban demotic enriched simply by his own learning and imagination instead of by the hidden treasures of Jamieson or MacTaggart, as in *Sink the Discovery!* or *Monsters from the Id*, he can produce contemporary Scots poetry of vigour, passion and commitment. In such poems his own statement, "In Scots I pretend that my basic speech – Dundonian – hasn't been atrophied by cultural neglect, and still has access to the broad vocabulary of the Scots dictionary",[1] emerges as a credible claim.

Finally, experimental writing of a very different kind is found in the work of Alison Kermack of Edinburgh, a younger poet who has developed Leonard's technique of quasi-phonetic spelling to produce an even more idiosyncratic medium than his, and applied it in less circumscribed fields than Mulrine. In a short note on her work, Kermack writes[2]: "Ah get loadzy ideaz fur poyumz jist by lisnin tay foak in barz an caffyz an that. foak ur olwaze sane reelly amayzin poetic stuff, ixpressin reelly hyooj complex ideaz inna singul sentins, jist in thi coarsy a convursay-shin. itz brillyint thi hole langwij thing". (This is the language of the entire note, as well as of her poetry.) This spelling system (if "system" is the appropriate word) is applied with unswerving consistency: scarcely a word in her writings has the conventional spelling; yet virtually her entire vocabulary is that of standard English. The poem *The Shadow Minister* illustrates her method:

> by meenzy a contrapshun
> like a perryscoap
> wi a tellyscoap
> attachd tay it
> while cashully stroalin
> aloang downin street
> ah chansd tay look
> in thi uppur windy
> i nummer ten
> ah seen thi pee em
> sittin inna big arrum chare
> in frunty a big coal fyur
> hoaldin a mappy scoatlin
> oan thi endy a toast foark
> funny thing wiz
> thoah kidny see it say cleerly
> kizzit happind tay faw
> oan thi oappisit waw
> thi shaddy i thi pee em

1. In *Dream State*, ed. Daniel O'Rourke, Edinburgh (Polygon) 1994, p. 144.
2. In *Dream State*, op. cit., p. 192.

    wiz dane igzackly
    thi same thing[1]

Say, tay, faw and *waw* clearly represent familiar Scots pronunciations;
dane for the present participle of *dae* is understandable; the reduction of
of to [e] (*meenzy, frunty*) is frequently heard in urban demotic; the raising
of short [ɔ] to [o] (*aloang, scoatlin*), the breaking of *fire* to something for
which *fyur* is a perfectly accurate spelling and the development of a prominent epenthetic vowel in *arm*, giving *arrum*, are conspicuous features of
most accents of the Central Belt conurbations. Those are among the few
cases where a non-standard spelling actually represents a definite dialectal
pronunciation: other orthographic idiosyncracies (*cleerly, happind,
igzackly*) are nothing more than mis-spellings, suggesting no pronunciation other than that of Scottish Standard English. (Kermack's mis-spellings are themselves, sometimes, so perverse as to be entertaining:
yoonyin, pollytishuns, conjuggles.) Grammatically, *ah seen* is clearly non-
standard; but though characteristic of Edinburgh and Glasgow demotic,
it is equally characteristic of several urban dialects in Scotland and elsewhere in the English-speaking world. And distinctive Scots vocabulary
items, whether associated with the traditional vocabulary or contemporary urban argot, are non-existent: even a search throughout her published work would reveal little more than an occasional *skeem*
("scheme", i.e. municipal housing estate) or *pish* (Scots form of "piss").
That is, if one looks for any of the traditional shibboleths of literary Scots
in the language of Alison Kermack's poetry, they are not to be found. On
the other hand, whereas the political orientation of Leonard's poetry is
socialist rather than nationalist, and Mulrine on his own showing selected
Glaswegian rather than literary Scots precisely to avoid the nationalist
overtones of the latter,[2] Kermack is unequivocally concerned to raise,
albeit by cryptic and caricaturing images, questions regarding the political
state of Scotland. *The Shadow Minister* uses a novel and startling imaginative conceit to encapsulate a disgraceful but unmistakable truth about the
attitude to Scottish affairs among London politicians; *Patriotic Pish* provides the ultimate ridicule of the "yoonyin jack" English jingoism of the

---

1. *Ibid.*, p. 193.
2. "Politically it [Lallans] is hung over with nationalism ...", "Poetry in Glasgow Dialect,"
op. cit., p.227.

Thatcher government; *Saltire* –

> when ah wiz it skule
> thur wiz loatsy flagz
> oan the frunty wur
> Text Books
>
> anna olwaze thot
> it wiz thi teechur
> hud pit a croass
> throo thi scoattish wun

– points the finger of blame (not for the first time by any means, but by a brilliantly original image) at the school system for the cultural alienation of Scottish children. If, as she claims, Kermack draws her inspiration from "lisnin tay foak in barz an caffyz an that", her poetry is a remarkable testimony to the fact that the vein of crazy fantasy in the Scottish imagination, often remarked on as it has emerged in the works of poets from Dunbar to MacDiarmid, is still alive.

The six poets discussed in this chapter form a heterogeneous group: the remark has often been made, in tones which depend on the individual observer's sympathy or lack thereof for the cause of Scots poetry, that *Scots* as a linguistic term must be an extraordinarily flexible one if it is to include a set of poetic media so diverse and idiosyncratic. Yet the fact that the Scots language not only is still so productive, but still attracts the enthusiastic and enterprising attentions of writers willing to experiment and innovate is surely grounds for rejoicing. It would be inappropriate to suggest that the language is in safe hands: those poets assuredly are not disposed to play for safety; and on a different level Scots cannot be safe, poetic experiments notwithstanding, while its social and educational status remain ill-defined and precarious. Yet the work of these six and many others confirms the irrepressible vitality of the Scots tongue, and its inexhaustible attractiveness to writers of creative talent; and it can be confidently predicted that they will continue to produce interesting and challenging Scots poetry well into the next century.

14
A Summing-Up

In 1995, Scots poetry endured the loss of two of the century's greatest figures, Tom Scott and Alastair Mackie. Scott's collected poems were published two years before his death; an important group of translations by Mackie[1] in the very month of his. Their achievement, and their influence, will last as long as Scotland lasts; but their deaths certainly evoked the sense of a great age gone: a sense which was heightened by the further losses, in that year and the next, of other Scottish literary giants – Norman MacCaig, Sorley MacLean and George Mackay Brown. One of the things which this book has demonstrated is that MacDiarmid and his Renaissance did not spring forth unheralded and unportended; yet the appearance of *Sangschaw* in 1925 will, rightly, always be seen as the seminal event which began the transformation of Scottish poetry, and with it the status of the Scots language and the entire cultural life of the nation. The years from 1925 to 1995 may therefore be taken as the great era of the Scottish Renaissance. Seventy years is a long lifespan for a literary movement, especially in our time; and it is certainly not at an end: there is no question of Scott and Mackie being the last poets, or even the last important poets, to write in Scots. The use of the Lowland tongue for poetry, in all its diversity of styles, registers and dialects, continues apace; and the vein shows no signs of exhaustion. Yet the year 1995 can, with some justice, be seen as an appropriate chronological landmark from which to take a retrospective view of the achievements of the Renaissance in relation to the Scots tongue.

These achievements have, in some respects, been nothing less than astounding. Not even the most optimistic of Scottish cultural patriots could have predicted at the beginning of the century that the current of

1. *"Giorno dopo Giorno* – Day Aifter Day (1943–1946)" Salvatore Quasimodo, owerset by Alastair Mackie. *Chapman* 80, 1995, 75–82.

Scots poetry would still be flowing boisterously at the end of it, the language having developed, matured and adapted itself to rapidly and radically changing social circumstances. Contemporary urban dialects and rural dialects both as spoken today and as remembered from the past, language suggestive of the eighteenth or the fifteenth century, language in which deliberate reminiscences of earlier literature are used for their evocative force: all, now, can be, and regularly are, employed in poetry. All registers and all modes of expression are available to a Scots poet: the language is no longer confined to the preoccupations of nostalgically-remembered rural communities; indeed, nostalgia and sentimentality are vigorously criticised whenever they appear in modern Scots verse. Linguistic experimentation is accepted as a principle: experiments may be successful or unsuccessful; but the mere fact of trying new things with Scots no longer raises any questions. Developments outwith the literary field have also materially affected the position of Scots. In addition to the progress in the educational and political fields mentioned in Chapter 2, advances in linguistic scholarship have, on the simplest and most general level, demolished for ever naive notions regarding the intrinsic inferiority of dialects and non-standard languages; and as a more specific achievement, have vastly increased the abundance and availability of reference material on Scots. Whereas the best source of Scots words available to MacDiarmid (besides, obviously, his reading of literature and his native knowledge of the Border dialect) was "Jamieson" – an admirable source skilfully employed, but produced in the intellectual context of 1808 – a poet writing in the '90s has the ten-volume *Scottish National Dictionary*, the *Concise Scots Dictionary*, the *Linguistic Atlas of Scotland* and – most helpful of all – the *Compact English-Scots Dictionary* and the *Scots Thesaurus* (all, be it noted, works which conform to the highest international scholarly standards of lexicography). And – perhaps the most encouraging fact of all – the growing energy and urgency of the debate surrounding Scots in the literary, educational and political domains is causing awareness and understanding of the issues to reach the general population: the actual and potential importance of the mither tongue is now something to which the querying and critical intelligence of lay individuals is being directed.

These are remarkable signs of progress. In one important field, however, such advances as have been achieved have been shamefully slow in arriving, are (so far) limited in scope, and owe little, if anything, to the century's literary successes. MacDiarmid was, of course, a single-minded Scottish Nationalist; so have been most of his poetic successors. Yet Scottish independence has not been regained; and despite the sudden exuberant rise now visible in the temperature of Scottish political activity, we cannot realistically believe that it is an immediate prospect. If MacDiarmid hoped that a revival of Scotland as a cultural entity, marked by a renaissance of internationally-respected poetry in Scots, would cause or be inseparably linked to the recovery of Scottish political independence, he has been proved wrong: the one has incontrovertibly come, but not the other. A semi-autonomous Scottish parliament has been established. This is the most revolutionary development in British politics since the achievement of independence by Ireland, and is in itself a cause for unequivocal rejoicing: all the more because of the suddenness and unexpectedness[1] with which it has followed a period when debate on Scotland's constitution among politicians continued to sink ever deeper to unsuspected abysms of sterile stupidity. But a Scottish parliament with severely restricted powers, the restrictions on which are being strongly emphasised by the London government, is not what MacDiarmid envisaged; though it is a major step towards it. Whether, or when, full independence will be achieved is a speculation which does not come within the scope of this book;[2] but it is certain at the very least that the SNP will continue to exist as an active and powerful force in Scottish politics, with its power-base greatly increased by the system of proportional representation established for the new parliament: indeed, a startling and – to the

1. The Labour party, while in opposition, had stated consistently for several years that they would establish a Scottish parliament if and when elected to form a government, but it can hardly be said that they gave a strong impression of commitment to the project, or that the total destruction of the party's credibility by the disgraceful fiasco of the 1979 devolution act had been redeemed by anything that had happened since.
2. Still less, of course, does any discussion of the meaning of "independence" in the context of contemporary Europe, with its advancing economic and monetary integration. Suffice it to note that though some people seem to think they are producing an argument against the aims of the SNP by reiterating the fact that no nation is fully independent in the contemporary world, that Scotland can attain to the same international status as, say, Sweden or the Netherlands, either of which is generally considered to represent what is meant by an independent state, is a perfectly realistic and perfectly comprehensible political aim.

government – profoundly unsettling effect of the constitutional change has been a dramatic rise in the level of expressed support for the SNP. And already the continuing campaign for independence is being conducted in a new context: whereas in, say, the 1940s and '50s the choice for Scotland was generally seen as being between independence and incorporation, and in the '70s and '80s between those two and some intermediate state of semi-autonomy, the choice now and for the future is a dual one between independence and devolution: the incorporating Union is finally and irrevocably at an end.

For the entire twentieth century, the course of Scottish political history has shown a seemingly interminable, and bitterly frustrating, sequence of waxings and wanings in the popular and political support for Home Rule. Time and again, with weary regularity, success or some measure of it seemed to be within reach, only to recede each time into the realms of dream. MacDiarmid's lyric *Lourd on my Hert* provides an exact encapsulation of the despairing mood which this sequence was liable to engender; and it was to continue for many more years and several more cycles:

Lourd on my hert as winter lies
The state that Scotland's in the day.
Spring tae the North has aye come slaw,
But nou dour winter's like tae stay
  For guid –
  And no for guid.

Wae's me on aa thae weary days
When it is scarce grey licht at noon.
It maun be aa thae stupid fowk
Diffusin dullness roun and roun
  Like soot,
  That keeps the sunlicht oot.

Nae wonder if I think I see
A shaddaw lichter nor the neist
I'm fain tae cry "The dawn, the dawn –
I see it brakin in the east!"
  But ah –
  It's jist mair snaw.

And as one of the strangest ironies in the history of the movement, the success which has now been achieved has come not during the period when the revolutionary clarion-calls of MacDiarmid and the other great Renaissance makars were at their height but long after that, when both Scots as a poetic language and Scottish nationalism as a political movement have become simply part of the normal scene. This carries an implication, perhaps a disconcerting one, for the Scots language: since it has indisputably come of age as a medium for modern poetry, to the extent that its use is now non-controversial, it can no longer serve as a political counter as it could from, say, the 1920s to the '50s. A poet who writes in Scots is certainly *ipso facto* proclaiming his Scottish nationality and his allegiance to a distinct Scottish identity; but a Scottish literary culture expressed in Scots is by now thoroughly "establishment": many, indeed most, of the Scottish literary coterie are fully as committed to Scottish political autonomy as they were in MacDiarmid's time; but they can no longer expect that the mere fact of writing in Scots is an active contribution to the cause of political independence; or even a necessary expression of radical socialism, as it was for MacDiarmid and (as the next most impressive example) Tom Scott. A political dimension is certainly still conspicuous on the Scottish literary scene in the sense that many writers are committedly nationalist and socialist; but it is now clear that the association of this with a Scots voice is contingent rather than inherent.

A further sobering fact is this: if proof were necessary that a literary movement, of whatever scale and distinction, cannot by itself bring about fundamental social or political change, that proof has been furnished by the history of the Scottish Renaissance. The Scots language has in the twentieth century become the vehicle for a national poetic literature of extensive scope and unchallengeable merit: MacDiarmid, Soutar, the two Mackies, the two Scotts, Garioch, Young, and all the other poets who have (and the many more who have not) been examined in this book have restored Scots to a position of dignity among the literary languages of the world that it has not held since the Union of the Crowns. If its restoration, in addition to this, to a recognised status in such fields as education, commerce and politics was not within the power of that company, then it was not within the range of human possibility – or its achievement by poets alone was not. On the other hand, if Scots should acquire this status in the future (which will require a sustained effort by linguists and educationists as well as men of letters), then it will surely be said that the work of the poets was one of the things which proved that this effort deserved to be made. And another and more hopeful aspect to the issue is this: a literary movement, particularly one which has been the target of such sustained hostility as the Scots Renaissance, could hardly have remained active for upwards of seventy years if it had not been able to find support on a bedrock of sympathy at some level in the collective national psyche.

This sustained hostility is itself worthy of discussion; for it is, on any showing, a most strange phenomenon. Scots is a living community speech; and its status as the vehicle of one of Europe's great national literatures, unassailable by the beginning of the century, has in the course of it been further enhanced by a fascinating and stimulating body of new work. Those are facts; yet powerful and protracted efforts have been, and are still being, made to conceal or deny them as facts. In 1948, Maurice Lindsay, in a short but perceptive essay on the Scottish Renaissance,[1] referred contemptuously to "a certain clique of West of Scotland journalists" who persistently ridiculed the new developments in Scots poetry. In 1964, Sydney Goodsir Smith produced an incisive and forceful critique of the "anti-Scots lobby", calling attention[2] to the fact that whereas in the 1920s MacDiarmid's literary, linguistic and political aims seemed "merely funny" to the contemporary establishment, by the '30s nearly every writer in Scotland was proclaiming support for the revival of Scots (and Gaelic) as literary languages and the recovery of Scottish political independence. Many were also radical socialists. By the '60s, however, a reaction had become evident, and the Scottish Renaissance was being attacked by "the old (who have never liked it), the middle-aged (who never like anything), and the young (who generally like the latest thing – and the Scottish thing was definitely old hat)". Smith proceeded to quote from several literary scholars (men of unassailable learning for the most part) from James Beattie in 1771 to Maurice Lindsay himself in 1962 (by which time he had abandoned his own earlier attempts at writing in Scots) who seemed bent on proclaim-

---

1. *The Scottish Renaissance*, Edinburgh (Serif Books) 1948.
2. *"Trahison des Clercs* or the Anti-Scottish Lobby in Scottish Letters", in *Studies in Scottish Literature* 2 (1964), 71 – 86.

ing, in defiance of plainly observable facts, that Scottish literature was essentially negligible in quality and quantity, and in particular that the Scots tongue, if it still existed at all, had long ceased to be of any use as a means of literary expression. More than thirty years later – thirty years in which the flow of interesting, challenging and often by any standards excellent Scottish writing has proceeded unchecked – precisely the same wearisome pronouncements are still being made.[1]

Besides this persistent denigration of Scots and its literature by critics, the field has been almost entirely neglected in Scottish schools. Routinely, generations of children have passed through the Scottish educational system in almost total ignorance of the national literature: for many, a perfunctory introduction to Burns represents the sum total of their "official" acquaintance with the vast and fascinating corpus of Scottish literature; and some have not even that. Teachers who regard it as their duty to give their charges at least a sampling of modern English and American poetry have often made no attempt to make them aware that any modern Scottish poetry even exists. In view of the extent and quality of the Renaissance literature, this can be regarded as nothing else, and nothing less, than a fully-developed conspiracy of silence.

What is it, we are certainly entitled to ask, in the soil, air or water of Scotland that makes its citizens, including some of the most prominent and most respected of them, so determinedly opposed to the development of a national literature in one of the national languages? It is normally taken as a matter of course that children in German schools study German literature. If in the United States, or Australia, literature courses in schools were devoted exclusively to the works of English writers, most Scots would surely find this surprising. If in the Languedoc a large and vociferous coterie of influential scholars and educationists maintained, with determined consistency and over many decades, that Provençal was incapable of being used for respectable literature and had no place in the region's educational curriculum, in spite of the achievements of

---

1. A week before this paragraph was written, the journal *Education in the North* (Vol.5, 1997: 5–10) printed a rebuttal by the present writer of an article by Tino Ferri (vol. 4: 1966, 13–16) criticising Scottish, especially Scots, literature and proposals to increase the amount of time devoted to it in the schools. Except for assumptions made regarding the political state of Scotland, Ferri's arguments and my counter-arguments could have been, and often have been, rehearsed at any time in the last fifty years.

Frédéric Mistral, his fellow-poets of the Félibrige and the entire school of Provençal poetry which they initiated and in defiance of the continuing vitality of Provençal as a community speech, this would surely be seen as a curious anomaly, and one which reflected no credit on Provence. Yet in Scotland, that is precisely the situation that still prevails: in the simplest terms, a corpus of literature outstanding in both quantity and quality has been deliberately prevented from reaching popular knowledge. Such mass deceptions are by no means unique to Scotland; but when they are recognised in other countries, or at other times in history, they are generally condemned. And recently this paranoid fear of anything Scots has taken a new and peculiarly base and shameful turn: opponents of any degree of Scottish political autonomy or cultural distinctiveness have taken to using the word "nationalism" as if it referred to something monstrous and terrifying. Poets, scholars and educationists who argue for a due degree of attention to be given to the Scots language and its associated literature in the school curriculum are routinely accused of "nationalism" as if this were a triumphant exposure of those individuals as agents of some crypto-fascist conspiracy: even when the individuals concerned are figures well known in the cultural or political life of the nation, with public and private lives which make this suggestion self-evidently ludicrous. In all conscience, what can be said of a country where the fantasy that teaching the national literature in the schools is one step away from instituting Serbian-style ethnic purges is expressed as if it were not even surprising; and what rational arguments can be used against people morally and intellectually crooked enough to talk in this way?

Evidence of this kind shows that the Unionist bias which has prevailed in Scottish education for most of this and the last century has had profound and profoundly damaging effects. The novelist Fionn MacColla exposed with an eloquence worthy of the passion which his insights aroused the sustained attempts by the Scottish teaching profession not only to wipe out the Gaelic language but to destroy, or distort beyond recognition, all popular memory and understanding of the entire Gaelic cultural achievement.[1] *Mutatis mutandis*, the Scots tongue has been sub-

---

1. This is a central theme in all his works, but see as an introduction his autobiographical sketch *Too Long in This Condition* (Caithness 1975).

ject to the same systematic undermining. It goes without saying that the situation has parallels in many countries: all over Europe languages and dialects other than those with official status in their respective homelands have been actively discouraged as spoken tongues and reduced to a position of inferiority, even insignificance, in the educational systems. What is unusual in Scotland is, firstly, the startling contrast between the abundance and merit of the body of Scots literature and the wilful blindness of those who have continued over centuries to deny its worth or even its existence; and secondly, the ability of those who persist in their entrenched anti-Scots position to persuade themselves that they are acting like patriotic Scots. For nobody, be it noted, ever advocates that the nominal distinctiveness of Scotland should be abandoned – that we should regard ourselves as English, or even as "British" *instead of* (not *as well as*) Scots – we are still Scots, citizens of a proud, ancient and distinctive country, even though any emphasis placed on the things that *make* us distinctive lays the proponent open to charges of anarchism or terrorism.

If this almost pathological state of confusion has any rational explanation at all, the only one which suggests itself is that Scots in speech and in literature is seen by some people as the kind of threat to the Union to which lifetimes of ingrained Unionism have engendered a conditioned reflex of fear and loathing. For there is no question that any promotion of the Scots language is in itself an assertion of Scotland's individual identity, and therefore, *ipso facto*, a challenging of the political system in which that identity is insufficiently recognised. Still less can it be questioned that most Scottish literature of the present century, and especially that part of it which is in Scots, is vigorously nationalistic, emphasising all that is distinctive in the national life, and calling with conviction and with persuasive eloquence for the restoration of the full political independence in which Scotland's culture may develop unchecked. In political debate, statements of the case for independence have regularly been answered with assertions which, when measured against observable facts, are merely contemptible: the country's resources are insufficient or its population too small to enable it to function as an independent state, or its people would simply not be capable of governing themselves. The rejection, in defiance of both reason and observation, of Scots as a spoken and literary medium is a manifestation of this same mindset.

Yet the signs are increasingly clear that this poison is at last working itself out of the collective Scottish psyche. On the political level, Home Rule is now a fact: the first and most fundamental break with the Unionist past has been made. On the educational, the gradual and unremitting efforts of literati, language scholars and a few enlightened teachers and directors over decades are at last bearing fruit: the place of Scots in the schools has increased, if not to a satisfactory level, then at least to a point from which a regression to the old ways is virtually inconceivable. The advances in scholarly research have both increased the international prestige of the language as a field of study and augmented the range of available knowledge relating to it; and both these developments are certain to continue. And there is no reason to doubt that Scots will survive for the foreseeable future as a poetic medium: we need not expect another MacDiarmid, but the many young and gifted poets now experimenting with the language will still further enhance the national literary achievement over the next few decades; and as the educational and cultural climate becomes increasingly favourable to the reception of Scots poetry, their work will reach a larger and more appreciative audience. To that extent, the hopes for Scots which were expressed in the early days of the Renaissance will be fulfilled.

A continuing flow of fine poems in Scots, however, is not enough. Excellent though the work of our contemporary poets often is, they are doing no more than what we now know can be done: MacDiarmid and his immediate successors did things of which nobody, until they happened, knew Scots to be capable. The achievements of the Renaissance Makars must, and surely will, continue to inspire poetry worthy of its antecedents; but events have demonstrated that Scots will not be restored to full health by merely adding to the existing poetic corpus. Scots must now develop in new fields, and become what it was within sight of becoming in the Stewart period: a national language. Not, obviously, *the* national language: English, the language in which not only many Scottish creative writers but all Scottish philosophers, economists, historians, and scientists in all fields have presented their thoughts to the world, will continue to be a Scottish language for the indefinite future; and Gaelic, which like Scots is currently demonstrating a new vitality after seemingly endless oppression, will shortly have its status enhanced by the (disgracefully belated) granting of official recognition. But until Scots is taught, and used, in every school in the land; until people of all classes can and do converse in it without embarrassment; until its literature enjoys the same degree of general familiarity as that of England or America – until MacDiarmid's question

> Are my poems spoken in the factories and the fields,
> In the streets o' the toon?[1]

can be answered in the affirmative – then the promise of the Renaissance remains unfulfilled.

Maurice Lindsay's essay on the Scottish Renaissance, referred to earlier, ends as follows:

> Scots and Gaelic poetry are moving slowly but surely back to the people. The people are not fully aware of this yet, just as they are still sunk in ignorance and apathy about the deplorable state of Scotland's affairs. But when the Scottish people do become completely conscious of the new poetry which has grown up out of them, the Scottish Renaissance will have achieved fruition, and new life may come to Scotland the nation. If this synthesis between poets and people is not achieved, then the Renaissance will be the last bright flicker of a guttering flame. Scotland will die in all but name, and the world will be the poorer because a proud and ancient light will have gone out in Europe.

The fifty years since that was written have seen many developments from the circumstances of the time; but not precisely those which could have been predicted. The synthesis between poets and people remains to be achieved; yet the cultural Renaissance has continued in full vigour. And Scotland most certainly has not died: on the contrary, Scotland is currently reclaiming a measure at least of control over its own affairs. Scottish independence in arts and letters is now an established fact. Scottish political autonomy is beginning to catch up. Will the third link in the chain – the restoration to full health of the national languages, and with that a rediscovery of the national cultural achievement – now follow, and with it the final goal of a comprehensive re-awakening of Scotland's national identity? The chance is here, and the omens are more favourable than ever since the Union. We must not fail to seize the opportunity.

1. *Second Hymn to Lenin* (1940).

Bibliography

References to the works of the poets discussed, and to many other books and articles in which relevant themes are developed, are given in the footnotes.

The basic reference work on the Scots language in the first part of the period discussed is, of course, *The Scottish National Dictionary* (ed. W. Grant and D. D. Murison, Edinburgh: Scottish National Dictionary Association, 1931–76). *The Concise Scots Dictionary* (editor-in-chief Mairi Robinson, first edition (1985) Aberdeen University Press, later reprints Oxford University Press) includes, in its introduction, an excellent encapsulation of the history of Scots. However, more than twenty years have passed since the last volume of the *SND* was published, and a much longer period since the collection of the data. The *CSD* includes some words found in more recent researches, but even it could make no claim to completeness as a record of the vocabulary of the second and third waves of Scots Renaissance poets. A full-scale lexicon of contemporary literary Scots is a desideratum for future researchers.

The most comprehensive short general history of Scots is the present author's "English in Scotland", Chapter 2 of *The Cambridge History of the English Language Vol.* V, ed. Robert Burchfield, Cambridge University Press, 1994. Three popular handbooks, designed to introduce the topic to the intelligent general reader, are *The Guid Scots Tongue* by David Murison, Edinburgh (Blackwood) 1977, *Scots: the Mither Tongue* by Billy Kay, Edinburgh (Mainstream Publishing) 1986, and *Why Scots Matters* by the present writer, Edinburgh (Saltire Society) revised edn. 1997. All of these, in their limited compass, make at least some reference to the modern literary language. The multi-author *Edinburgh History of the Scots*

Language, ed. Charles Jones, Edinburgh University Press 1997, of course treats the subject in far greater detail; but despite the excellence of most of the individual chapters, it is seriously defective in making no attempt to examine the literary development of Scots in the twentieth century (nor, for that matter, in the nineteenth or eighteenth). Conversely, Volume 4 of the *Aberdeen History of Scottish Literature*, ed. Cairns Craig, Aberdeen University Press, 1987, treats the language issue only incidentally in its (likewise excellent) studies of modern and contemporary poetry. *Scottish Literature since 1707* by Marshall Walker, London (Longman) 1996, is more satisfactory in this respect. A most welcome attempt to integrate linguistic analysis with literary criticism is provided by *Language and Scottish Literature* by John Corbett, Edinburgh University Press, 1997.

Only MacDiarmid, among twentieth-century Scots-writing poets, has had anything remotely like a respectable amount of scholarly and critical attention. *Hugh MacDiarmid and the Scots Renaissance* by Duncan Glen, Edinburgh (Chambers) 1964, is still the fundamental work, placing him in his literary, intellectual and political context. Two more recent books which pay attention to the linguistic interest of his poetry are *Thistle and Rose* by Ann Edwards Boutelle, Loanhead (Macdonald) 1980 and *To Circumjack MacDiarmid* by W. N. Herbert, Oxford (Clarendon) 1992. Albert Mackie's essay 'MacDiarmid and the Scottish Language', in *Hugh MacDiarmid: a Festschrift*, ed. K. Duval and Sydney Goodsir Smith, Edinburgh (K. Duval) 1962, pp. 165–186, is very good; David Murison's 'The Language Problem in MacDiarmid's Work', in *The Age of MacDiarmid*, ed. P. H. Scott and A. C. Davies, Edinburgh (Mainstream) 1980, pp. 83–99, is outstanding.

Index

Index

Index

Index

Index

Index